Corporate Finance

FOR

DUMMIES®

A Wiley Brand

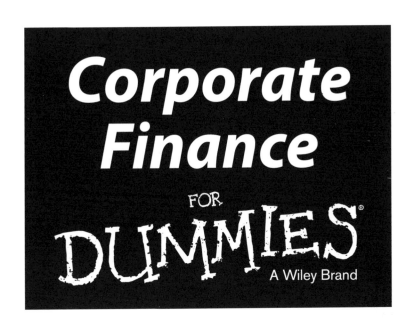

Corporate Finance

FOR

DUMMIES

A Wiley Brand

by Steve Collings and Michael Taillard

Corporate Finance For Dummies®

Published by: **John Wiley & Sons, Ltd.,** The Atrium, Southern Gate, Chichester, www.wiley.com

This edition first published 2013

© 2013 John Wiley & Sons, Ltd, Chichester, West Sussex.

Registered office

John Wiley & Sons Ltd, The Atrium, Southern Gate, Chichester, West Sussex, PO19 8SQ, United Kingdom

For details of our global editorial offices, for customer services and for information about how to apply for permission to reuse the copyright material in this book please see our website at www.wiley.com.

For general information on our other products and services, please contact our Customer Care Department within the U.S. at 877-762-2974, outside the U.S. at (001) 317-572-3993, or fax 317-572-4002. For technical support, please visit www.wiley.com/techsupport.

For technical support, please visit www.wiley.com/techsupport.

A catalogue record for this book is available from the British Library.

ISBN 978-1-118-74350-8 (paperback); ISBN 978-1-118-74348-5 (ebk); ISBN 978-1-118-74347-8 (ebk)

Printed in Great Britain by TJ International, Padstow, Cornwall

10 9 8 7 6 5 4 3 2 1

Contents at a Glance

Table of Contents

Introduction

*I*n case you didn't already know, this book is about corporate finance. If you were looking for dog grooming, we're afraid you've picked up the wrong book.

Corporate finance is the study of how groups of people work together as a single organisation to provide something of value to society. If a company is using up more value than it's producing, it loses money and goes bust. So the job of people in corporate finance is to manage the organisation so that it uses resources efficiently (to the best advantage of the company), pursues the most valuable projects, remains competitive and people get to keep their job. You can accomplish this task through an easy process: measuring. In corporate finance, you measure value using money, because the final goal of all companies is to make money. When a company makes money – that is, when it's profitable – it's making sales that have more value than the things it buys and it's adding value to society rather than sucking the life out of it. Ensuring that a company is financially successful, however, is far more complicated than simply ensuring that it's profitable.

In this book, we discuss a wide range of topics in corporate finance. Think of it as a sampler or a greatest-hits album – an introductory book that provides everything you need to understand what corporate finance is and how to begin functioning at a basic level in the world of finance.

About This Book

This book is a little different from other corporate finance books. First of all, it's better! More useful than that, though, is that this book is written and organised so that people with absolutely no understanding of corporate finance can use it as a reference guide. It's also a wonderfully interesting read.

Everything in this book is written as if you're a complete newbie. The little details are pointed out, and when stuff gets complicated we just summarise the topic. We also explain – or at least clarify – everything, in down-to-earth language, without sounding technical. This book is all about making the subject of corporate finance accessible to everyone, while keeping it from being too dry. Corporate finance books can be really boring, which is sad because they don't need to be.

This book is organised to be used as a reference book. We still recommend reading it all, of course, but we break down and structure everything carefully to give the book what we like to call a disjointed continuity. This organisation makes looking things up without reading the entire book easy, while maintaining enough fluid continuity to make sense if you want to read the book from start to finish.

Foolish Assumptions

While writing this book, we did our best to assume that you know absolutely nothing. That being said, no one is perfect and we forgive you for failing to live up to the expectation that you're a complete dummy. In return, we'd appreciate it if you forgive us for the assumptions we made throughout this book. What we can do for you, though, is give you a heads up regarding some things you need to be aware of, know or perhaps prepare yourself with.

Unavoidably, this book involves a bit of maths. Yes, we know, maths is hard; we never liked it, either. That's why we supplement the majority of the maths with explanations of how to do the calculations that are simple enough to spare you from needing to know how to study maths. In other words, you can often skip over the majority of the equations and just read the paragraph(s) following them to get an understanding of what you're supposed to do. That's not always the case, though. To understand this book – to understand corporate finance at all – you do need a basic understanding of arithmetic (addition, subtraction, multiplication, division) as well as algebra (how to find x). We talk a bit about statistics and calculus in this book as well, but we provide you with careful, step-by-step instructions or simple summaries for that. We don't discuss anything that's very difficult. As long as you know arithmetic and a little algebra, you'll be fine – nothing's harder than $4 + x = 10$.

You can also supplement the information in this book by checking out *For Dummies* books on accounting. The two subjects have some overlap, and we bring up accounting subjects occasionally. Looking at *Accounting For Dummies* by John A. Tracy (Wiley), for example, can help give you more background about these topics. We try to include only those details relevant to the subject of corporate finance.

Other than that, if you're reading this right now, you're prepared to begin reading *Corporate Finance For Dummies!*

Icons Used in This Book

We scatter a few icons around the book to help you find relevant material. These icons highlight bits of information that are of particular importance to you. Here's what to look for.

Professionals get good at what they do by making stupid mistakes and learning from them. Now you can benefit from these stupid mistakes without the unfortunate side-effects of making them yourself. Just look for the Tip icon.

Whenever you see this icon, it means that you may one day need to remember the information included. You may want to consider keeping it in mind.

When you see this icon, we're talking about something that may pose a serious threat. We're not being facetious, either. Corporate finance is a study in money, and this is an introductory book, and so in some instances you need to talk to a professional before you get yourself or others into financial or legal trouble.

This icon clues you into the fact that the paragraph contains some interesting but not essential-to-know information. If you prefer, you can skip this material secure in the knowledge that you aren't missing anything vital. But then again, if you want to gain that extra edge. . . .

Beyond the Book

As you walk your journey of discovery into the world of corporate finance, you can augment what you read here by checking out some of the access-anywhere extra goodies that we've hosted for you online.

You can find the book's e-cheat sheet online, at `www.dummies.com/cheatsheet/corporatefinanceuk`. The at-a-glance tips and info that we offer in this cheat sheet can help you to make room for the basic skills you need in order to understand corporate finance, to understand how behaviour affects corporate finance, and more.

Additionally, you can also find bonus content online, at `www.dummies.com/extras/corporatefinanceuk`, which includes an extra Part of Tens chapter – 'Ten Key Points about Islamic Finance' – and some great bonus articles.

Where to Go from Here

We didn't write the chapters in order and you don't have to read them in order. If we can make a recommendation, though, you may want to begin with the chapters in Parts II and III before attempting Parts IV and V. At least flip through the earlier pages to make sure that you're familiar with how to read financial statements and the time value of money before you attempt to move on to Parts IV and V. As long as you're familiar with those things (financial statements and the time value of money), nothing in this book is going to be out of your grasp.

Part I

Getting Started with Corporate Finance

In this part . . .

✔ Bone up on the basics of corporate finance and become proactive with your corporate finance know-how.

✔ Navigate your journey through the complex world of corporate finance, stopping off at the major organisations and visiting the major roles involved along the way.

✔ Get to grips with how companies raise money by incurring debt and by selling equity.

Chapter 1

Introducing Corporate Finance

In This Chapter
▶ Understanding the meaning of money
▶ Looking at the study of corporate finance
▶ Seeing the role corporate finance plays in your life
▶ Making corporate finance work for you

Corporate finance is more than just a measure of money. In fact, as you discover in this chapter – where we talk about the nature of money, how it applies to corporate finance and how it connects to you and your life – money is somewhat incidental to finance. When you're discussing corporate finance, you're looking at the whole world in a brand new way that measures it and what it contains so as to make the information useful to people. You can calculate things in terms of corporate finance that you simply can't measure accurately in any other way.

Part of the role of this chapter is also to introduce you to the book as a whole. Therefore, as part of helping you become proactive with your corporate finance know-how, we clue you into other chapters to allow you to follow your personal interests quickly and easily.

Considering Corporate Finance and the Role of Money in the World

Corporate finance is the study of relationships between groups of people that quantifies the otherwise immeasurable. (Corporate finance can also refer to a department, such as the corporate finance department in an investment bank that deals with advice given to companies about financial arrangements.) To understand how this rather wordy definition makes any sense at all, you have to take a quick look at the role of money in the world.

According to Adam Smith, an 18th century economist, the use of money was preceded by a *barter system,* in which people exchanged goods and services of relatively equivalent value. For example, if you worked growing hemp and making rope out of it, you'd give that rope to people in exchange for food, clothes or whatever else you needed that the people around you were offering.

But what happens when someone wants rope but that person has nothing you want, or you need food but no one needs rope? These times caused people to start using a basic form of money. So, you sell your rope to someone with nothing you want and he gives you a credit note for his services that you're free to give to anyone else. You decide to go and buy some beer, giving the brewer the credit note, ensuring that the person who bought your rope would provide the brewer a service in exchange for giving you beer. Thus, the invention of money was born, though in a very primitive form.

Looking at money in this way, you come to realise that money is in fact debt. When you hold money, it means that you've provided goods or services of value to someone else and that you're now owed value in return. The development of a standardised, commonly used currency among large numbers of people simply increases the number of people willing to accept your paper or coin IOUs. Therefore, that currency becomes easier to exchange among a wider number of people, across greater distances and for a more diverse variety of potential goods and services (for additional gloss on this account, read the nearby sidebar 'Taxes started early').

Put simply, money is debt for the promise of goods and services that have an inherent usefulness, but money itself isn't useful except as a measure of debt. People use money to measure the value that they place on things.

Imagine that you're living in Ancient Egypt and you want to know the value of a goat. You can say that one goat is worth five chickens, but that doesn't help you much. You can say that a bricklayer's labour is worth half that of a brewer of beer, but you can't measure that mathematically. Using these methods, you have no real way to establish a singular, definitive measurement for the value that people place on different things.

Taxes started early

According to 21st century anthropologist David Graebner, early money was probably something closer to bartering with the government as a taxation, which meant providing goods and services to the government (for example, the emperor) and then being provided units of 'currency' worth product rations. So you can say that money was invented for the first government contractors as a method for the government to acquire resources in return for units of early currency worth specific amounts of resources, rather than a true barter.

So, how can you measure value? By determining the amount of money that people are willing to exchange for different things. This method allows you to determine very accurately how people interact, what they value and the relative differences in value between certain things or certain people's efforts. Much about the nature of people, the things they value and how they interact together become clearer when you develop an understanding of what they're spending money on and how much they're spending.

Eight millennia on from Ancient Egypt, in the modern era of money – well after the establishment of weighted coins to measure an equivalent weight of grain, the standardised minting of currency and after the origins of money were forgotten by the vast majority of the world's population (welcome to the minority) – money begins to take on a more abstract role. People use it as a way to measure resource allocations between groups and within groups. They even begin to measure how well a group of people are interacting by looking at their ability to produce more using less. Success is measured by their ability to hoard greater amounts of this inter-personal debt. The ability to hoard debt in this manner defines whether the efforts of one group of people are more or less successful than the efforts of another group.

People use money to place a value on everything, which allows them to compare different items. Which one is better, apples or oranges? The answer is the one on which people place more value based on the total amount of revenues. Higher revenues tell you that people place greater value on one of those two fruits, because they're willing to pay for the higher costs plus any additional profits.

When we say that corporate finance is the study of the relationships between groups of people, we're referring to measuring how groups of people are allocating resources among themselves, putting value on goods and services, and interacting with each other in the exchange of these goods and services. Corporate finance picks apart the financial exchanges of groups of people, all interconnected in professional relationships, by determining how effectively and efficiently they work together to build value and manage that value after it's acquired. The organisations that are more effective at developing a cohesive team of people who work together to build value in the marketplace are going to be more successful than their competitors.

In corporate finance, you measure all this information mathematically in order to assess the success of the corporate organisation, evaluate the outcome of potential decisions and optimise the efforts of those people who form economic relationships, even if for just a moment, as they exchange goods, services and value in a never-ending series of financial transactions.

Identifying What Makes Corporate Finance Unique

Corporate finance plays an interesting role in all societies. Finance is the study of relationships between people: how they distribute themselves and their resources, place value on things and exchange that value among each other. Therefore, all finance is really the science of decision-making. We're talking about studying human behaviour and how people make decisions regarding what they do with their lives and the things they own.

Corporate finance, as a result, studies decision-making in terms of what groups of people do when working together in a professional manner. This definition guides you in two primary directions connected to what makes corporate finance unique:

- ✔ Understanding that corporate finance is a critical aspect of human life as an intermediary that allows people to transfer value among themselves.

- ✔ Discovering how groups of people interact together as a single unit, a company, and how decisions are made on behalf of the company by its managers.

Money is just the unit of measure people use to calculate everything and make sense of it numerically, to compare things in absolute terms rather than relative ones. In contrast, corporate finance is a unique study that measures *value*. When you accept that fact, you see that everything in the world has value. Therefore, you can use corporate finance to measure everything around you that relates to a company, directly or indirectly (which, in the vast majority of the world, is everything).

Serving as an intermediary

The easiest way to understand how corporate finance acts as a critical intermediary process between groups of people is to look at the role of financial institutions in the greater economy. Financial institutions, such as banks and credit unions, have a role that involves redistributing money between those who want money and those who have excess money, all in a manner that the general population believes is based on reasonable terms.

Now, whether financial institutions as a whole are fully successful in their role is no longer a matter of debate: they aren't. The cyclical role being played out time and again prior to the Great Depression, prior to the 1970's economic troubles and prior to the 2008 collapse are the legacies of a systematic operational failure yet to be resolved.

For the most part, however, the role that financial institutions play is necessary. They facilitate the movement of resources across the entire world. They accept money from those who have more than they're using and offer interest rate payments in return. Then they turn around and give that money to those seeking loans, charging interest for this service. In this role, financial institutions are intermediaries that allow people on both sides of these sorts of transactions to find each other by way of the bank itself. Without this role, investments and loans would very nearly come to a total halt compared to the extremely high volume and value of the current financial system.

Corporate finance plays a similar role as an intermediary for the exchange of value of goods and services between individuals and organisations. Corporate finance, as the representation of the value developed by groups of people working together towards a single cause, studies how money is used as an intermediary of exchange between and within these groups to reallocate value as is deemed necessary.

We'd like to backtrack for a moment. What on earth is an investment, anyway? An *investment* is anything that you buy for the purpose of generating greater value than you spent to acquire it. Yes, yes, shares and bonds are good examples; you buy them, they go up in value and you sell them. But no doubt you can think of other examples that work in different ways. A house that you buy to generate income is a good example of an investment: you buy it, generate revenue as its tenants pay their rent and after the house goes up in value, you sell it. (In contrast, your own home usually isn't considered an investment.)

Analysing interactions between people

Money places an absolute value on transactions that take place, and so you can measure easily not only these transactions, but also all the several potential options in a given decision. In other words, you can measure the outcome of a decision before it's made, thanks to corporate finance.

That's the second thing (after its role as an intermediary process) that makes corporate finance a unique study: it analyses the value of interactions between people, the value of the actions taken and the value of the decisions made, and then compiles that information into a single collection based on professional interconnectedness in a single company.

This analysis allows you to measure how effectively you're making decisions and optimise the outcome of future decisions you have to make. The decisions that companies make tend to have far-reaching consequences, influencing the lives of employees, customers, suppliers, investors and the greater national economy, and so ensuring that a company is making the correct decisions is of the utmost importance. Corporate finance allows you to do this. So if you have a favourite company, hug the financial analysts next time you see them (or maybe just send a box of chocolates; you may freak someone out if you just randomly starting hugging people).

Recognising How Corporate Finance Rules Your Life

Unless you're in the rare minority and live as a secluded and self-sufficient recluse, practically every aspect of your life is strongly influenced, directly or otherwise, by corporate finances. For instance, the price and availability of the things you buy are decided using financial data and the chances are high that your job relies heavily on decisions made using financial data, as do your savings and investments. Your house, car, where you live and even the laws in your area are all determined using financial information about companies.

From the beginning, a company needs to decide how it plans to fund its *start-up:* the time when it first begins purchasing supplies to start operating. This single decision decides a significant amount about the company's costs, which, in turn, decide a lot about the prices it's going to charge. Where it sells its goods depends greatly on whether the company can sell them at a price high enough to generate a profit after the costs of production and distribution, assuming that competitors can't drive down prices in that area. The number of units that the company produces depends entirely on how productive its equipment is, and the company only purchases more equipment if doing so doesn't cost more than the organisation can make in profits.

These factors affect your job, too; the company recruits more people who add value to the company only if doing so is profitable. Where your job is located depends greatly on where in the world it's cheapest to locate operations related to your line of work. The decision to outsource your job to another nation depends entirely on whether that role within the company can be done more cheaply elsewhere, without incurring risks that are too expensive. That's right, even risk can be measured mathematically in financial terms.

As well as affecting your work life – controlling how much you make, what you can afford, what your job is and where you work – corporate finance also influences your personal life, because companies have this habit of financially assessing government policy.

When a proposed law (called a *bill*) is introduced, companies determine what its financial impact is going to be on them. They also assess whether a law that exists (or one that they think should exist) has a financial impact on companies. If the impact is greater than the cost of engaging a lobbyist in London, they hire one to pressure politicians into doing what they want. This effort includes making campaign contributions, marketing on behalf of the politician and more. It can even rise to the level of international relations between nations, where a single large company can bring a global industry to a stop by convincing the right people that one nation is selling goods at a price lower than cost, which causes political conflict between nations. This scenario happened many times in the past, with the majority of claims being made by US companies, and it can easily happen again.

Every aspect of your life is influenced in some way by the information derived from corporate finance. Money is a measure of value, and you're valuable, and so nearly everything that makes you who you are can be measured in terms of money. And if it can be measured in terms of money, decisions are going to be made in terms of money.

If you're not the one making those decisions, you probably need to ask yourself who is.

Becoming Proactive about Corporate Finance

Corporate finance plays such a critical role in your life (the proof is in the preceding section) that you need to ask how you can be more proactive about understanding and, if at all possible, managing corporate finance to your own benefit. Asking how to manage those influences on your life is a fair question if ever there was one. Ignoring the obvious conflict of interest, you're on the right path by beginning to read this book. We don't mean simply owning it; thrilled as we are that you've bought this book – and we certainly hope you decide to buy many more copies for friends and family – you have to read it in order to find out stuff!

The point is that before you can become financially proactive for yourself, your business or a company, you first have to understand the basics. That's where this book comes into play: this is an introductory book designed to help you develop an understanding of how corporate finance works.

To discover some preliminary information with which you need to be familiar, read Chapter 2 (on the types of organisations and people involved in corporate finance) and Chapter 3 (on how companies raise money). In Chapters 4–8, we talk about understanding the different corporate financial records and statements and using the contained data effectively to make them useful. If you want to know how to measure the value of just about everything, including the amount of uncertainty involved in your financial actions, turn to Chapters 9–13, as well as Chapters 14–17 on risks and to discover innovative financial tools of all sorts. We also cover using this information to manage a business properly in Chapters 18–20. Don't forget Chapters 21 and 22, which discuss two increasingly prominent issues for companies: international and behavioural finance.

After you grasp the corporate finance basics, you can begin to apply the information to your own life. You can find out what specific companies (possibly the one where you work) are doing that influence your life, measure how well they're doing and predict what may happen in the future. Corporate executives work with methods and tools that are freely available to the public, and so understanding exactly what they're looking at and the actions they're likely to take in response helps you anticipate what's going to happen. It also gives you the tools to manage your own professional life, as well as your personal finances, more effectively. Maybe not quite as well as the professionals – not without a more advanced understanding and some practice – but you're definitely on your way.

Chapter 2

Navigating the World of Corporate Finance

*W*elcome to the wondrous world of corporate finance, where your wildest fantasies come true (assuming that your wildest fantasies have something to do with analysing financial data!). Unfortunately, getting lost in Finance Land is all too easy, considering that it's filled with a variety of organisations and people whose exact roles are rather specialised and unfamiliar to those outside the inner circles of corporate finance.

Therefore, we design this chapter as a road map to help you navigate your way through the complex world of corporate finance. We discuss the different organisations and many of the different jobs involved. Plus, in our aim to be ever-helpful, we also include a list of resources you can check out for more information on the basics of corporate finance.

Visiting the Main Attractions in Finance Land

Finance Land is filled with a surprisingly large and diverse number of organisations, each one specialising in a different area of financial goods or services and many of them being quite narrow in their focus. Regardless of how limited or unlimited in offerings any particular organisation may be, they're all interconnected, with each one playing a vital role in the wider economy.

All the organisations in Finance Land influence each other and the individuals working for them in several important ways that vary depending on which type of organisation you're talking about.

The following sections introduce you to some of the more common financial institutions and related organisations and explain how each one plays a role in the world of corporate finance.

Investigating the incorporated entity

Incorporated entity refers to *limited liability companies* (those with 'Limited' or 'Ltd' after their name) or *public limited companies* (those with 'PLC' after their name). Companies are this book's primary focus (when we write 'company' or 'firm', we mean this type of organisation), and so we start your journey through the world of corporate finance with them.

Companies are a special type of organisation whereby the people who have ownership (the shareholders) can transfer their shares of ownership to other individuals without having to reorganise the company legally. This transferring of shares is possible because the company is considered a separate legal entity from its owners, which isn't the case for other forms of entities such as sole traders or traditional partnerships. This characteristic has a few significant implications that influence the financial operations and status of companies compared to other forms of organisations:

- ✔ **Professional managers typically run companies rather than the owners.** This situation leads to questions about a type of moral hazard called the *agency problem* – the conflict of interest that occurs when managers make decisions that benefit themselves rather than the owners of the organisation they're managing. Often, an individual who holds a very large proportion of a company's shares (usually referred to as the company's *ultimate controlling party*) is also a manager or a director, but generally speaking, companies have the resources at their disposal to hire highly experienced professionals.

- ✔ **The company is taxed on its profits separately from the owners.** In most organisations, the profits are considered the owners' income and they're only taxed as such. In companies, however, the business itself is taxed on any profits it makes and the owners are taxed on any income they receive by owning shares (called *dividends*). The shareholders can also be subject to another tax when they come to sell their shares in the company (called *capital gains tax*).

Noting not-for-profits

In most cases, profits are the aim of a company. The one exception is the not-for-profit organisation, which includes organisations such as Oxfam, many public universities and other organisations that operate within the parameters of a tax-exempt status. Although not-for-profit organisations can still be profitable, their profits must be for the public benefit, and so they can't distribute any profits as a dividend like for-profit companies can. Many not-for-profit organisations choose not to generate any revenues, relying instead on donations. (The complicated process and structure of many not-for-profit organisations, and the rigmarole they have to go through to achieve such a status, means that we don't discuss them in this book.)

  ✔ **Companies have limited liability, meaning that the owners can't be sued for the actions of the company.** Oddly enough, this characteristic also frequently protects managers, though to a lesser extent if the company has been trading to the detriment of its creditors (those to whom it owes money). This type of trading is known as *wrongful* or *fraudulent* trading, which holds managers more accountable.

  ✔ **Companies are required to disclose all their financial information in a regulated, systematic and standardised manner.** These records are available not only to the government and the shareholders, but also to the public, because companies have to file their financial information with Companies House. Shareholders can also request specialised financial information.

The primary goal of companies is to provide goods or services in exchange for money; their underlying objective is to generate a profit. The management of a company is required to act in the best interest of shareholders by increasing shareholder wealth as much as possible (within the boundaries of the law of course), and also to act in the interest of third parties such as creditors, banks and financiers, Her Majesty's Revenue and Customs (HMRC) and other such interested stakeholders.

Discovering depository institutions

Whenever you give your money to someone with the expectation that the person is going to hold it for you and give it back when you request it, you're either dealing with a depository institution or acting very foolishly.

Depository institutions come in several different types, but they all function in the same basic manner:

- ✔ They accept your money and typically pay interest over time, though some accounts provide other services to attract depositors instead of paying interest payments to the account holder.

- ✔ While holding your money, they lend it out to other people or organisations in the form of mortgages or other loans and generate more interest than they pay you.

- ✔ When you want your money back, they have to return it. Fortunately, they usually hold enough deposits so that they can give you back what you want. That's not always true, as everyone saw during the Great Depression in the 1930s, but it's almost always the case. Plus, safeguards are now in place to protect against another Great Depression (at least one that occurs because banks lend out more money than they keep on hand to pay back to their lenders).

The three main types of depository institutions are commercial banks, savings institutions and credit unions.

Commercial banks

Commercial banks are by far the largest type of depository institution. They're for-profit organisations that are usually owned by private investors (though some banks have become owned by the taxpayer of late, such as Royal Bank of Scotland). They often offer a wide range of services to individuals and companies around the world.

Often the size of the bank determines the exact scope of the services it offers. For example, smaller community or regional banks typically limit their services to consumer banking and small-business lending, which includes simple deposits, mortgages and consumer loans (such as car, home equity and so on), small-business banking, small-business loans and other services with a limited range of markets. Larger national or global banks often also perform services, such as money management, foreign exchange services, investing and *investment banking* (investment banks are financial institutions that assist individuals and companies to raise capital), for large companies and even other banks (such as overnight interbank loans). Large commercial banks have the most diverse set of services of all the depository institutions.

Savings institutions

Savings banks are financial institutions that have a primary focus on consumer mortgage lending. Sometimes savings institutions are designed as companies; other times they're set up as *mutual co-operatives,* whereby paying cash into an account buys you a share of ownership in the institution. Companies don't use these institutions frequently, however, and so we don't cover them in the rest of the book.

Credit unions

Credit unions are financial co-operatives. Paying cash into a particular credit union is similar to buying shares in it and offers members flexible savings and loans. The profits of that credit union are distributed to everyone who has an account in the form of dividends (in other words, depositors are partial owners).

Credit unions are highly focused on consumer services, and so we don't discuss them extensively here or elsewhere in this book. However, their design is important to understand because this same format is very popular among the commercial banks in Muslim nations (called Islamic Banks), where Sharia law forbids charging or paying traditional forms of interest (for more on Islamic finance, check out our online bonus chapter at `www.dummies.com/extras/corporatefinanceuk`). Credit unions are also known to charge much lower rates of interest on loans to its customers.

Covering yourself: Insurance companies

Insurance companies are a special type of financial institution that deals in the business of managing risk. A company periodically gives them money and, in return, they promise to pay for the losses the company incurs if some unfortunate event occurs (such as a flood or a fire), causing damage to the wellbeing of the organisation. Here are a few terms you need to know when considering insurance companies:

- ✔ **Benefits:** The money the insured receives from the insurance company when something goes wrong

- ✔ **Claim:** The act of reporting an insurable incident to request that the insurer pay for coverage

- ✔ **Co-payment:** An expense that the insured pays when sharing the cost with the insurer

- ✔ **Deductible:** The amount that the insured must pay before the insurer pays out anything

- ✔ **Indemnify:** A promise to compensate the insured for losses experienced

- ✔ **Premium:** The periodic payments the insured makes to ensure that insurance cover is maintained

You're probably thinking to yourself, 'Hang on. You pay the insurance company to indemnify your assets, but then it makes you pay a premium, deductible and a co-payment and caps your benefits. What's the point?' Yeah, we know. Insurance companies can calculate the probability of something happening and then charge you a price based on the estimated cost of insuring you. They generate profits by charging more than your statistical cost of making claims. Think of it like this: as a nation, people in the UK overpay for everything that's insured by an amount equal to the profits of the insurance companies.

Originally, this set-up allowed companies and individuals to share the risk of loss; each person paid just a little bit so that no person had to face the full cost of a serious disaster. Unfortunately, this situation is rapidly becoming less common, as insurance companies grow in profitability and incur unnecessary overhead costs.

You can insure just about anything on the planet. (Lloyd's of London can insure the hands of a concert pianist or the tongue of a famous wine taster!) The following sections outline three of the most common (and relevant) types of insurance companies as far as firms are concerned.

Public liability insurance companies

Public liability insurance is the most critical type of insurance for companies to have. It covers the potential harm that can befall a company or anyone on property owned by the company when an accident occurs. If a meteor falls from the sky and smashes your head office building, that's insurable!

Health insurance companies

Companies deal a lot with health insurance companies, because they often provide their employees with health insurance as a perk – not to mention that healthy employees tend to be more productive. Health insurance is a popular benefit for employees, because being insured as a part of a large group is generally less expensive than trying to find individual insurance:

- ✔ Group insurance is cheaper than individual insurance, because the probability of large groups of people being rewarded more than they pay in premiums is lower than that of individuals.

- ✔ Group insurance is frequently the only option that allows for coverage on *pre-existing conditions* (conditions that people develop before receiving insurance).

Many companies subscribe to organisations such as BUPA for things like critical illness cover; this can often be invaluable in terms of time in the unfortunate event of an employee becoming seriously ill, because waiting lists on the NHS can be quite long.

Life insurance companies

Life insurance (often referred to as *life assurance*) companies work in a similar way to other types of insurance companies, except that the only time they pay benefits is when you die. Organisations sometimes take life insurance policies on critical employees who have specialist skills or knowledge that can't be easily replaced without significant financial losses. Many companies also offer group life insurance which, like health insurance, is cheaper than individual insurance.

Life insurance comes in two basic flavours: whole and term. Each one has a wealth of variations and additional options. The primary distinction is that term life insurance is paid for a set period and is only valid as long as it's being paid, whereas whole life insurance is considered permanent and builds value over time.

Spotting securities firms

Securities firms provide transaction services related to financial investments, which are quite distinct from the services provided by traditional depository organisations (check out the earlier section 'Discovering depository institutions'). However, many commercial banks have separate departments that offer the services of securities firms, and some merge or partner with securities firms. Other securities firms are completely independent of any depository institution. Exactly what services a securities firm provides depends on the type of institution it is.

Investment banks

Investment banks deal exclusively in companies and other businesses as clients as well as products. In other words, they offer a wide range of services, including underwriting services (see the later section 'Understanding underwriters') for companies that issue stocks and shares on the *primary market* (the market that issues new shares), broker-dealer services for buyers and sellers of stocks and shares on the primary and *secondary markets* (secondary markets deal with shares that have previously been issued), merger and acquisitions services (the subject of Chapter 20), assistance with corporate reorganisations and liquidation procedures, general consulting services for organisations large enough to be able to afford them and other such services related to raising or transferring capital.

Broker-dealers

In case you can't tell from their name, *broker-dealers* perform the services of brokers and dealers:

✔ **Brokers:** Organisations that conduct securities transactions on the part of their clients – buying, selling or trading for the investment portfolio of their clients.

✔ **Dealers:** Organisations that buy or sell securities of their own portfolio and then deal those securities to customers who are looking to buy them.

✔ **Broker-dealers:** Organisations that do a combination of these services. They perform pretty much all the intermediary functions of providing securities services to companies and individuals alike, and they've all but eliminated the need for organisations that specialise in broker or dealer services.

✔ **Discount brokers:** Perform similar functions to broker-dealers, except that they only perform the transactions, whereas broker-dealers often provide assistance by offering advice, analysis and other services that can help their customers make investment decisions. Discount brokers don't perform these additional services.

Understanding underwriters

Underwriters are a special type of insurance company that deal only with other insurance companies. They analyse applications for insurance, determine the degree of risk and associated costs with issuing insurance, and calculate eligibility and price. Some insurance companies have their own internal underwriting departments, whereas others outsource to external companies that specialise only in underwriting.

Here are two special sorts of underwriters:

✔ **Banking underwriters:** They assess the risk and potential of loan applicants to pay back their loans, assisting banks in determining what interest rate to charge and whether applicants are even eligible for a loan.

✔ **Securities underwriters:** They assess the value of a particular organisation or other asset for which securities are being issued. In other words, if a company wants to become listed on the London Stock Exchange, one step in that process is to determine the value of the company, the number of shares to issue and the amount of money the company is liable to raise. Securities underwriters also help with the distribution and sale of the original shares of stock to raise money for the company to become listed.

Finding out about funds

During the early days of the Christian Church, groups often pooled all their assets together and allowed them to be managed for the good of the group. *Funds* are basically the free-market-investor version of this collective idea. Individuals pool their money together in a fund, that money is managed as a single investment portfolio and the individuals contributing to that portfolio (the fund) receive returns on their investments in proportion to their ownership from the returns generated by the entire portfolio.

The point of pooling assets is to make professional investments and investing strategies available to people who otherwise don't have the resources on their own to pursue such investments. Funds are popular options for companies to provide for the retirement of their employees, but companies themselves also frequently trust their investment management to a fund.

Generally speaking, each fund has its own investing strategy, and so investors choosing between funds need to pick one that has a strategy they believe is going to benefit them the most.

Funds come in two types – hedge funds and mutual funds – and although they both have the same fundamental principles, each type has some unique traits, processes, regulations and variations. Table 2-1 provides a quick guide to the main differences.

Table 2-1	Differences between Hedge Funds and Mutual Funds	
	Hedge Funds	*Mutual Funds*
Strategy	Managers have more freedom in their use of investment tools and an ability to change strategy as they see fit.	Managers must adhere strictly to the strategy described when the fund was established and must choose from a rather limited range of investment types.
Fees	Hedge funds typically charge a fee based on the performance of the fund; the better the fund performs in the market, the more the investors pay in fees.	Mutual funds are highly regulated in terms of the amount they can charge in fees and the types of fees they can charge.

(continued)

Table 2-1 *(continued)*

	Hedge Funds	*Mutual Funds*
Shares	Hedge funds pool the assets of the investors collectively and invest them.	Mutual funds sell shares from a pool and they come in two types: *open-end* and indefinite (no restrictions apply on the number of shares issued and the fund buys back shares as they're sold by investors); or *closed-end* (traded like shares).

Obtaining other loans: Financing institutions

Financing institutions are a bit like banks in that they lend money, but they're different in two main ways:

- ✔ They tend to give different types of loans than banks do.
- ✔ They get their funding by borrowing it themselves instead of through deposits. They earn a profit by charging you higher interest rates than they're paying on their own loans.

Sales financing institutions

Sales financing institutions work with individuals and companies making large purchases.

If you've visited a car dealership, a furniture or jewellery shop, or some other retailer that deals in expensive goods, the chances are that you've been offered a loan that you can use to purchase an item immediately and then pay it off in instalments. Well, the shop itself isn't offering you the loan; a type of financing institution called a *sales financing institution* works with the store to give you the loan.

Personal credit institutions

Personal credit institutions are companies that offer small personal loans and credit cards to individuals. They don't have much to do with corporate finance – unless the personal credit institution itself is a company or you're using your personal line of credit to invest in a company (in which case, as long as your returns exceed the interest you're paying, good for you) – and so we don't cover this topic in this book.

Business credit institutions

Commercial organisations can get credit cards and credit loans just as you can, and those credit loans come from a type of financing institution called a *business credit institution.* Business credit loans differ from standard business loans in that they're a line of credit in the same manner as your credit card. These loans can be freely increased or gradually paid off within certain limits as long as the company makes periodic minimum payments on the balance.

A special type of business credit institution, called a *captive financing company,* is a company that's owned by another organisation and handles the financing and credit for that organisation only, instead of for any applicants. For example, GMAC, the financing arm of General Motors, which changed its name to Ally Bank, is the captive financing company for the company General Motors.

Loan sharks and subprime lenders

All the lending we discuss in this chapter is at the *prime rate,* which is the interest rate charged to customers who are considered to be at little or no risk of defaulting. In the UK, the prime rate is about 3 per cent above the interest rate that banks charge each other (called the London Interbank Offered Rate, or LIBOR). But companies and people who are considered higher risk often qualify only for loans considered *subprime,* which are offered at interest rates higher than the prime rate.

For a period between the 1980s and 1990s, subprime mortgage lenders were very common. In fact, they contributed to the 2007 financial collapse, when many commercial banks were venturing into the subprime market with little or inappropriate risk management.

Another form of high-interest loan is called the *payday loan,* which basically makes *loan sharks* legal (organisations that offer loans at rates above the legal level and who often have heavy-handed tactics). The payday loan company gives you money for a short period, usually only one to two weeks, and charges several hundred (sometimes thousand) per cent in annual percentage rate, in addition to fees and penalties. Rather than breaking your knees, as the stereotype would have it, these lenders simply annihilate your credit score and financial wellbeing. As a result, the UK is currently targeting these types of lenders with a view to making them more responsible in their lending tactics by placing onerous regulations on them.

The bottom line is: avoid loan sharks and subprime lenders at all costs, or else they ruin your finances and the greater economy.

Buying and selling shares: Stock markets

Stock markets (or *exchanges*) such as the FTSE 100, NASDAQ, Nikkei and others are globally renowned for being open forums for ferocious trading. In stock and commodities exchanges, the most recognised space is called the *pit,* or trading floor, where large numbers of brokers and dealers shout and scream at each other, buying, selling and trading shares of this or that.

Of course, computers are now replacing much of this in-your-face activity. Even on the trading floor itself, computers are becoming ever-present, while the number of people who vigorously declare their intentions to anyone within a two-mile radius is rapidly shrinking.

The function of the exchanges themselves is more about providing a place for these trading activities to occur than anything else, making them increasingly irrelevant, with modern technological advances in investing transactions making trading easier.

Setting the rules: Regulatory bodies

Numerous regulatory bodies oversee corporate finances and financial institutions, and each one warrants its own book (in fact, the roles and regulations encompassing each regulatory body span volumes of books of information). We obviously can't fit all that information in this book, and so we just cover the basics of the main UK regulatory bodies here (you can use their names and main purposes to do a quick online search to find out more about the ones that interest you most):

- **Bank of England:** Sets interest rates and decides on levels of *quantitative easing* (an unconventional monetary policy where the Bank of England buys financial assets from commercial banks and other private institutions to increase the monetary base) in times of economic difficulty (such as a recession). Check out the next section 'Banking on the Bank of England' for details.

- **Chartered Financial Analyst Society United Kingdom:** The professional organisation that regulates all chartered financial analysts.

- **Consultative Committee of Accountancy Bodies:** A collective group of five Chartered professional accountancy bodies as follows: Association of Chartered Certified Accountants; Chartered Institute of Public Finance and Accountancy; Institute of Chartered Accountants in England and Wales; Chartered Accountants Ireland; and Institute of Chartered Accountants in Scotland.

A profusion of bodies

We're not sure what the collective term is for finance regulatory bodies (a 'forfeit', perhaps, or a 'mulct'), but undoubtedly plenty provide oversight and regulation around the world. Although many nations are beginning to adopt international financial reporting standards (IFRS), which may limit the need for individual national accounting standards, the standards boards are likely to remain in most countries even after they adopt IFRS.

Looking at all the regulatory bodies that regulate other regulatory bodies, we believe that the industry as a whole may welcome some streamlining – not less regulation, necessarily (that's a far more complicated debate), but less bureaucracy.

✔ **Financial Conduct Authority:** A quasi-governmental organisation employing 3,000 people that's in charge of setting and enforcing regulations among its member groups (who directly employ over one million people between them), which include brokerage firms and exchange markets.

✔ **Financial Reporting Council:** An organisation that creates the UK's Generally Accepted Accounting Practice (GAAP), which is used for preparing financial statements in the UK.

✔ **HMRC:** Handles all tax reporting, tax accounting, tax collection and pretty much all taxation issues (other than determining the tax rates).

✔ **HM Treasury:** A government department responsible for developing (and executing) the government's public finance and economic policy (flip to the later section 'Governing policy: HM Treasury' for more).

✔ **Institute for Fiscal Studies:** Britain's leading independent research institute on public finances, tax and welfare policy, tax legislation, inequality and poverty, pensions, productivity and innovation, consumer behaviour and the evaluation of policies designed to promote development in poor countries.

✔ **London Stock Exchange:** Sets the standards for corporate public financial reporting, the rules for investment and the regulations for securities exchanges.

Banking on the Bank of England

The Bank of England is what we call a *central bank* and is owned by the Treasury Solicitor (the largest in-house legal organisation in the UK's Government and Legal Service) on behalf of the government and is an independent public organisation authorised to print money in the UK. Its current headquarters are situated on Threadneedle Street in London.

The Bank of England accepts deposits, makes loans to member banks and facilitates loans between banks using the deposits. It also determines interest rates for certain key loans and the *bank reserve requirement,* which is the proportion of total deposits that commercial banks must keep available as liquid cash. Bank reserve requirements are used to manage bank liquidity for customer withdrawals and to manage the supply of money in the nation as a whole.

The Bank also sets the UK's interest rate through its Monetary Policy Committee (MPC) and each month it announces whether the rate of interest in the UK is going to rise, fall or remain static. At the time of writing this book, the UK's interest rate remains at 0.5 per cent (which has been stable for a few years following the collapse of the economy). The Treasury also has the power to give orders to the MPC in extreme economic circumstances if such orders are considered to be in the public interest (though such orders have to be endorsed by Parliament within 28 days).

Companies need to know that one of the main functions of the Bank (among performing the usual functions of a central bank) is to maintain price stability (by controlling inflation) and support the economic policies of the UK's government, which in turn promotes economic growth. When the economy is growing, businesses tend to do well; when the economy shrinks, trouble looms for companies.

The Bank of England tries to strike a balance between inflation and interest rates, because when interest rates are low it encourages people to go out and spend their money. But this spending promotes growth and feeds inflation (the by-product of a growing economy). If the Bank of England decides that the economy is growing at such a pace that demand is going to exceed supply, it can raise interest rates to slow down the amount of cash that enters the economy.

Governing policy: HM Treasury

The Treasury is a division of the UK government and is, quite possibly, the simplest arm of the government to understand, at least regarding finance. The Treasury is responsible for developing and executing the government's public finance and economic policy. The Chancellor of the Exchequer is the Minister responsible for the Treasury.

The Treasury is responsible for maintaining the Combined Online Information System (COINS), which contains a detailed analysis of departmental spending under loads of category headings (see http://data.gov.uk/dataset/coins).

Meeting the Inhabitants of Finance Land

Of course, corporate finance people are tall (even the short ones), attractive, well-dressed and smell positively delightful. You may not notice because they tend to be hidden away number-crunching all the time, but you can take our word for it.

A wide variety of positions are available in corporate finance; we cover some of the more common ones in the following sections.

Starting at entry-level positions

The entry-level positions in corporate finance are typically the same as the ones you see in accountancy:

- **Accounts clerks and other paperwork processing:** People who work on data entry; think Charles Dickens's character Bob Cratchit from *A Christmas Carol.*
- **Credit control:** The people who process incoming payments and money owed.
- **Payroll:** The people who make sure that you (and the rest of your company) get paid.
- **Purchase ledger clerks:** The people who process outgoing payments and money owed to others.

Typically, you don't get to do any calculations, offer recommendations or make decisions until you're out of these entry-level positions.

Researching the analysts

Analysts have the best job in the financial world, as far as we're concerned. They get to do vast amounts of research and analysis to generate useful information from data or to investigate as yet unstudied scenarios.

Normally, analysts receive budget information or corporate financial information and are told to do the calculations necessary to make recommendations. Often these projects are fairly broad, and analysts have to model new forms of calculations, assess market trends and make other similar efforts that require a degree of creativity and innovation.

Checking the auditors

As you're typing on the computer and spell a word incorrectly, the spell-checker more than likely corrects you. *Auditors* are a bit like the spell-checkers for corporate finance. They go back and check the work of all the other finance professionals, making sure that everything is accurate, correct and done properly.

They're also sometimes the ones who discover cases of fraud or theft. A special type of auditing, where auditors do their calculations for the purpose of presenting them in court, is called *forensic accounting.*

If forensic accounting interests you, why not get hold of *Forensic Accounting For Dummies* by Frimette Kass-Shraibman and Vijay S Sampath.

Assessing loss adjusters

Loss adjusters are people who work for insurance companies and analyse your insurance claim to determine how much the insurance company is going to pay for damages and whether your claim is fraudulent or real. Any claim large enough for a company to file is guaranteed to attract a loss-adjuster inspection.

Taking in the view from the top: Executives and managers

Executives and *managers* are the people who make the final decisions based on the recommendations that all the other financial professionals make. In other words, these people take recommendations from analysts and then follow the recommendation or do something else completely.

Although companies frequently try to keep someone from each department in executive positions (in the case of corporate finance, the Chief Financial Officer (CFO) is supposed to be a financial professional in executive management), that isn't always the case. In the UK, the CFO role is often carried out by the finance director.

Making money: Traders

The term *trader* refers to anyone who makes a living by buying and selling investments with great frequency. Unlike investors, who purchase investments with the intention of holding onto them for an extended period of time with the expectation of them rising in value, traders hold onto investments just long enough for their value to rise a little bit and then sell them at a profit.

Any Tom, Dick or Harry can try to be a trader; some will succeed and others fail. The only requirement is that you have some starting capital (in other words, money) or are lucky enough to get a job using someone else's money.

Taking financial responsibility: Treasury officers

Treasury officers are in charge of managing financial assets; that is, for keeping track of cash management, foreign exchange and capital structure. Don't worry – we discuss these topics in greater detail in Chapters 7, 14 and 17.

Often treasury officers are also in charge of risk management, although this responsibility is sometimes given a separate position, depending on the company. (Check out Part IV for more on risk management.)

Considering other finance positions

Every company has a number of positions that are strongly related to finance but different enough to warrant their own categorisation. Economics, for instance, is far broader than finance. In fact, finance is only one sub-discipline of economics. Economists, as a result, do similar work to financial analysts but on a much broader scale and encompassing more than money-related items.

Accountants also have a heavy overlap in finance, but whereas accountants are generally more responsible for recording and reporting, financial analysts deal more in analysis and planning.

Visiting the Finance Land Information Resources

If you're feeling all at sea in Finance Land, like a 2-year-old lost at the market, you can go to plenty of places for additional information. Think of this section as your information desk, pointing you in the right direction for more exploration.

Using Internet resources

The Internet, with its seemingly unlimited ability to provide free, reliable information, has become a great resource tool for people involved in corporate finance.

Be careful when using online sources, because some of them don't verify their accuracy, and you definitely don't want to be misled or lied to.

Here are just a few sources that you can trust:

- ✔ **AllExperts:** This website allows you to ask volunteer experts questions about a wide range of subjects. You post your question and an expert who's been lightly screened for legitimacy answers your question. Check out `http://www.allexperts.com/cl1/17/smallbusiness` for more information.

- ✔ **Companies House:** The UK's database website, which provides easy access to a huge number of financial reports by public companies listed in the UK. Check it out at `http://www.companieshouse.gov.uk`.

- ✔ **Investopedia:** This online encyclopedia focuses exclusively on issues related to corporate finance and investing. Go to `www.investopedia.com` for more details.

- ✔ **Publisher websites:** Many book publishers, particularly for textbooks, provide supplementary information and resources on their websites.

- ✔ **Tutor2U:** Provides simple explanations and introductory information for a wide range of topics, including finance. The info on this site is the kind you'd find in an introductory class, though, and so don't expect anything advanced. Head to `http://tutor2u.net` for more.

✔ **University websites:** Many publish beginner's guides, course supplements and other information useful for people with a range of understanding in corporate finance. These resources can be difficult to find on the websites themselves, though, and so your best bet is to find them using a search engine.

Just type a search for the concept you're researching; if a website has an .ac domain, it's probably a good reference.

Reading print resources

A number of different print sources are available to help you find out more about corporate finance:

✔ **Books:** The one you're reading right now is a great place to start! You can also find several other useful books in the *For Dummies* range. If you're looking for more, ask your librarian to point you in the right direction. In particular, librarians at universities can be extremely helpful because they have lots of books geared toward students who are studying the same things as you.

✔ **Financial reports:** All financial reports made by companies publicly listed in the UK are available for free on request or at many libraries.

✔ **Journals:** Academic and professional journals are an amazing source of information and are particularly reliable because the work is all peer-reviewed for accuracy and legitimacy. The problem is that they also tend to include extremely advanced information – not for the beginner!

✔ **Magazines:** *CFO, Corporate Financier, Global Finance, Project Finance, Finance, Islamic Banking & Finance, Money, Strategic Finance* and many others are great resources. The topic of corporate finance seems to sell a lot of magazines.

Hunting out human resources

Finding the right people to talk to about corporate finance can be difficult, especially when the people who talk the most are the ones who know the least and the ones who know the most are the hardest to find. Here are a few hints to help you get the best, most useful information from the finance people you talk to:

✔ Never trust someone giving you a tip on stocks and shares!

✔ Understand the nature of people's jobs, and don't trust anyone who keeps trying to give you information outside of that job's area.

✔ Make sure that the person you're talking to has credentials of some sort (in other words, they know about corporate finance).

Some people who are frequently willing to chat and who have knowledge of a wide range of finance topics include university professors, financial advisers and qualified accountants who specialise in corporate finance.

Chapter 3

Raising Money for Business Purposes

In This Chapter

▶ Finding money for your business

▶ Borrowing funds

▶ Selling equity to raise cash

*N*o doubt you've heard the saying 'it takes money to make money', which confirms the fact that you need to have capital available to start a business and make more money. Unfortunately, this little saying fails to mention exactly where to get that much-needed capital. Surely some rich entrepreneurs didn't buy the multi-billion-pound business Sony in full from the exorbitant amounts of cash they just happened to carry around in their back pockets? (Hint: the answer is no!) Like nearly all businesses, Sony was paid for, at least in part, with someone else's money.

Companies raise finance in two primary ways: by incurring debt or by selling equity. In both cases, the goal is for the company to acquire things of value, starting with cash and then using that cash to purchase other items such as equipment, supplies and so on. This chapter explores the different methods that companies use to raise money, and who the magical money-fairies are.

Raising Capital

Everything that makes up a company and everything a company owns, including the building, equipment, office supplies, brand value, research, land, trademarks and so on, are considered *assets*. Believe it or not, when you start a company, the firm's assets aren't just given to you; you have to go out and acquire them. Generally speaking, you start off with cash, which you then use to purchase other assets.

For most new companies, this cash consists of a combination of the following:

- ✓ **Owner's personal money:** Money that the owner has converted to equity by issuing himself shares in the company.
- ✓ **Small loans:** This money includes business loans from banks and financiers and government loans. The money obtained through loans is considered a *liability,* because the company has to pay it back at some point. In other words, these loans are a form of debt.

The combination of these two funding sources reveals the most fundamental equation in corporate finance:

Assets = Liabilities + Equity

The total value of the assets a company holds is equal to the total liabilities and total equity that it holds. Because the total amount of debt a company incurs goes into purchasing equipment and supplies, increasing debt through loans increases a company's liabilities and total assets. As the firm's owners contribute their own funding to the company's usage, the total amount of company equity increases along with the assets.

After a company raises the original capital, or cash, it exchanges that cash for more useful forms of capital, such as goods to sell to make sales.

Unlike liabilities, equity represents ownership in the company. So if a company owns £100,000 in assets and £50,000 was funded by loans, the owners still hold a claim over £50,000 in assets, even if the company goes bust, requiring them to give the other £50,000 in assets back to the bank. For companies, an alternative way of raising money other than incurring liabilities such as loans varies a bit because the owners of a company are the shareholders. The equity funding of companies comes from the initial sale of shares, which exchanges shares of ownership for cash to be used in the company. (For more on equity funding see the later section 'Selling Equity to Raise Cash'.)

Acquiring Debt to Raise Funds

When a company needs money, one of the primary options it has available is to borrow some. Now, we're not talking about borrowing a few hundred quid from a friend or family member; we mean borrowing an amount of money sufficient to fund the start-up of a new company, the expansion of an existing company, the purchase of expensive equipment, the acquisition of another company or, if you're the executive of a large bank, huge parties that would put Caligula to shame.

Regardless of what the money's for, when a company wants a loan, it starts by putting together a proposal. For new start-up companies, this proposal comes in the form of a business plan, but whenever a company receives a loan significant enough to influence its capital structure (not lines of credit) it has to present a proposal for the use of the funds. This proposal contains financial information about the company, including detailed predictions for future financial wellbeing, called *projections,* which prove that the company can pay back the loan on time and without risk of default.

For more information about business plans, which you can use in many forms of proposals, you may want to read *Business Plans For Dummies* (Wiley) by Paul Tiffany and Steven D. Peterson.

The following sections explain what a company has to do after its proposal is ready to go, including where to go to ask for money and how to evaluate the worth of a loan and its terms.

Asking the right people for money

After the proposal is in place, companies have a few options as to where to go for the money they need:

- ✔ **Commercial banks:** Banks are common sources for corporate debt financing. These loans work in similar ways to any other loan, where the bank evaluates your ability to repay and planned use of the funds in detail before agreeing to offer the loan. The findings of its investigation determine, in part, the interest rate the bank charges, the amount it's prepared to lend and the duration of the loan. Banks may also include *covenants,* which are conditions that a borrower must comply with (for example, keeping assets at a certain threshold), in loan agreements.

- ✔ **Government loans:** These loans are frequently available, but they're often reserved for special types of companies (usually in a field that the government is trying to promote), firms with a special role in the nation (such as defence contractors) or especially large companies facing the truth that they've been poorly managed for decades and must now resort to begging the government for money (yes, we're talking about the likes of Northern Rock and so on).

✔ **Issuance of bonds:** Bonds, which basically act as IOUs, are a popular form of debt financing. A company goes through an underwriter to have bonds issued, and then private investors purchase those bonds. The company keeps the money raised as capital with a promise to repay the bondholders' money with interest. Bonds come in many different flavours; turn to Chapter 11 for more details.

After a potential moneylender receives the company's loan application, an interview process typically occurs, along with an underwriting process during which the potential lender assesses the borrower for risk, financial ability to repay the loan, credit history and other variables. If the lender approves the loan application, the money is transferred to the company's bank account, making it available for use by the company in a manner consistent with the original proposal.

Making sure the loan pays off in the long run

The responsibility for ensuring that a particular loan is beneficial to a company lies with that company. Every loan (except for those rare *government-subsidised loans* in which the government pays for the interest) incurs interest, meaning that you and your company pay more money back to the lender than the lender originally gives you. (We talk more about the reasons behind interest in Chapter 9.)

Here's a quick look at how interest works:

$$B = P(1 + r)^t$$

This equation says that the balance *(B)* is equal to the principal amount *(P)* times the rate *(r)* exponentially multiplied by time *(t)*. So if your company borrows £100 at an interest rate of 10 per cent for one year without making any payments, the amount of money it owes at the end of that one year is as follows:

$$B = 100(1 + 0.1)^1$$

Therefore, the answer is £110 (because £10 is 10 per cent of £100 and interest is accrued annually for only one year).

When accepting a loan, the goal of every company is to make absolutely sure that it can generate more returns from spending the money borrowed than the interest rate being charged. After all, by keeping the loan, the company agrees to pay back interest as well as the principal (sometimes referred to as *capital*).

So if your company spends the money it borrows in the preceding example on a new machine, it has to generate more than 10 per cent profitability from that single machine in order to make the loan worth the 10 per cent interest rate. Of course, this example is simplified and doesn't take into consideration several real-life variables.

If a company absolutely must raise capital but can't generate enough value to pay back the interest rate, it ends up losing money on the loan. As a result, it may want to pursue an alternative option for raising capital, such as selling equity (which we discuss in the later section 'Selling Equity to Raise Cash').

Looking at loan terms

You have a few different options available when choosing a loan for your company. To make the best choice for your company, you need to be aware of the pros and cons of each loan type. If you're not sure which one is best for you, ask a professional such as your financial adviser or accountant – but not the person trying to sell you the loan. Here are some terms you need to be aware of:

- ✔ **Fixed versus variable rate:** When you take out a *fixed rate loan,* the percentage interest you pay is always the same. For example, if you take out a loan with 5 per cent APR (annual percentage rate, which is your annual interest rate and which must be disclosed in any advertising the bank may do), you're always charged 5 per cent interest per year. With a *variable rate loan,* however, the interest rate you pay changes; the amount of change depends on the type of loan. Variable rate loans come in many types, changing their rates based on another interest rate, a stock market index, your income or another indicator. Some of these loans increase gradually over time and others start low and jump after a period of time (called *teaser rates*).

    Although the wide variety of variable rate loan options is great news for the financially savvy, it can be highly dangerous for beginners.

- ✔ **Secured versus unsecured:** *Secured loans* are tied to an asset, which becomes collateral. In essence, you tell the bank that if you fail to pay back your loan, the bank can keep and/or sell that particular asset to get its money back. With *unsecured loans,* no assets are directly considered to be collateral to which the lender has automatic rights upon the borrower's default of the loan. But default can still hurt the credit history of the company, and a lender can still sue to get its money back.

- ✔ **Open-ended versus closed-ended:** *Closed-ended loans* are standard loans. After your company gets one, it makes periodic payments for a predetermined time period and then the loan is paid back and the business between you and the lender is complete. Think of a closed-ended loan as being like a mortgage, except that it's not used to buy a house. *Open-ended loans* are more similar to credit cards. Your company can draw upon an open-ended loan until it reaches a maximum limit, and it continues to make payments as long as it has a balance.

✔ **Simple versus compounding interest:** *Simple interest* accrues based only on the principal loan. In other words, if a loan for £100 charges 1 per cent interest, the lender makes £1 every period. On the other hand, *compounding interest* pays interest on interest. So if the borrower doesn't make any payments on a loan of £100 with 1 per cent interest in the first year, the lender charges 1 per cent interest on £101 rather than the original £100 in the second year. This type of interest is far more common with bank accounts than loans. (Turn to Chapter 9 for more on these two types of interest.)

If a company goes out of business, any money raised by selling its assets goes first to pay lenders.

Selling Equity to Raise Cash

Raising money by selling shares of equity is a little more complicated in theory and in practice than borrowing money using loans. When you sell equity, in essence you're selling bits of ownership in a company. Ownership of the company is split up into shares and the people who buy these shares are called *shareholders*.

When you own shares in a company, you own a part of that company equal to the proportion of the number of shares you own compared to the total number of shares in issue. For example, if a company has 1,000 shares issued (meaning that this is the total number of shares that make up the entire company) and you own 1 share, you own 0.1 per cent of that company, including any profits or losses it experiences (because profits belong to the owners of the company).

When you sell equity to raise cash, you're really selling the rights to a certain amount of control over how the company is managed in addition to your rights to the future profits of that company.

Selling shares to the public

When a company is getting ready to *go public,* meaning that it's opening up the purchase of equity to the public (or become a *listed company,* meaning that the company is *listed* on a stock exchange), it must first put all its records and reports in the proper format. The London Stock Exchange requires that all UK public companies follow specific criteria for keeping track of financial information and reporting it to the public. The company also has to meet a number of accountability and other requirements. In other words, before becoming a listed company a business needs to act like a listed company. Often this requirement includes hiring a consultant or an investment banker to help make sure that everything is in order. Then, finally, the company can go through the process of becoming established as a listed company and sell shares.

The easiest way to become a listed company is to go through a full-service investment bank. Often this bank can take a company through all the steps, including reorganising it legally as a listed company, registering with the proper regulatory authorities, underwriting and selling shares on the primary market. The legal reorganisation process alone is well beyond the scope of this book; we recommend that you consult a lawyer.

During the underwriting stage, an underwriter evaluates the value of the company and estimates how much the firm needs to raise, how much it should raise to meet its requirements and how much it's likely to raise given the company's current financial health (for example, it may need a loan of £100,000 but a bank might only be prepared to offer £50,000). That same person verifies that the company meets all the requirements for being a listed company and selling shares to the public. After that, the company can have its first Initial Public Offering (IPO).

An IPO occurs when a company sells shares to the public, and so it's the stage that raises money for the firm. After all, the company is going to use the money that people pay to own its shares to purchase things the company needs to operate or expand. The people who buy shares from the company during the IPO make up the *primary market,* because they take part in the initial sale of shares.

After the initial shares are sold to the public, they can be resold over and over again, but the company itself doesn't make any more money. The subsequent selling of shares is just an exchange of ownership between investors for a price negotiated between those same investors. The exchange of shares between investors is called the *secondary market;* it doesn't raise additional money for the company.

Any company, old or new, can have an IPO. All it means is that new shares have been created and registered and are being sold for the first time. If an old company decides that it wants to raise more money and it thinks investors are willing to pay for more shares, it can have another IPO to sell new shares that simply add to the total amount of shares the company has on the market.

Looking at the different types of shares

Like most aspects of corporate finance, shares come in many varieties, but no matter which type of shares your company has, its value increases or decreases based on its performance. Here are three of the main share types, along with their distinguishing characteristics:

- **Ordinary shares:** If you hold *ordinary shares* in a company, you're a partial owner, so that you get to vote in any decisions regarding company policy, the board of directors and many other issues.

  Keep in mind that to be brought to a vote, an issue usually needs to be instigated by one shareholder and then supported by others, at which point a voting form goes out to all shareholders of that company to fill out and return.

  Holding ordinary shares may also give you rights to a share of *dividend payments* (profits returned to the company owners) when they're issued, although this is optional. In the case of company *liquidation* (selling assets after going out of business), ordinary shareholders get whatever value is left over after the lenders and preference shareholders (see the next bullet point) get what they're owed. Finally, holding ordinary shares gives you the right to receive full financial reports from the company.

- **Preference shares:** If you hold preference shares in a company, you get your dividend payment in full before the ordinary shareholders get a penny. That holds true for liquidation as well. As with ordinary shares, being a preference shareholder gives you the right to get information from a company. But the key difference between ordinary and preference shareholders is that preference shareholders don't have voting rights and hold preference shares purely for investment potential. So although you have a right to the ownership and success of a company, you have no voice or control over the actions the company takes.

- **Treasury shares:** When a company issues ordinary shares, it has the opportunity to repurchase those shares on the secondary market as any investor would. When a company does so, those ordinary shares become *treasury shares.* The shares themselves haven't changed at all; they're just owned by the company that the shares represent, so, in essence, the company owns itself. Companies tend to do this (buy treasury shares) because they can generate income in the same way that many investors do, but buying treasury shares also allows them to manage their share price more effectively.

Another share-related term you need to know, although it isn't a type of share as such, is *share split.* A share split occurs when a company takes all its ordinary shares and splits them into pieces. For example, say that a person has 1 share worth £10 before a share split. After the split, that person has 2 shares each worth £5 each. Companies use share splits to increase the liquidity of shares, making them easier to buy and sell and, in the long run, driving up the total value.

This process can easily backfire if demand for a company's shares doesn't already exist from people willing to buy it at the cheaper post-split rate. You may also come across scrip issues (also known as *bonus issues*) and rights issues. A *scrip issue* is the process of creating new shares that are given free of charge to existing shareholders. A company would usually give free shares to existing shareholders instead of paying them a dividend, thereby preserving cash in the business. A *rights issue,* however, is a way for a company to raise cash by selling additional shares to existing shareholders in proportion to their current shareholding. As an incentive for the shareholder to take up a rights issue, the shares are usually sold at a discount (in other words, at a price set lower than the current share price), but this isn't prescriptive and companies can offer a rights issue to existing shareholders at market value if they so wish.

Part II
Reading Financial Statements as a Second Language

Five Types of Financing Activity that Show Up in the Cash Flow Statement

- **Sale of shares:** When a company sells another company's shares, the sale is considered an investing activity. When a company sells its own shares, however, the sale is considered a financing activity. The difference is that a company purchases another company's shares in the hope that it will increase in value, whereas a company sells its own shares to generate income meant to finance the purchase of assets. So when a company sells its own shares, it contributes to a positive balance of cash in the financing activities.

- **Dividend payments:** A company that makes money instead of losing it has to give that money back to the shareholders at some point. It may hold on to that money in the profit and loss account reserves (or retained earnings) to reinvest that money back into the business. If the company does this, the shareholders will get their money back when they come to sell their shares. Alternatively, it might pay out the cash held now in the form of dividends to the shareholders. Whenever a company pays out dividends, the amount of cash the company has available decreases by the total amount of dividends paid.

- **Purchase of treasury shares:** *Treasury shares* are those shares in the possession of the company that the shares represent. In other words, a company purchases its own shares, and those shares become treasury shares. If the company uses cash to purchase these shares, the total amount of cash the company has decreases as a result of financing operations.

- **Loans received:** Companies often accept loans as a way of financing operations or expansion. In some cases, they receive the loan in the form of cash, which increases the total amount of cash they have available. Accepting a cash loan, therefore, translates as an increase in cash from financing activities.

- **Loans paid:** Companies need to pay back the loans they accept, an action they typically do by using cash (banks don't often accept anything other than repayment in cash these days). So when a company gives cash to someone to repay a loan, that cash no longer belongs to the company and the company must deduct the amount from the cash flows from financing activities.

Find out about the problem of companies misleading their stakeholders by manipulating financial statements in a free bonus online article at www.dummies.com/extras/corporatefinanceuk.

In this part . . .

✔ Examine the balance sheet to understand how the value of a company is allocated so that the directors, managers, investors and other stakeholders can assess how effectively a firm's assets are being managed.

✔ Assess a company's profitability by taking a look at the profit and loss account.

✔ Watch with wonder as the cash flow statement tells you about the movement of cash into and back out of a company, and understand the reasons why these cash flows occur.

✔ Turn financial statements' data into numbers that show how a company is performing financially through the wizardry of ratio analysis.

✔ Get to grips with the best ratio and financial calculations for measuring a company's asset management and financial wellbeing.

Chapter 4

Seeing What You're Worth with the Balance Sheet

In This Chapter

▶ Discovering what's what on the balance sheet

▶ Taking a closer look at assets, liabilities and shareholders' funds

▶ Understanding how you can use the balance sheet

*T*he balance sheet is a record of how the value of a company is allocated so that the directors, managers, investors and other stakeholders can assess how effectively the firm's assets are being managed. In this chapter, we explain what each section of the balance sheet means – assets, liabilities and shareholders' funds – and touch briefly on how you can use it.

Introducing the Balance Sheet

The *balance sheet* (sometimes referred to as the *Statement of Financial Position*) is a financial report that's useful to anyone with even the slightest interest in a business, including management, investors, banks, Her Majesty's Revenue and Customs (HMRC) and all other stakeholders. In short, the balance sheet includes loads of important stuff, and so eyes front and pay attention!

The Companies Act 2006 requires that all limited companies maintain a balance sheet and in fact all businesses are highly recommended to keep one. Its main purpose is to show the financial position of the business at a particular point in time (usually a month- or year-end). Unlike other financial reports, the balance sheet doesn't compile financial information over a period of time. Instead, it reports the value of all the assets the company currently has, divided into relevant categories, and also includes the value of the company's liabilities and shareholders' funds, each divided in a manner similar to assets.

Here's the basic formula for the balance sheet:

Assets = Liabilities + Shareholders' funds

So the total value of all assets equals the total value of all liabilities plus all shareholders' funds. If the two sides of the equation don't balance, someone did something wrong and you need to dig around to find the mistake.

Knowing the Weights on the Balance Scale

Everything of value in a company falls into three main categories, each representing a section of the balance sheet:

- ✔ **Assets:** Includes anything of value that currently belongs to the company or is currently owed to or controlled by the company.

  The company purchases all assets by using capital acquired by incurring debt (such as bank loans) and selling shares in the company, and so the total assets must balance with the cumulative totals of the other two sections of the balance sheet (see the next two bullet points).

- ✔ **Liabilities:** Includes the value of all the company's debt that needs to be repaid.

- ✔ **Shareholders' funds:** Includes all the value that the company holds for its shareholders.

Each section of the balance sheet begins with what's least liquid. In other words, the top of each section includes the things that take the most time to be converted to cash. As you make your way down each section, the items included gradually become increasingly liquid or require repayment for shorter periods of time. Stock, for example, is sold to a customer on credit and so it turns into a *debtor* (money the customer owes to the company for the stock it has bought on credit); the debtor pays their debt, which turns it into cash. Therefore, the order of liquidity is stock, debtors and cash.

Assessing Your Assets

Assets include the value of everything the company owns and everything the company is owed. Assets fall into two main categories:

✔ **Current assets:** Those assets that a company expects to turn into cash within one year from the balance sheet date – for example, stock and work-in-progress.

✔ **Long-term assets:** Those assets that will take more than one year to turn into cash from the balance sheet date or that are otherwise not intended to be sold yet (but can be sold, if necessary).

Considering current assets

We now outline the subsections of the current assets section of the balance sheet from least to most liquid.

Stock and work-in-progress

This category includes the value of all supplies that a company intends to use up during the process of making and selling something. It includes the raw materials used in production, the work-in-progress products (partially completed products), finished goods ready for sale and even basic office supplies and goods consumed in production (such as stationery used in offices, oil carried on delivery trucks for regular maintenance and so on).

Tax assets

Tax assets includes two forms of taxes:

✔ **Corporation tax returns:** When a company is set to receive money back on its corporate taxes, that money becomes a short-term asset until the company receives it, at which point it becomes cash.

✔ **Deferred tax:** Occurs when a company meets the requirements to receive a tax benefit but is yet to receive it. For example, a company that experiences trading losses one year can offset those losses against profits made in the next financial year rather than the current year, so that the tax value of its losses is a deferred tax asset that would decrease any corporation tax owed the next year.

Prepayments

When a company pays for some expense in advance, the value of that advance payment becomes an asset (called a *prepayment*) for which the company will receive services in the future.

Insurance is an example. If a company prepays its insurance for a full year, the full sterling amount paid adds to the value of the company's prepayments. Every month the company decreases $\frac{1}{12}$ of the value of that prepayment (each month the company uses up one month's worth of value). In other words, the company uses up its prepaid amount as the service it paid for is provided.

Other current assets

The *other current assets* category is a common one to find on the balance sheet, but it means different things to different companies. Generally, it's an all-inclusive category for any assets that are expected to turn into cash within a one-year period but that aren't listed elsewhere on the balance sheet. Other current assets may include restricted cash, certain types of investments, collateral and pretty much anything else you can think of.

Trade debtors

The *trade debtors* category includes the value of all money owed to a company within the next year.

You need to make the important distinction between money that's owed in the next year and money that's likely to be paid. Unfortunately, sometimes people refuse to pay what they owe, or can't pay due to cash flow problems. In these cases, the debtor remains receivable until the money is paid or the company suspects that the debt is about to become bad (in other words, not recoverable).

If the company thinks that a debt may become bad, it subtracts the value of the account owed from trade debtors and transfers it to a subaccount called *bad debt provisions*. This subaccount includes the value of the money that's still owed and overdue but has yet to be written off as uncollectible (which is considered an expense). Usually, the trade debtors entry appears along the following lines:

Trade debtors (net) + Bad debt provision = Trade debtors (gross)

Cash and cash equivalents

Cash and cash equivalents are the most liquid assets a company has available. In other words, they're the assets that the company can turn most easily into cash because, well, they're already cash.

Cash refers to the money a company actually has on hand, while *cash equivalents* refers to savings accounts and such, from which the company can withdraw cash quite easily (though at times the bank may be able to restrict access temporarily).

Finding out about fixed assets

The fixed assets section includes three main categories, which we describe here.

Investments

The *long-term investments* category typically includes equities and debt investments held by the company for financial gain, for gaining control over another company or in funds such as pension schemes. It can also include facilities or equipment intended for lease or rent. In any case, all the investments in this section are meant to be held for more than one year.

Tangible fixed assets

The *tangible fixed assets* category includes nearly every major physical asset a company has that it will use for more than one year (*tangible* means that you can touch the asset physically). Buildings, machinery, land, major furniture, computer equipment, company vehicles and even assets under construction all qualify as tangible fixed assets. Basically, if you can touch it and plan to use it for more than a single year, it contributes to the value of tangible fixed assets.

Depreciation

The long-term tangible fixed assets used by a company don't last forever. With age and usage, every fixed asset is subject to *depreciation* (a decrease in value). Different companies measure depreciation in different ways, but regardless of the method the total shows up on the balance sheet as a subtraction from the total value of tangible fixed assets. It looks something like this:

Cost price – Depreciation = Net book value

We discuss two of the most common methods for calculating depreciation in the next two sections.

The straight-line method

The easiest type of depreciation to use is called *straight-line depreciation.* Straight-line depreciation is cumulative, meaning that if you report a value in depreciation for a piece of equipment one year, that same amount gets added to the next year's depreciation, and so on until you get rid of the equipment or its value drops to zero.

For example, if you buy a piece of equipment for £100 and each year it has a depreciation of £25, you report £25 of accumulated depreciation the first year and £50 of accumulated depreciation the next year, while the asset's value would go from £100 the first year to £50 the next.

To calculate straight-line depreciation, you start with the original purchase price of the equipment, subtract the amount you think you can sell it for as scrap (known as the asset's *residual value*) and then divide that number by the total number of years for which you estimate the equipment will be in

use. The answer you get is the amount of depreciation you need to apply each year. So a piece of equipment bought for £110 that lasts four years and can be sold as scrap for £10 has a depreciation of £25 each year.

The reducing balance method

The second most common method of depreciation used by UK companies is known as the *reducing balance* method (sometimes referred to as the *diminishing balance* method). This approach works by charging a fixed percentage on the remaining *net book value* (the value of the asset after depreciation has been charged).

For example, an asset costing £10,000, depreciated at 25 per cent each year, depreciates by £2,500 in Year 1, but by 25 per cent multiplied by £7,500 (£10,000 – £2,500) in Year 2, to equal £1,875. Therefore, you charge more depreciation in earlier years and less in later years to reflect the fact that more repair and maintenance costs will be incurred in later years.

This method is most commonly applied to motor vehicles, which depreciate faster in earlier years but require more routine service and maintenance in later years, so that the reducing balance method reduces the depreciation charge in later years to reflect the additional maintenance costs.

Investigating intangible assets

Intangible assets are things that add value to a company but don't exist in physical form (in other words, you can't kick them!). Intangible assets primarily include the legal rights to some idea, image or form. Here are just a few examples:

- ✔ The big yellow 'M' that McDonald's uses as its logo is worth quite a bit because people recognise it worldwide. Imagine if McDonald's simply gave that 'M', which it calls the 'Golden Arches', away to another restaurant. Just imagine how much business it would attract.

- ✔ The curved style of the Coca-Cola bottles, as well as the font of the words 'Coca-Cola', are worth a lot of money because, like the Golden Arches, they're easy to recognise across the globe.

- ✔ The owned patent to new forms of medication can be worth a lot to pharmaceutical companies, simply because the patent gives them the right to produce that medicine while simultaneously restricting other businesses from producing the same drug.

You can't touch any of these examples physically, but they contribute to the value of the company and are certainly considered long-term assets.

Gathering the rest: Other assets

Any assets not otherwise listed in the assets section of the balance sheet go into an all-inclusive portion called *other assets*. The exact items included can vary quite a bit depending on the industry in which the company operates.

Looking at Liabilities

Liabilities include those accounts and debts that a company needs to pay back. Like assets, liabilities usually fall into two main categories:

- ✔ **Current liabilities:** Those that must be paid back, fully or in part, in less than one year from the balance sheet date.
- ✔ **Long-term liabilities:** Those that have to be paid back in a time period of one year or more from the balance sheet date.

Calculating current liabilities

This section lists the current liabilities you find on the balance sheet, in the order from those that must be paid in the shortest period from when they were incurred to those that can be paid off in the longest period from when they were incurred.

Trade creditors

Trade creditors includes any money that's owed for the purchase of goods or services that the company intends to pay within a year. Say, for instance, that a company purchases £500 worth of stationery supplies and plans to pay that amount off in six months. The company adds £500 to the value of its trade creditors. But after the company pays an invoice for the money it owes, it removes the value of that invoice from the trade creditors list.

Deferred income

When a company receives payment for a product or service but hasn't yet provided the goods or services for which it was paid, the value of what the company owes the customer contributes to its *deferred income*. Imagine a customer buying some goods from a catalogue company and the catalogue company doesn't have the goods in stock. The customer pays in advance for the goods but the catalogue company is yet to supply those goods. The catalogue company classes the value of the payment from the customer as deferred income, because it hasn't yet provided the goods to its customer.

Accrued payroll and accrued expenses

As a company uses resources, such as labour, utilities and the like, it must pay for them eventually. But most companies make such payments once every week, two weeks, three weeks, a month and so on, and not upon receipt of the resource.

Accrued payroll refers to the amount of money that employees have earned by working for the company but haven't been paid yet. Not that the company is refusing to pay, necessarily, just that people tend to get paid once every one to four weeks. So until these people receive their pay, the amount that the company owes them is considered a liability.

Accrued expenses works in a similar way and is applied to such things as rent, electricity, water and any other expenses that a company incurs and pays at regular intervals.

Current portion of long-term debt

Often companies pay long-term debt in small portions over the course of several years. The *current portion of long-term debt* that a company has to pay in the next year is subtracted from long-term liabilities (see the later section 'Exploring long-term liabilities') and added as part of the current liabilities.

Other creditors

Companies include any liabilities that they have to pay within the next year and that they don't specify elsewhere on the balance sheet in the liability category creatively called *other creditors*. This category can include a wide variety of things from royalties to interest to rebates and everything in between.

Exploring long-term liabilities

This section outlines the categories you see in the long-term liabilities section of the balance sheet.

Long-term loans

When a company owes money that it expects to pay in a time period that's longer than one year, the value of that money goes into a category called *loans due after one year*. Often this category includes all loans and debt that the company is expected to pay in the long run. Other forms of finance such as mortgage instalments due after more than one year are also shown within this category.

Finance lease obligations

When a company leases an asset through a finance lease, the total capital amount owed on that lease adds to the value of the *finance lease obligations* category of liabilities. As the company gradually pays the lease, each payment causes a deduction from this liability.

Preference shares

Company ownership is measured in shares, but the types of shares vary (see the later section 'Valuing the Company: Shareholders' Funds'). Despite the word 'shares' appearing in the title of *preference shares,* in the vast majority of cases these types of shares are treated as a liability because they entitle the holder of the shares to cash (by way of a dividend or because the holder charges the company interest).

Whenever the shares entitle the holder to cash, or they contain any sort of redemption feature, they're considered a liability in the UK. The dividends paid to preference shareholders are classed as interest payments in the profit and loss account and not as a dividend, because the *substance* (the commercial reality) of the transaction is reported in the accounts and not the legal form of the arrangement.

The *substance* of the transaction in this context is that the preference shareholder is entitled to receive cash from the company and therefore the company has a liability, hence such shares are recognised as liabilities. Where payments to preference shareholders are concerned, they rank higher than ordinary shareholders and also get their full share value in the liquidation of the company if it goes out of business before holders of ordinary shares receive anything.

For more information about shares, check out Chapter 3.

Other long-term liabilities

Any other debts that a company has to pay in a time period of one year or more and that don't fit elsewhere on the balance sheet fall into the category called *other long-term liabilities.* As you may have already guessed, financial statements are designed to be easily understood, not creatively labelled.

Deferred tax

Deferred tax is an accounting concept that aims to smooth out the differences between the accounting treatment of certain items against the tax treatment of the same items. You find deferred tax liabilities in the *provisions for liabilities* section of the balance sheet after long-term liabilities.

Deferred tax balances that are assets (in other words, temporary differences that will reduce next year's corporation tax liability) are shown within current assets in the company's balance sheet.

You see, *accounting profit* (profit before tax) is often, if not always, different to *taxable profit* (the profit on which a company pays tax). This difference arises because some stuff that makes up accounting profit isn't allowable for tax purposes and so gets added back, and events in the current year can have a tax consequence in the future periods.

The most frequent cause of a transaction that's recorded in the current year but has a future tax consequence (giving rise to a long-term deferred tax liability) is the acquisition of a new fixed asset, because sometimes a company can claim generous allowances from HMRC (known as the *Annual Investment Allowance*) that allow a company to claim the entire cost of a qualifying asset in the year of acquisition against its profits. These generous allowances are often (if not always) different to the rate at which the same asset is being depreciated for accounting purposes.

As a result, a difference arises between the *net book value* of the asset (cost less depreciation) and the asset's value for tax purposes (which can sometimes be nil due to the Annual Investment Allowance). This difference is known as a *temporary difference* and gives rise to a deferred tax liability, because the company won't receive the same tax benefit in the next year and so the corporation tax bill will be higher.

Valuing the Company: Shareholders' Funds

The shareholders' funds section of the balance sheet breaks down exactly what value the company has to its owners (the shareholders) and how that value is allocated to them. The amount of value that investors have in a company is equivalent to the amount of total assets the company has minus its total liabilities.

In all cases, regardless of any other variables, creditors always get their cut in a company's assets before investors. Just as you have to take into consideration all the money you owe when calculating your personal net worth, every company must do the same. Owners don't receive anything until creditors (suppliers, financiers, HMRC and so on) get what's owed to them.

This section describes the subsections that fall under the shareholders' funds section of the balance sheet. The first two cover different types of shares, while the next three go over other types of earnings and income.

Ordinary shares

Ordinary shares often give their holders the right to receive dividends and obtain company information upon request. Ordinary shares also come with voting rights that can influence company policy. The balance sheet requires ordinary shares to be shown at their issue price and additional notes are made in the financial statements showing the number of shares in issue and the face value of each share.

Treasury shares

Treasury shares are shares that the issuing company has repurchased. Companies often hold on to treasury shares in an attempt to drive up their own share price with the goal of reselling the shares at a profit. Companies aren't required to list as much information about these shares on the balance sheet, but they do have to include the total value of shares.

Share premium

The *face value* (known also as the *par value*) of a share is originally set by companies and then the shareholders purchase shares as an investment. Sometimes a company issues shares for more than they're actually worth, an act known as issuing shares *at a premium*.

If the company makes an issue of shares at a price that's higher than the shares are worth, a *share premium account* takes the excess of the price paid over the price the share is worth. So, for example, if a company's shares are worth £1 but the company decides to issue shares at £1.50, the premium is the difference between the par value and the price paid (£1 minus £1.50): in this case, £0.50.

Profit and loss reserves

When a company makes money, that money goes to the owners of the company as a dividend or is reinvested in the company. In either case, the money belongs to the company's owners and needs to contribute to the value of their ownership in the company.

For companies, any money that doesn't go to the shareholders in the form of dividends is reinvested in the value of the company as *reserves*. Profit and loss reserves consist of the money that a company makes after all expenses, which it reinvests instead of giving to shareholders.

Using additional notes for the balance sheet

Sometimes actions occur that impact the reported value of a company or some section of the balance sheet. If these actions need more explanation to be understood fully, the company can include them in the notes to the financial statements.

Revaluation reserve

If a company has, say, a building that it subjects to an independent revaluation on a regular basis, any change in that building's valuation is taken to the *revaluation reserve* subsection.

For example, if the building increases in value by £10,000, you increase the asset by £10,000 and put the corresponding entry into the revaluation reserve account (as a credit balance). If in the next year the building's value goes down by £2,000, you can reduce (credit) the asset by £2,000 and reduce (debit) the revaluation reserve by £2,000.

Making Use of the Balance Sheet

The information compiled in the balance sheet is arguably the most important information available for investors and other owners of the company, as well as lenders who need to determine the financial position of the company in order to decide whether to issue loans. The balance sheet's information allows you to work out the financial position of a company at a particular point in time, as well as to whom that value is allocated as the company thrives or fails in its pursuits.

When you apply the information in the balance sheet in the equations we cover in Chapters 7 and 8, you can determine a company's ability to pay back loans, the value of the company's shares and the expected return for investors. Plus, you can use the values you get from these equations to evaluate whether the company is worth any loans issued, how efficiently management is allocating resources, how efficiently the company's production department is working, how effective a company is at managing stock, how efficiently it sells its products, how effective it is at collecting debt and much more.

By itself, the balance sheet shows only analyses related to value. But when you use it together with information from the profit and loss account and the cash flow statement, you can determine how effectively a company is using its assets to generate income, as well as how well it may use income to pay its debts.

Chapter 5

Getting Paid with the Profit and Loss Account

In This Chapter
▶ Surveying the parts of the profit and loss account
▶ Evaluating a company's ability to make money

*H*ow can you tell whether a company is successfully generating wealth beyond the wildest dreams of its owners – providing them with the depths of luxury understood only in terms of ancient mythology – or whether it's dooming them to a life of desperate poverty from which they'll never escape? The answer is by looking at the company's profit and loss account, which explains all about the revenues that a company makes and the costs it incurs, therefore allowing you to evaluate its profitability. Or put simply, the profit and loss account describes whether your company is thriving in its pursuit of income or flushing money down the proverbial toilet.

In this chapter, we break down the profit and loss account in the order that it's completed, covering the total amount of money made, all the additional revenues and all the costs, until you arrive at a profit (or loss, if your company isn't doing so well).

Adding Income and Subtracting Costs: What's on the Profit and Loss Account

Profit and loss accounts come in two types, usually referred to as Formats One and Two (Formats Three and Four also exist but are beyond the scope of this book because they're rarely used):

✔ **Format One** is the most commonly used profit and loss account in the UK and reports the classification of expenses by *function* (cost of sales, distribution costs and administrative expenses).

✔ **Format Two** reports the classification of expenses by *type* (raw materials and consumables, staff costs and depreciation).

A company's profit and loss account works a lot like your personal finances: you start with the amount of money you make and then subtract all your costs to find out how much you have left to put in the bank, buy a new car or go on the holiday of your dreams.

The main difference is that a company's profit and loss account includes more information than your personal income and expenditure account. In fact, a company's profit and loss account breaks down how much money it's making versus how much it's spending into six main groups. Together, these six categories detail the company's costs and revenues, separating them by their source operations. We cover each of these categories in the following sections.

Calculating profitability: Gross profit

The first section of the profit and loss account, called *gross profit,* seeks to calculate the profitability of a company's operations after *direct costs.* (*Direct costs* are referred to as a company's *cost of sales* and we take a look at these costs in the later section 'Cost of sales'.) Its ultimate goal is to determine the company's gross margin.

Imagine that you're a self-employed window cleaner. In this case, your margin (which is usually expressed as a percentage; we look at this number in the later section 'Gross margin') is all the money you make for cleaning windows, minus the cost of the materials you use to wash those windows (for example, soap, water and other supplies), but *not* the cost of your ladder because you use it over and over again.

Sales

Sales is all the money that a company makes from its primary operations. If the company is a retailer, sales includes all the money the company generates from selling retail goods. If the company provides gardening services but also offers tree trimming, sales includes the money it makes from both services. But it doesn't include any money the company makes from other activities outside of its core operation(s). So, no counting the extra money made from selling an old lawnmower.

To get sales, don't subtract any costs yet. Sales includes every last pound a company makes from sales; the costs come into the mix later (see the next section 'Cost of sales').

Some companies refer to sales as *turnover, revenue* or other similar terms. Just remember that the sales figure is always the very first item in the profit and loss account, regardless of what a company calls it.

Cost of sales

To make a product or provide a service, a company has to purchase supplies. For example, a tool manufacturer needs to buy steel; a window-cleaning company needs to buy soap and water, and a tuition provider needs to pay its tutors. Whatever its primary operation, every company adds up all the direct costs it incurs as a result of making its product or providing its service, not including indirect costs (sales costs, administrative costs, research costs and so on), and includes them under *cost of sales* (COS) in the profit and loss account. The very nature of this section lies within its name: it's the cost a company incurs in making or buying the goods that it sells.

Just as the price of petrol changes at the forecourt from time to time, the costs of those things a company purchases can also change. In this situation, it needs to choose how to measure the COS. Here are the three primary ways in which a company can account for the costs of goods sold:

- ✔ **FIFO (first-in, first-out):** With this method, a company uses the costs of those things it purchased *earliest* when accounting for COS. In other words, the first stock items made or bought are the first items to be sold.

- ✔ **LIFO (last-in, first-out):** With this method, a company uses the cost of those things it purchased *most recently* when accounting for COS. In other words, the most recent stock items made or bought are the first items to be sold.

 Be careful with this method! When the new UK accounting standard (FRS 102) comes into play for accounting periods commencing on or after 1 January 2015, this method is no longer permissible.

- ✔ **AVCO (weighted average cost):** Using the AVCO method, the weighted average cost of items held at the beginning of the period is calculated using the following formula:

 Weighted average cost = Total cost of goods in inventory ÷ Number of items in inventory

 The weighted average cost is then used to value COS. But a new weighted average cost must be calculated every time further items of stock are bought during the year.

The value of stock minus costs influences all other financial statements, and so a company has to choose to use FIFO or LIFO accounting or AVCO and stick with that method for everything. If a company chooses to switch from one method to another, it must describe the change, including the calculated change in value resulting from the change in method, in the supplementary notes to the financial statements (see the later section 'Completing the picture: Supplemental notes').

Gross margin

The last part of the gross profit section of the profit and loss account is the *gross margin,* which you get by subtracting the COS from the sales figure. The gross margin is all the money a company has left over from its primary operations to pay for overheads and indirect costs, such as the sales staff, building rent, stationery supplies and everything else that's not directly related to the production or purchase of goods.

When you divide gross margin into sales, you get the percentage of sales that isn't spent on producing the inventory. This percentage is extremely important in evaluating a company's ability to fund supporting operations, plan growth and create budgets. The gross margin, sometimes just called *margin,* also comes into play in a number of ratio analyses that we describe in Chapters 7 and 8.

Finding the costs of doing business: Operating profit

Operating profit is the second section of the profit and loss account and takes into account a company's costs of doing business other than the costs of sales (check out the earlier 'Cost of sales' section). Think of it as a way of breaking down the overhead costs associated with all the standard operations without including any infrequent revenues or costs.

The overall goal of the operating profit is to determine how much money a company is making after taking into consideration all the costs the company incurs during its primary and supporting operations. Here's what goes into the calculation of operating profit:

✔ **Selling expenses:** Includes everything a company spends on selling the products it buys or makes, such as advertising, sales wages or commissions, shipping and the cost of retail outlets. A selling expense may be the advertising cost of opening an entire new retail outlet or perhaps just the cost of a sales team – anything at all related or attributed exclusively to the sales process, whether entirely or in part.

✔ **General and administrative costs:** Covers all the expenses of running a company. The salaries of the finance, marketing, human resources and management staff fall into this category, as do the salaries of everyone who isn't directly associated with making or selling the company's products. Other costs that come under this category include the costs of buildings, utilities, office supplies, insurance, office equipment, repairs and maintenance, and a wide variety of other stuff.

Any time a company spends money on an expense that keeps the company going but isn't related to production or sales, it goes into the general and administrative costs category.

✔ **Depreciation and amortisation:** This category doesn't reveal anything about a physical transition of money from one party to another, but instead simply recognises the use of items that will lose value. The amount of depreciation included in the profit and loss account is the same as the amount incurred during a single accounting period that gets added to the balance sheet (we discuss balance sheets in Chapter 4). Depreciation applies to *tangible* fixed assets (that is, assets you can touch) whereas amortisation applies to *intangible* fixed assets (those you can't touch).

Note, however, that the depreciation and amortisation value in the profit and loss account isn't the same value that appears on the balance sheet, because the balance sheet is cumulative whereas the profit and loss account includes only depreciation incurred that year. But the amount of depreciation incurred in the year does go into the balance sheet's cumulative total.

To arrive at the operating profit figure, you just add up all the costs listed in these bullet points and then subtract that number from the gross profit. Because the operating profit represents the amount of money a company has left over after it pays for all its standard operations, firms need to consider it when planning whether or not to expand, whether to use equity or debt to fund expansion and how much money they can borrow and safely pay back using their primary operations. Operating profit is also useful in other financial analyses, such as liquidity, which we cover in Chapter 7.

Accounting for other costs and revenues: Earnings before interest and taxes

Over the course of doing business, a company incurs costs or generates income from a number of activities that aren't related to its normal operations. The goal in this section of the profit and loss account is to account for all these other costs and revenues, so that the company can make smart financial decisions on debt and knows how much to pay in corporation tax. The final calculation in this portion is called *earnings before interest and taxes, depreciation and amortisation* (EBITDA) and includes the following elements:

- ✔ **Other income:** Includes anything the company does other than its main business that generates income. For example, a company that has an extra office in its building that it isn't using can rent that office out to others, thereby generating other income. Similarly, a company can sell snacks through a vending machine. The money it makes in this way falls into the other income category.

- ✔ **Other expenses:** Includes anything the company does other than its main business that incurs costs. As with other income, other expenses can vary widely. If a company spends or loses money that doesn't belong in any other category, it's included here. Payments for things such as tea and coffee are one of the most common other expenses a company incurs that are usually included in this category.

- ✔ **Profit/loss on discontinued operations:** Whenever a company decides to stop pursuing one or more of its operations, the amount of profit or loss experienced from stopping, as well as the amount generated from running those operations up until that point, goes in this category. In other words, if a company is losing money on an operation and decides to stop it halfway through the period, the amount of money the company lost up until that period is included here. In addition, any money the company receives from selling the equipment for that operation or paying off legal fees for the operation is also included here.

You calculate EBITDA by taking gross profit and then subtracting or adding the different sources of costs and revenues associated with non-primary business operations.

Essentially, EBITDA is the total amount the company makes before lenders and the government get their hands on the company's profits. It's an important value for firms and investors to consider, because this profit and loss account item shows how much money the company is making before it has to pay taxes. For example, a company that's making less money this year than last year generally pays less taxes. So, all in all, EBITDA determines whether a company is able to make money the way it's currently operating.

Considering tax and interest to arrive at net profit

The *net profit* section of the profit and loss account is the last to list costs and revenues and is arrived at after taxes and interest are taken into account. A company pays tax on its profits after interest charges from lenders have been included in the profit and loss account. As a result, the company has to account for all other expenses and revenues and then it can include these final items and determine the company's total profit.

Here's a breakdown of the final items that go into calculating net profit:

- ✔ **Interest income:** A company can earn interest when it has certain types of bank accounts, when it owns bonds or other forms of debt on individuals or companies, or when it purchases money-market investments such as certificates of deposit. All this interest falls under the category of *interest income* in the profit and loss account.

- ✔ **Interest expense:** A company generates interest expense when it borrows money from a bank or other organisation or when it issues bonds. All the interest that a company pays, regardless of where the expense comes from, goes into the *interest expense* portion of the profit and loss account.

- ✔ **Tax on profits:** Companies have to pay corporation taxes on the income they generate. The amount of corporation tax a company pays is based on its EBT (earnings before tax). So if a company has taxable profit of £10,000 in a financial year and it needs to pay 20 per cent in corporation tax, it has to hand over £2,000.

Net profit is calculated by subtracting all interest, tax, depreciation and amortisation expenses from EBITDA (check out the preceding section). Simply put, the net profit is the final amount that a company walks away with after it considers all costs. It includes all revenues and all costs and represents the final profits that a company generates during the period. The company has to choose whether to distribute the money from net profit as a dividend to its shareholders (who own the company) or to reinvest it into the company for improvements and expansion. Either way, the money from net profit belongs to the company owners and must contribute to the value of their ownership in the company.

Including earnings per share

In this section of the profit and loss account immediately following net profit, companies have to include the amount of earnings each individual share they have outstanding and owned by the shareholders has generated. Here are the two main components of this section, aptly called *earnings per share* (EPS):

- ✔ **Basic earnings per share:** Companies calculate the basic EPS by dividing net profit attributable to shareholders by the total number of ordinary shares outstanding. This calculation tells investors how much money each share they own earns during the period. For example, if a company makes £1,000 during a year and has a total of 1,000 ordinary shares in issue, everyone who owns that company's shares makes £1 per share.

✔ **Diluted earnings per share:** A company can issue a number of options that can eventually turn into shares. For example, company employees may be given share options or convertible debt (debt that contains an option to convert into shares at a later date if the owners of the loan note so desire) that may be converted into shares.

The diluted earnings per share does the same thing as basic EPS except that it assumes that all these different holding options have been turned into shares. So a company that makes £1,000 and has 1,000 shares in issue has an EPS of £1. But if that company also has 1,000 shares of convertible debt, its diluted earnings per share is £0.50.

Completing the picture: Supplemental notes

Sometimes events occur that alter a company's profit, but these either don't have a place in the profit and loss account or they require additional disclosures to be made so that the reader of the accounts can see the full picture. Anything of this sort goes in the supplemental notes section of the profit and loss account. Examples include the following:

✔ A switch from LIFO cost accounting to FIFO cost accounting for stock (flip to the earlier section 'Cost of sales' for definitions of these approaches).

✔ An unusual or infrequent event, such as a fire in one of the warehouses after the year-end, where the costs of repairs are significant.

✔ Any discontinued operations or unusual earnings from subsidiaries.

Putting the Profit and Loss Account to Good Use

The profit and loss account is probably the most fundamental of all financial reports. Although other financial reports provide important information, the profit and loss account is the final test of whether a company is succeeding or failing in the pursuit of success – that is, making money.

By itself, the profit and loss account provides valuable information for tracking expenses and revenues, corporate revenue management and dividend policy. But you can discover even more by comparing the same company's profit and loss accounts over a series of years. In fact, by watching for trends in a company's profit and loss accounts, you can identify successes or problems with specific operations that generate costs relative to the amount that the operations contribute to generating revenues.

You can also compare the profit and loss account of one company to the profit and loss accounts of other companies in the same industry to determine how competitive that company is within the industry as well as how it needs to position itself regarding price and volume of output.

When used in conjunction with other financial statements, the profit and loss account contributes to a number of ratio analyses (which we discuss in Chapters 7 and 8) that measure how effectively a company's management manages its assets and how well the company yields returns on those assets. Investors can use these ratio analyses to determine whether the company is generating income and wealth on their share of the ownership in the company and whether it's holding excessive levels of debt that may endanger the value of their ownership sometime in the future.

Chapter 6

Easy Come, Easy Go: Understanding the Cash Flow Statement

In This Chapter

▶ Identifying what makes up the cash flow statement

▶ Putting the cash flow statement to good use

*W*ithout doubt, cash is extremely useful. In fact, everyone likes having some cash available. Sometimes people use it to purchase things of value, such as homes, investments and so on. At other times they take things of value and turn them into cash to use for other purposes, such as selling their time and efforts (both of which have value) to employers for cash so that they can then turn that cash into a mortgage payment (or perhaps a weekend away on holiday).

In this chapter, we discuss the cash flow statement, which is the financial record that tells people about the movement of cash into a company *(inflows)* and out of a company *(outflows),* and the reasons why these cash flows occur.

Piecing Together a Puzzle of Cash Flows

Cash and cash equivalents hold a special place in the hearts of managers, investors and lenders. No wonder companies write about cash (and the way they use it) in the form of a financial statement called the *cash flow statement* (sometimes called the *Statement of Cash Flows*). Having assets and value is great, but it's all meaningless unless you can turn it into cash, because cash is the universal medium for transferring all the value a company generates. (Chapter 1 discusses the role of money as a medium of transferring value.)

In Chapter 4, we explain that the phrase *cash and cash equivalents* refers to any money that's currently in the possession of the company or can almost instantly be put in the company's possession by way of withdrawals on bank accounts. Any transaction that appears in the balance sheet or profit and loss account and that influences cash must also appear in the cash flow statement. Not all transactions alter a company's cash flows, but every transaction that does must be part of this statement.

To create the cash flow statement, companies divide cash flows into three separate categories based on the type of business activity that caused the transaction to take place:

- **Operating activities** (check out the following section for a discussion).
- **Investing activities** (the later section 'Buying and selling: Investing activities cash flows' examines this category).
- **Financing activities** (flip to 'Raising capital: Financing activities cash flows' later in this chapter for details).

Each cash flow statement starts with a section on operating activities that lists the transactions that increase cash flow, followed by the transactions that decrease cash flow. The end of each section lists the net cash flow as positive or negative. For example, if a company makes revenues from its primary operations, it would have a positive net cash flow in the first section of its cash flow statement.

Together, the three sections of the cash flow statement determine how a company's different financial operations influence its total cash flows. Management can then use this info to better manage its cash and identify any potential problems that may result from having a lack of cash.

A company can have a lot of assets, but unless it can turn those assets into cash, it can still have cash flow and liquidity problems that may spell the end of the life of the company if management doesn't act quickly to sort out the problems.

Earning or spending cash: Operating activities cash flows

Q: What do you call the situation when a company earns or spends money in the form of cash by performing its primary operations?

A: Operating activities cash flows, of course!

In essence, *operating activities cash flows* include any increases or decreases in cash that result from the primary functions of the company (for example, for a company selling cars, the primary function of the business is the sale of vehicles and cash from the sale of vehicles is cash flow from the company's *operating activities*). Here are some of the most common changes in cash you may see in the operating activities portion of the cash flow statement:

- ✔ **Cash received from customers:** When a customer pays in cash (including via an electronic transfer made between accounts), you count that transaction as a cash increase in the operating activities cash flows. The ultimate purpose of any company that makes something is eventually to trade that something for money, and when that trade happens as a cash transaction, it qualifies as a cash flow.

- ✔ **Cash paid to suppliers and employees:** To make the products being sold to customers, companies have to pay their employees, as well as any other companies that provide supplies. The cash paid to employees and suppliers counts as cash flow, but it doesn't include only cash paid for direct labour. It includes cash paid to everyone involved in keeping the company in business.

- ✔ **Income taxes paid:** Income taxes (such as corporation tax) are considered a part of operations because they're the taxes that result from selling goods at a profit. Companies have to subtract this number from the cash flows from operating activities.

The total amount of cash gained or lost by operations is the *net cash flow from operating activities.* To calculate it, add up the positive values from the preceding list of cash flows from operations and subtract the negative values.

Buying and selling: Investing activities cash flows

Whenever a company purchases or sells any form of investment, including large, long-term assets, the cash flows result in a gain or loss in cash from the total cash and cash equivalents (although they can also *break even,* which is the point of balance between a gain or a loss). Any of these cash flow changes that result from the purchase or sale of investment assets belongs in the *investing activities cash flows* portion of the cash flow statement. Some of the most common transactions that show up in this section are as follows:

- ✔ **Purchases of investments:** When a company buys an investment with cash, the price of that purchase decreases the amount of cash available to the company. No matter what type of investment it is (shares, bonds or something else), the impact on cash influences the cash flows from investing activities.

✔ **Proceeds from sale of investments:** When a company sells the investments it already owns for cash or partially for cash, whatever cash increase the sale generates is considered proceeds from investing activities. Even if the company sells the investment at a net loss (the company paid more for the investment originally than what it's sold for), overall the sale still increases cash relative to the company's cash levels before the sale, because the company already accounted for the cash decrease when it purchased the investment.

The cash flow statement focuses only on cash levels, not company value.

✔ **Purchase of fixed assets:** This term refers to the times when a company purchases long-term assets, usually of a large and/or expensive nature (such as a machine to be used in a company's manufacturing process). Because companies often make fixed asset purchases *on credit* (buy now, pay later), the impact on cash usually happens a little at a time over several periods. For example, when a company purchases a ₤100,000 piece of equipment and plans to pay it off over the course of ten years (with no interest), the annual impact on cash flows is a ₤10,000 annual reduction as the company makes its payments.

✔ **Proceeds from the sale of fixed assets:** Companies can usually sell any used machinery and equipment they don't need anymore (at least for scrap if not whole), and they can even sell land and buildings at a profit as property values increase. The proceeds companies make from these types of sale go into the investing activities cash flows.

✔ **Interest received:** Savings accounts, certain types of short-term money-market investments and a number of other accounts generate interest. This interest comes in the form of cash (whether or not it is actually posted out to the holder, or just written up in a record), and so contributes to a positive net cash flow from investing activities.

This category doesn't include interest generated from investments, because investing isn't part of the company's primary operations (unless the company is a bank or some other financial institution). Holding cash in an account, on the other hand, is a necessity of business operations, and so the interest generated in that regard counts as an operational cash flow.

✔ **Interest paid:** A number of transactions related to operations influence a company's cash balance, including interest financing for the purchase of equipment and stock or other short-term loans or repayment plans. As long as the company isn't a bank or other financial institution, interest paid contributes to the value of cash that must be subtracted from investing cash flow.

When you add up all the positive values from the investing activities portion of the cash flow statement and then subtract the negative values, the answer is the total amount of change in cash the company has had as a result of its investing activities (called the *net cash flow from investing activities*). This number usually appears at the end of the investing activities portion of the cash flow statement. Some people use the analogy of a bucket of water, with the idea being that net cash flow is the amount you've spilled out, or topped up, in the period.

Raising capital: Financing activities cash flows

Financing refers to the process of acquiring capital to fund a start-up (a *start-up* is a brand new company), an expansion, basic operations and so on for which the company needs the extra funds. Most of the time changes in *liabilities* (the debt a company uses to fund asset purchases) and *shareholders' funds* (the ownership purchases whose proceeds are used to fund asset purchases) impact cash, regardless of whether the company is acquiring or repaying the cash. Thus, the following types of financing activities show up in the cash flow statement (yep, you guessed it – in the financing activities portion):

- ✔ **Sale of shares:** When a company sells another company's shares, the sale is considered an investing activity (see the preceding section). When a company sells its own shares, however, the sale is considered a financing activity. The difference is that a company purchases another company's shares in the hope that it will increase in value, whereas a company sells its own shares to generate income meant to finance the purchase of assets. So when a company sells its own shares, it contributes to a positive balance of cash in the financing activities.

- ✔ **Dividend payments:** A company that makes money instead of losing it has to give that money back to the shareholders at some point. It may hold on to that money in the profit and loss account reserves (or retained earnings) to reinvest that money back into the business. If the company does this, the shareholders will get their money back when they come to sell their shares. Alternatively, it might pay out the cash held now in the form of dividends to the shareholders. Whenever a company pays out dividends, the amount of cash the company has available decreases by the total amount of dividends paid.

- ✔ **Purchase of treasury shares:** *Treasury shares* are those shares in the possession of the company that the shares represent. In other words, a company purchases its own shares, and those shares become treasury shares. If the company uses cash to purchase these shares, the total amount of cash the company has decreases as a result of financing operations.

- ✔ **Loans received:** Companies often accept loans as a way of financing operations or expansion. In some cases, they receive the loan in the form of cash, which increases the total amount of cash they have available. Accepting a cash loan, therefore, translates as an increase in cash from financing activities.

- ✔ **Loans paid:** Companies need to pay back the loans they accept, an action they typically do by using cash (banks don't often accept anything other than repayment in cash these days). So when a company gives cash to someone to repay a loan, that cash no longer belongs to the company and the company must deduct the amount from the cash flows from financing activities.

When you add up the positive values of the items in the preceding list and subtract the negative ones, you get the *net cash flow from financing activities.* This value shows up at the end of the financing activities portion of the cash flow statement. As with the other sections in the cash flow statement, a positive balance here means that the financing operations are positively contributing to cash, whereas a negative balance means that they're reducing the total amount of cash available.

Combining the three types of operations to find net change in cash

When you add up all the net cash provided by the three types of company operations (see the preceding three sections), you get the total amount of change to the company's cash and cash equivalents, as follows:

- ✔ **Positive net change:** The company increased its total amount of cash.

- ✔ **Negative net change:** The company decreased its total amount of cash.

In each case that change appears on the balance sheet under the cash at bank and in hand line item in the assets portion (or liability portion if the bank accounts are overdrawn).

A reduction in cash isn't necessarily a bad thing, as long as the operations are positively contributing to the company's overall value. If a company is experiencing negative cash flows consistently, however, the management has to ensure that it manages the company's cash and other assets carefully so that the firm can continue to pay its bills. The *reduction* in cash is the change in cash from one period to the next, but of course the actual cash balance is also important. A *shortfall* in cash is known as a *cash deficit* whereas an increase in the cash is known as the *cash surplus.*

Using the Cash Flow Statement

The cash flow statement is a big deal for lenders who are considering whether or not to lend money to a company. Even if a firm is making money, lenders still want to make sure that it will have the cash available to make payments on its loans. So lenders commonly use the cash flow statement to assess a company's financial health, particularly its ability to maintain consistent positive cash flows to the degree required to pay off any potential new loans.

Lenders, managers and investors frequently use data from the cash flow statement to carry out the following tasks:

- ✔ Measure a company's *liquidity* (the ability of the company to pay its debts and bills)
- ✔ Measure the strength of a company's profitability
- ✔ Evaluate how efficiently a company is using its assets
- ✔ Evaluate a company's financial management regarding its costs of capital

We cover these analyses and others in detail in Chapters 7 and 8.

When comparing data from the cash flow statement for the same company over a period of years, you can evaluate effective cash management and track the sources of cash flows to assist financial efficiency and optimise asset use.

Chapter 7

Making Financial Statements Useful with Ratio Analysis

In This Chapter

▶ Determining whether a company can pay all its bills on time

▶ Evaluating company efficiency

▶ Measuring the ability to generate and manage profits

▶ Using debt ratios to discover how well companies manage debt

*A*lthough accountants may try to convince you that a lot of different things go into building financial statements, by themselves they're really quite useless (the statements, that is, not the accountants). Unless you know what to look for, you can stare at a financial statement for hours and accomplish little more than high levels of boredom. Fortunately, you can overcome this problem by using *financial ratios* (analysis equations) that turn the financial statements' data into numbers that explain how well a company is performing financially. In other words, you take all the data that an accountant compiles and convert it into something that's practically helpful.

Don't worry if financial ratios sound complicated; in fact, they're pretty simple. All you have to do is pick out a few numbers from the financial statements we cover in Chapters 4 and 5 (the balance sheet and the profit and loss account, respectively) and apply some basic maths from your primary school days (nothing more involved than addition, subtraction, multiplication and division).

In this chapter, we break down the most useful financial statement equations into three primary categories that any company can use to analyse its own performance: liquidity, profitability and activity analysis.

The ratios in this chapter are most useful when you compare the results from one company to the results of other companies in the same industry, and to the past results of that same company. When we discuss the variation of the values calculated in these ratios, we use phrases along the lines of 'as the value increases' or 'as the value goes higher', which just means that you can use that interpretation as a general rule, if everything else is the same. Of course, the interpretation of each value is highly dependent on the individual company.

It makes no difference how good your maths skills are when it comes to interpreting financial information – all these ratios are only going to prove as useful and reliable as the information on which you base them. If the financial information on which they're based is meaningless, the ratios will be useless too. Also, bear in mind that you can calculate some ratios in different ways to arrive at alternative conclusions, so some ratios can be quite flexible in the way they are calculated.

If you're involved with businesses that operate in specific industries or have distinct financial requirements, check out Chapter 8, which covers some common special-use equations that help you discover how such companies are performing.

Being Able to Pay the Bills: Liquidity Ratios

Liquidity ratios measure a company's ability to pay its bills. Firms use the equations in this category to measure their ability to pay for the costs of doing business with the assets they currently have available to them.

Look at it this way: if you pay your electricity bill with a cheque that bounces, you can't expect to be able to use the lights in your house for much longer. Similarly, a company that can't pay its bills has to stop output in the near future.

This scenario doesn't necessarily mean that the company is losing money; it just means that it has bills due before it receives its earned money.

Current ratio

You can use the *current ratio* to look at a company's liquidity for the next 12 months. This ratio calculates the number of times a company can pay off its current liabilities, using its current assets. Here's what the ratio looks like:

$$\frac{\text{Current assets}}{\text{Current liabilities}} = \text{Current ratio}$$

Here's how to use it:

1. **Find current assets and current liabilities on the balance sheet (which we discuss in Chapter 4).**

2. **Divide current assets by current liabilities to get the current ratio.**

So if a company has twice as many current assets as current liabilities, its current ratio equals 2.0. If a company has half as many current assets as current liabilities, its current ratio is 0.5.

 The current ratio includes stock in addition to other forms of current assets, and so although a low current ratio may indicate that a company is at risk, it can also simply mean that it's very good at managing a low stock level (great for keeping costs down). In other words, you need some context to make this ratio really useful.

Acid test ratio

Some companies that sell very large or expensive items have a difficult time selling stock. To see whether these companies would be able to pay off their debts due within the next year, you can use a ratio analysis called the *acid test ratio* (sometimes known as the *quick ratio*). This ratio uses all current assets except stock and divides their value by the current liabilities, as you can see in this equation:

$$\frac{\text{Current assets} - \text{stock}}{\text{Current liabilities}} = \text{Acid test ratio}$$

Follow these steps to put this equation to work:

1. **Find the current assets value from the assets portion of the balance sheet (check out Chapter 4 for details of the balance sheet).**

2. **Subtract the value of the stock from the current assets figure in Step 1 (stock will be included in the current assets section).**

3. **Find the current liabilities figure in the balance sheet and divide the current assets less stock figure calculated in Step 1 into current liabilities to get the acid test ratio.**

This ratio shows how many times a company would be able to pay off the debt that's due within the next 12 months using current assets other than stock.

This value is smaller than the current ratio (because it doesn't include stock), but it's still important to consider because it shows whether a company has enough cash and other assets to turn quickly into cash to pay off debts owed and so avoid insolvency. Even so, a low acid test ratio may mean that the company is at risk or that the company is very effective at managing its trade debtors by collecting them quickly.

The moral of the story: be sure to interpret this ratio in the context of the company's trade debtors management.

Analysing Efficiency with Activity Ratios

Activity ratios (also known as *efficiency ratios*) look at how efficiently a company has managed its short-term assets and liabilities (its *working capital*), and they're very closely linked with the liquidity ratios of the preceding sections. Each ratio is calculated on a consistent basis and so you need to use year-end or average values when performing activity ratios.

Trade debtors' days

As a company collects the money it's owed, the total amount the business is owed on average goes up or down depending on how quickly it collects its money. As a result, companies like to know how many days they take to collect an amount equivalent to the average total amount they're owed. They can calculate this number by using *trade debtor days,* which looks like this:

$$\frac{\text{Average gross trade debtors}}{\text{Net credit turnover} \div 365} = \text{Gross trade debtors turnover in days}$$

You follow these steps to employ this equation:

1. **Use the balance sheets (check out Chapter 4) of the current year and the previous year to calculate the average gross trade debtors.**

   Add the trade debtors from both years and divide that number by 2.

2. **Find the turnover (or sales) figure at the top of the profit and loss account for the current year (we discuss this account in Chapter 5).**

3. **Divide the turnover by 365: the answer is the average number of sales the company is making per day in the current year.**

4. **Divide the answer from Step 1 by the answer from Step 3 to get the number of days needed to collect as sales a total value that's equivalent to the average amount of money the company is owed as trade debtors.**

Often year-end trade debtor balances are used rather than working out averages – however the principle is still the same whichever method you use. This tip can apply to other ratios found in this chapter.

Days sales in trade debtors

When a company sells a product and the person who buys it doesn't pay right away, the money that the company collects in the future is called a *debtor*. To calculate the number of days required for a company to finish collecting the money a customer owes it, the firm can use the *days sales in trade debtors* equation, as follows:

$$\frac{\text{Trade debtors}}{\text{Sales} \div 365} = \text{Days sales in debtors}$$

To use this equation, follow these steps:

1. **Find the trade debtors figure in the asset section of the balance sheet (refer to Chapter 4) and turnover (sales) at the top of the profit and loss account (Chapter 5).**

2. **Divide turnover by 365 (the number of days in the year): the result is the average amount of income after costs that the company is making per day in a given year.**

3. **Divide the trade debtors by the answer from Step 2 to get the number of days on average for the company to collect a single debtor.**

The company knows how many sales it made during a year and what percentage of those sales were debtors meant to be collected in the future, and so it can calculate the average debtors per year. As the value of this ratio goes up, the company is taking longer to collect its money. If it goes down, the company is collecting its money more quickly.

Although any sale made on credit becomes a debtor, companies usually collect money for cheap products very quickly. Thus, this particular calculation is really meant more for companies selling expensive products, such as machinery or vehicles. These companies like to plan ahead so they don't spend too much money producing stock before they collect on their existing sales.

Trade debtors turnover

Companies like to know that they're collecting the money that customers owe them. To find out exactly how effectively a company is making sales to collect in the future and how well it's collecting the money that people owe it, you can use the *trade debtors turnover* equation, which you calculate as follows:

$$\frac{\text{Turnover}}{\text{Average trade debtors}} = \text{Trade debtors turnover}$$

Here are the steps for putting this equation to use:

1. **Find the turnover (sales) figure in the profit and loss account (refer to Chapter 5).**

2. **Use the balance sheets (refer to Chapter 4) of the current year and the previous year to calculate the average trade debtors.**

   Add the trade debtors from both years and divide that number by 2.

3. **Divide turnover by the answer from Step 2 to get the trade debtors turnover.**

This equation is called a *turnover* because it measures the number of times the average value of a company's trade debtors turns over - in other words, the number of times the trade debtors have been collected as sales and started afresh with brand new debtors. Of course, the company is still acquiring debtors, and so the trade debtors account is never depleted; however, the average value can still be collected as sales. If the number is very low, the company may be having a difficult time collecting money it's owed.

Trade creditors ratio

When a company buys goods or services from a supplier for which it will pay later, it incurs a *trade creditor.* You can calculate the average number of days a company takes to pay its trade creditors with the following equation:

$$\frac{\text{Trade creditors}}{\text{Cost of sales}} \times 365$$

To use this equation, follow these steps:

1. **Find the trade creditors figure for the current and the previous year in the current liabilities section of the balance sheet (refer to Chapter 4).**

2. **Locate the cost of sales (COS) figure in the profit and loss account (usually the figure underneath the turnover (sales) figure: refer to Chapter 5).**

3. **Take the trade creditors figure and divide that into the COS figure and then multiply the result by 365 (days in the year).**

4. **Appraise the result, which is the average number of days the company takes to pay its suppliers.**

If the number is higher than the previous year, the company is taking more time to pay suppliers. If it's lower, the company is paying suppliers faster than the previous year.

Days sales in stock

Businesses like to know how long they take to turn their stock into sales. You can find the answer by using the following *days sales in stock* equation:

$$\frac{\text{Closing stock}}{\text{Cost of sales} \div 365} = \text{Days sales in stock}$$

Here are the necessary steps:

1. **Find the closing stock figure (the value of the stock listed at the end of the year) on the balance sheet (refer to Chapter 4) and the cost of sales (COS) in the profit and loss account (it's usually underneath the turnover (sales) figure: refer to Chapter 5).**

2. **Divide COS by 365: COS includes the costs of making a product without all the additional business costs (for example, the materials to make the product but not the cost of stationery), and so dividing this number by 365 tells you how much money a company is spending on average per day to make a product.**

3. **Divide the value of the closing stock by the answer from Step 2 to find out how many days a company takes to sell the total value of its stock.**

Of course, the company continues to produce more stock, but measuring the stock at the end of the previous year gives you the amount of turnover (sales) to which you're comparing the days sales in stock. A lower number means the company is selling its stock faster, whereas a higher number means the company takes longer to sell its stock.

Stock turnover

The number of times a company's stock is sold and replenished is called the *stock turnover*. In this context, the term *turnover* means that the total value of a company's stock has been completely depleted and recovered. A high number means that the company uses up its stock very quickly, whereas a low number means that the stock is used up very slowly. You calculate this magical value by using this equation:

$$\frac{\text{Cost of sales}}{\text{Average stock}} = \text{Stock turnover}$$

Follow these steps to put the equation to use:

1. **Find the COS figure in the profit and loss account (it's usually underneath the turnover (sales) figure: refer to Chapter 5).**

2. **Use the balance sheets (refer to Chapter 4) from the current year and the previous year to find average stock (from the assets section).**

   Add the two stock values together and divide the total by 2.

3. **Divide COS by the answer from Step 2 to get the stock turnover.**

Stock turnover in days

When a company makes a lot of a single product, it wants to have an idea of how long selling the entire quantity of that product is going to take. Knowing this fact can help the company estimate how quickly it's going to make money to pay off its bills and how much money it needs to spend on making more stock, so that it doesn't have too much stock or, even worse, run out altogether. Believe it or not, selling something you don't have is quite difficult, as is buying more supplies if you can't sell what you've already made. To avoid these mistakes, companies use the *stock turnover in days* calculation:

$$\frac{\text{Average stock}}{\text{Cost of sales} \div 365} = \text{Stock turnover in days}$$

Here's how to press this equation into service:

1. **Use the balance sheets (refer to Chapter 4) from the current year and the previous year to find average stock.**

   Add the two stock values together (find them in the assets section) and divide the total by 2.

2. **Find the COS figure in the profit and loss account (usually underneath the turnover (sales) figure: refer to Chapter 5).**

3. **Divide COS by 365.**

4. **Divide the answer from Step 1 by the answer from Step 3 to get the stock turnover in days.**

Operating cycle

Have you ever walked into your favourite shop and wondered how long the shop takes, from start to finish, to do everything it has to do to collect its money and complete a transaction? Probably not, but the shop's management and investors certainly have.

The period of time from the minute a company purchases its stock to the minute the final payment on the sale of that stock is made is called the *operating cycle.* You calculate a company's operating cycle by using this equation:

Trade debtors turnover in days + Stock turnover in days = Operating cycle

The two numbers that go into this equation come from calculations that we discuss earlier in this chapter (check out 'Trade debtors turnover' and the preceding section). So, unfortunately, you need to do some preliminary calculations before you can calculate a company's operating cycle, but the extra work is well worth it. After all, the end result is a number that tells you how well a company is managing its assets by calculating how long it takes to make money from start to finish.

As with many of the other equations in this chapter, you have to compare this one to other companies in the industry and against itself for it to be really useful. Aircraft carriers have longer operating cycles than a clothing retailer, for instance, and companies with longer operating cycles tend to have higher liquidity needs.

Working capital

If you were to pay off all your short-term debts, what would the value of your remaining short-term assets be? For example, if you paid off your credit cards, would you have any money left in your bank account? Companies care about this fact and measure it with the *working capital* equation, which tells them exactly what their net value is in the short run. Here's what this equation looks like:

Current assets – Current liabilities = Working capital

Here are the associated steps:

1. **Find current assets and current liabilities on the balance sheet in the assets and liabilities sections (refer to Chapter 4).**

2. **Subtract current liabilities from current assets to get the working capital.**

If a company has more short-term assets than short-term liabilities, its working capital is a positive number. Companies like to see positive working capital because it indicates that they're going to be able to pay off their debts for at least the next year or so.

Turnover (sales) to working capital

The appropriate level of liquidity varies depending on the individual company in question. But you can use the *turnover (sales) to working capital* ratio to help determine whether a company has too many or too few current assets compared to its current liabilities. This equation goes as follows:

$$\frac{\text{Turnover}}{\text{Working capital}} = \text{Turnover to working capital}$$

Here's how you use it:

1. **Find turnover (sales) at the top of the profit and loss account (refer to Chapter 5).**

2. **Calculate working capital by subtracting current liabilities from current assets (both of which you find on the balance sheet: refer to Chapter 4).**

3. **Divide the value of the company's turnover (sales) by its working capital to get the sales to working capital.**

A very high number may indicate that a company doesn't keep enough current assets available to maintain stock levels for the number of sales it's making. A very low number may mean that the company is keeping such a high proportion of its assets current that it isn't using its assets to generate sales.

Watching how a company's sales to working capital varies over time compared to that of its competitors can give context to the other liquidity ratios by measuring how effectively the company is managing its working capital.

Fixed asset turnover

A significant factor of a company's profitability is how well it manages fixed assets, such as production plants, properties, equipment and other assets that contribute to the company's potential output volume. A bigger plant may be able to handle greater production volume, but unless the company is able to turn that potential into actual sales, it's just a wasted expense. That's where the following *fixed asset turnover* equation comes into play:

$$\frac{\text{Turnover}}{\text{Average net fixed assets}} = \text{Fixed asset turnover}$$

To put this equation to use, follow these steps:

1. **Take turnover (sales) from the top of the profit and loss account (refer to Chapter 5).**

2. **Find average net fixed assets by using the balance sheets (refer to Chapter 4) of the current year and the previous year.**

   Add the net fixed assets of the current year and previous year together, and then divide the sum by 2.

3. **Divide turnover by the answer from Step 2 to find the fixed asset turnover.**

Trends in this ratio are a critical element when companies are deciding whether or not to expand their production volume. A high fixed asset turnover means that a company is using its fixed assets efficiently. If a company's fixed assets are already producing at capacity and it has a high fixed asset turnover, it may be able to expand by investing in more fixed assets to generate additional sales. A low fixed asset turnover may indicate that the company has invested in too many fixed assets and needs to increase sales or sell off those assets in order to reduce costs.

Measuring Profit Generation and Management with Profitability Ratios

The purpose of all companies is to generate profits. No matter what a public relations officer or CEO may say on television or to the Public Accounts Committee that's investigating allegations of tax avoidance, the ultimate reason anyone starts a company is to make profits. After all, profits are a company's income. Just as you wouldn't accept a job that doesn't pay wages, no company wants to run a business that doesn't make profits.

Of course, companies can't just charge any price they want and make masses of profits. If they charge too much, customers go to the competition, and so every company is limited in its profitability. The equations we describe in this section are ways to measure how well a company generates profits, as well as how effective it is at managing them.

Return on capital employed (ROCE)

This equation is a common ratio that relates the overall profitability of a company to the finance used to generate it. You calculate the ratio as follows:

$$\frac{\text{Profit before interest and tax}}{\text{Capital employed}} \times 100 = \text{ROCE}$$

Here's how you put this equation to work:

1. **Take the profit before tax figure from the profit and loss account (refer to Chapter 5).**

2. **Add the interest charges figure from the profit and loss account back onto the profit in Step 1 to arrive at a profit before interest and tax.**

3. **Locate the total assets (fixed assets plus current assets) and the current liabilities figure from the balance sheet (refer to Chapter 4).**

4. **Subtract the current liabilities figure from the total assets figure in Step 3 to arrive at the figure for capital employed.**

A company with a higher ROCE is doing better than a company with a lower ROCE and so the higher the percentage, the better.

Net profit margin

The most common measure of a company's profitability is the *net profit margin*. This calculation measures the percentage difference between net profit and turnover (sales). In other words, it measures the percentage of a company's sales revenues that don't go towards business costs. You measure net profit margin as follows:

$$\frac{\text{Net profit} \times 100}{\text{Turnover}} = \text{Net profit margin}$$

Here's how to use this equation:

1. **Find the net profit figure near the bottom of the profit and loss account and turnover (sales) near the top of the profit and loss account (we cover this account in Chapter 5).**

2. **Multiply net profit by 100: you use '100' here to form an answer that's a percentage rather than a decimal number.**

3. **Divide the answer from Step 2 by turnover to get the net profit margin as a percentage.**

The net profit margin tells you what percentage of the total money made by a company increases the value of the company for its owners instead of being spent on costs. But a low profit margin doesn't necessarily mean low profits. A company with a 1 per cent profit margin makes less money on every sale than a company with a 2 per cent profit margin, but the company with a 1 per cent profit margin may make up the difference with a greater volume of sales.

Many books say to divide net profit by turnover (sales) and then multiply the answer by 100. Don't worry, our preceding equation gives you the same answer. Test it for yourself.

Net asset turnover

A company may have plenty of assets, but it still needs to discover how effective it is at using those assets to generate sales. To find out this point, you use a ratio called *net asset turnover,* which uses the company's turnover (sales) figure. You find this figure in the profit and loss account. Here's how you calculate it:

$$\frac{\text{Turnover (sales)}}{\text{Capital employed}} = \text{Net asset turnover}$$

Follow these steps to put this equation to use:

1. **Find turnover (sales) at the top of the profit and loss account (refer to Chapter 5).**

2. **Use the balance sheets (refer to Chapter 4) from the current year and the previous year to find the capital employed figure.**

   Add together the fixed and current assets and take off the value of current liabilities to give a capital employed figure.

3. **Divide turnover by capital employed to get the net asset turnover.**

Assets that don't generate sales cost money. The simplest example is stock: If a company has assets in the form of stock that aren't being sold, it's paying for the storage of that stock without generating sales on it. The net asset turnover equation helps indicate how well a company manages its assets.

Gross profit margin

After a company works out how much it needs to cover the direct costs associated with making and selling a product, it has to discover whether it can cover all the indirect costs that it must pay (those not directly associated with the product itself). You use the *gross profit margin* to calculate the percentage of sales that are left over to cover these other expenses. Gross profit margin looks like this:

$$\frac{\text{Gross profit}}{\text{Turnover}} \times 100 = \text{Gross profit margin}$$

Here's how to use this equation:

1. **Find the gross profit and turnover (sales) figures in the profit and loss account (refer to Chapter 5).**

2. **Divide gross profit by turnover and multiply by 100 to get the gross profit percentage.**

A high gross profit margin is a good thing as long as a company isn't raising prices so high that people stop buying its products. A low gross profit margin may mean that the company is at risk of no longer being able to afford the costs of being in business. It may end up reducing the workforce or stopping operation entirely as a result of not being able to afford the necessary supporting functions to maintain its core operations.

EBITDA/capital employed

EBITDA stands for Earnings Before Interest Tax Depreciation and Amortisation. This equation relates EBITDA to the equity and debt finance used to generate it:

$$\frac{\text{EBITDA}}{\text{Capital employed}} \times 100$$

Here's how to use this equation:

1. **Take the operating profit figure (the profit before interest) from the profit and loss account (refer to Chapter 5).**

2. **Add back the depreciation and amortisation amounts that have been charged in the profit and loss account to find the EBITDA figure (you may need to ask the preparer of the accounts for these amounts).**

3. **Calculate capital employed by taking total assets (fixed and current) from the balance sheet (refer to Chapter 4) and deducting current liabilities from this figure.**

4. **Take the EBITDA figure calculated in Step 2 and multiply it by 100.**

5. **Divide the result from Step 4 by the capital employed figure from Step 3.**

The end result is the EBITDA/capital employed ratio. A higher percentage is a good thing!

Return on assets

Even if a company has loads of assets, the crucial point is how effectively it uses them to generate income. To find out, you use a ratio called *return on assets.*

You may think that this description sounds similar to that of net asset turnover earlier in this section, but the primary difference between return on assets and net asset turnover is that return on assets measures a company's ability to turn assets into profit rather than just sales. In other words, return on assets helps determine whether a company can use its assets to develop profitability, not just a volume of sales.

Here's the equation:

$$\frac{\text{Net profit}}{\text{Average total assets}} = \text{Return on assets}$$

Put this equation to use by following these steps:

1. **Find net profit near the bottom of the profit and loss account (refer to Chapter 5).**

2. **Use the balance sheets (refer to Chapter 4) from the current year and the previous year to find the average total assets.**

   Add together the total assets of the current year and the total assets of the previous year, and then divide that value by 2.

3. **Divide net profit by average total assets to get the return on assets.**

Operating profit margin

The *operating profit margin* measures the percentage difference between operating profit and turnover (sales). This equation differs from net profit margin (which we discuss earlier in this section) in that it concerns itself only with income from operations, excluding a number of costs and revenues (such as *discontinued operations,* which are divisions of a business the company has ceased) that go into measuring net profit. You measure operating profit margin with this equation:

$$\frac{\text{Operating profit}}{\text{Turnover}} = \text{Operating profit margin}$$

To put this equation to use, follow these steps:

1. **Find the turnover (sales) figure at the top of the profit and loss account (refer to Chapter 5).**

2. **Find the operating profit figure in the profit and loss account if it's listed; if it isn't, calculate it by subtracting operating expenses and depreciation from the company's gross profit.**

3. **Divide the operating profit by turnover to get the operating profit margin.**

You may prefer to measure operating profit margin rather than net profit margin, because it's more strictly reflective of how profitable a company's operations are and how competitive a company is in its primary purpose.

Operating asset turnover

How effectively is a company using its operating assets to generate sales? To find out, use the *operating asset turnover* ratio, which you calculate like this:

$$\frac{\text{Turnover}}{\text{Average Fixed Assets}} = \text{Operating asset turnover}$$

Follow these steps to use this equation:

1. **Locate turnover (sales) at the top of the profit and loss account (refer to Chapter 5).**

2. **Find average fixed assets by using the balance sheets (refer to Chapter 4) from the current year and the previous year.**

   Add together the fixed assets of the current year and the fixed assets of the previous year and divide that value by 2.

3. **Divide turnover by average fixed assets to get the operating asset turnover.**

This equation determines how well a company is using those assets used specifically in the company's primary operations to generate sales. Operating asset turnover is different from net asset turnover in that it doesn't take into consideration all assets and it may be more reflective of the company's competitiveness in its primary operations.

Return on operating assets

You use the *return on operating assets* ratio to find out how effectively a company uses its fixed assets to generate profit:

$$\frac{\text{Operating profit}}{\text{Average fixed assets}} = \text{Return on operating assets}$$

To use this equation, work through these steps:

1. **Use the profit and loss account (refer to Chapter 5) to find the operating profit.**

2. **Subtract operating expenses and depreciation from the company's gross profit.**

3. **Use the current year's and the previous year's balance sheet (refer to Chapter 4) to find the average fixed assets.**

   Add together the fixed assets of the current year and the previous year and divide that value by 2.

4. **Divide operating profit by average fixed assets to get the return on operating assets.**

The primary difference between return on operating assets and operating asset turnover (from the preceding section) is that return on operating assets measures a company's ability to turn operating assets into profit rather than just sales; that is, return on operating assets determines whether a company is using its operating assets to develop profitability rather than just a volume of sales. Like other measures of operating assets, this one differs from return on assets in that it focuses on the company's core operations instead of giving an overall picture.

Return on total equity

Imagine that you own equity in a company. As a shareholder you probably want to know how much value the company is making for you. The good news is you can calculate the amount of income a company is able to generate with the equity you invest in it by using the *return on total equity* equation:

$$\frac{\text{Net profit after tax}}{\text{Average total equity}} = \text{Return on total equity}$$

To put it to work for you, follow these steps:

1. **Locate the net profit after tax from near the bottom of the profit and loss account (refer to Chapter 5).**

2. **Find the average total equity by using the balance sheets (refer to Chapter 4) from the current year and the previous year.**

   Add the total equity from the current year and the previous year, and then divide the sum by 2.

3. **Divide the current year's net profit after tax by the average total equity to find the return on total equity.**

Regardless of whether a company has ordinary shares only or preference shares as well (we define the differences in Chapter 3), this ratio takes all equity into account. So if you're a preference shareholder, this is the return on equity you want to be concerned about.

Return on investment

When a company raises funds, whether by incurring debt or selling equity, it invests those funds in purchasing the things necessary to make the company operate. The *return on investment* (ROI) is an extremely common measure that determines how well a company is using those investments to generate profits. In other words, ROI determines whether raising those funds was worth the company's time and effort in the first place.

Here's the equation for calculating ROI:

$$\frac{\text{Net profit}}{\text{Average long-term liabilities} + \text{Average equity}} = \text{Return on investment}$$

To put this equation to work, follow these steps:

1. **Find net profit from near the bottom of the profit and loss account (refer to Chapter 5).**

2. **Use the balance sheets (refer to Chapter 4) of the current year and the previous year to calculate average long-term liabilities and average equity.**

   Add up the long-term liabilities and the total equity from the current year and the previous year, and divide the total sum by 2 to get the total average long-term liabilities plus average equity.

3. **Divide the current year's net profit by the answer from Step 2 to get ROI.**

Make sure that net profit has already taken into account interest expense, to avoid ending up with an artificially high return (interest expense is a cost of capital that doesn't add value to the company).

Evaluating a Company's Debt Management with Debt Ratios

Debt is a big deal - such a big deal that companies value their capital structure based on how effectively they manage debt. Debt is so important compared to equity for three main reasons:

✓ A company can have more debt than assets. Unlike equity, where the maximum equity is the value of all the company's assets, debt can exceed assets.

> ✔ Debt incurs interest that needs to be paid off; equity doesn't.
>
> ✔ As far as the capital structure goes, using debt as a measure usually provides important information about equity as well.

Interest cover

When evaluating a company's debt structure, you need to know whether a company can pay the interest it owes on the debt it has incurred. To find out, you use *interest cover,* which looks like this:

$$\frac{\text{Earnings before interest and taxes (EBIT)}}{\text{Interest expense}} = \text{Interest cover}$$

Here are the steps for using this equation:

1. **Find EBIT (sometimes called *operating profit*) near the middle or bottom of the profit and loss account (refer to Chapter 5) and interest expense somewhere below that.**

2. **Divide EBIT by interest expense to calculate the interest cover.**

An interest cover of more than seven times is generally regarded as safe, with an interest cover of more than three times usually regarded as acceptable. A low interest cover may mean that the company is at risk of defaulting on its debt obligations, which is a bad sign for its level of earnings. But a very high interest earned may mean that the company isn't fully using its available capital and could possibly generate additional sales by acquiring more debt to expand its production capacity, particularly if earnings have reached a plateau with the company already producing at full capacity.

Fixed charge coverage

Interest is only one form of fixed charge on which a company can default. Leases are another particularly common form, but many others also exist. To determine whether a company is going to default on any of these charges, you use the equation *fixed charge coverage.* Although this equation has a few variations, here's the most common:

$$\frac{\text{EBIT} + \text{Fixed charges before tax}}{\text{Interest} + \text{Fixed charges before tax}} = \text{Fixed charge coverage}$$

Follow these steps:

1. **Find EBIT, fixed charges before tax and interest expense in the profit and loss account (refer to Chapter 5).**

2. **Add EBIT and fixed charges before tax.**

3. **Add interest and fixed charges before tax.**

4. **Divide the answer from Step 2 by the answer from Step 3 to calculate the fixed charge coverage.**

This equation is extremely similar to interest cover (in the preceding section), but adding the same value (fixed charges before tax) to the top and bottom of the equation is guaranteed to change the end value.

Fixed charge coverage is particularly important for companies that have a high portion of fixed charges other than interest.

Debt to equity ratio

When measuring a company's capital structure, you need to calculate the *debt to equity ratio,* which tells you the ratio that liabilities compose of a company's funding compared to equity. Here's what this equation looks like:

$$\frac{\text{Total liabilities}}{\text{Shareholders' funds}} = \text{Debt to equity ratio}$$

To use this equation, follow these steps:

1. **Find total liabilities in the liabilities portion of the balance sheet (refer to Chapter 4) and shareholders' funds in the shareholders' funds portion (nothing like stating the obvious!).**

2. **Divide total liabilities by shareholders' funds to find the debt to equity ratio.**

A high debt to equity ratio can mean two different things. If a company also has a low interest cover (see the earlier section 'Interest cover'), it was probably a bit too reliant on funding operations with debt and will have a hard time paying its interest. If the company also has a very high interest cover, it was probably incurring debt to generate funding beyond what it could earn selling debt to generate sales. As long as the extra ratio of debt increases a company's interest earned, the difference in earnings increases the value of equity, balancing out the debt to equity ratio in the long run.

Chapter 8

Measuring Financial Wellbeing with Special-Use Ratios

*N*o one watches a company's finances closer than the people who give that company money. Like a loan shark or the singer Sting, the people and organisations that invest in your company know 'every move you make, every breath you take, they'll be watching you'.

Therefore, you may not be surprised to hear that many of the best ratio and financial calculations available have been developed (and are used) by people with a financial stake in the success of one or more companies. The same information used by many of these specialists is now the gold standard for individuals who want to do some personal investing, corporate management and business analysts wanting to know how well their company is performing for external stakeholders, and employees wondering whether they're likely to have a job tomorrow.

Although some of the calculations in this chapter are *special use,* meaning that they're intended for companies in particular industries (that is, investors, banks and companies with large capital investments), many of them double as measures of a company's asset management and financial wellbeing.

Focusing on Earnings and Dividends with Investor Ratios

The ratios and financial calculations developed and used by investors are some of the most useful for businesses. After all, owning shares in a company is the same as owning a portion of the company, and so investor ratios often relate to profitability in earnings, efficient use of capital and effective asset management.

In addition, because a company's managers are obliged to maximise the wealth of the shareholders (the people who own the company), executive pay is often tied to the performance of the company as measured by the equations that investors use. The following sections walk you through how to use these calculations.

Return on equity

Return on equity is the measure of a company's profitability as a percentage of the shareholders' funds. The equation is similar to return on capital employed (ROCE), which we look at in Chapter 7, but return on equity instead compares the profit that belongs to the ordinary shareholders with the book value of their investment in the business. Therefore, it's an important tool for shareholders. Here's how the ratio looks:

$$\frac{\text{Earnings after tax and preference dividends}}{\text{Shareholders' funds}} = \text{Return on equity}$$

Here's how you use the equation:

1. **Find the profit after tax and preference dividends at the bottom of the profit and loss account (refer to Chapter 5).**

2. **Locate the section called 'Capital and Reserves' or 'Shareholders' Funds' at the bottom of the balance sheet (refer to Chapter 4).**

3. **Divide the profit after tax and preference dividends in Step 1 by the shareholders' funds figure in Step 2.**

4. **Appraise the result, which is the return on equity: a higher percentage is a good thing.**

If you see the return on equity increasing year on year, more profit is being generated as a percentage of the shareholders' funds in the company.

Earnings per share

When you own a company by yourself, the amount of money the company makes is the amount of money you earn. In contrast, when you own a share in a company, you still own a part of the company, but you have to split the amount of money the company makes with everyone else who owns the remaining shares.

To discover how much money an investor makes when owning a share in an organisation, you determine the *earnings per share* (EPS):

$$\frac{\text{Net profit less preference dividends}}{\text{Average ordinary shares in issue}} = \text{Earnings per share}$$

Follow these steps to use this equation:

1. **Find the net profit figure in the profit and loss account (refer to Chapter 5) and preference dividends paid, which may be in the notes to the financial statements or as a reconciliation of equity.**

2. **Use the balance sheets (refer to Chapter 4) to get details of the issued number of ordinary (not preference) shares: if ordinary shares have been issued in the year you need to calculate a weighted average number of shares (*weighted average* means the average number of shares in issue during an accounting period). (For more info on how to calculate a weighted average number of shares see the nearby sidebar 'Calculating weighted average'.)**

3. **Divide the profit after tax, less preference dividends, into the number of shares in issue in the year to find the EPS.**

 Companies always report their EPS near the bottom of their profit and loss account, but having this ratio available isn't helpful unless you know what it means. For investors and companies alike, this ratio is a measure of the distribution of value that the company is generating, and in the UK listed companies are required to disclose EPS in their financial statements.

The EPS ratio doesn't give any indication of the quality of a company's earnings. Two companies with the same EPS may generate their earnings using different amounts of capital, making one more efficient than the other. But EPS is often tied to executive pay, and so management has an incentive to generate low-quality earnings in the short term - just one reason why you don't want to rely on only one or two equations to analyse a company. We discuss the quality of earnings in Chapter 18.

Calculating weighted average

On 1 January 2013, Breary Bricks PLC has 10,000 shares in issue. On 1 July 2013, it issues another 7,000 shares. Say that you need to calculate the weighted average number of shares in issue during the year to 31 December 2013. Here's how you do it:

Date	No. of months	No. of shares in issue	Time fraction	No. of shares in issue x the time fraction
1.1.13 to 30.6.13	6	10,000	6/12	5,000
1.7.13 to 31.12.13	6	17,000	6/12	8,500
				13,500

So Breary Bricks PLC had a weighted average number of 13,500 shares in issue from 1 January 2013 to 31 December 2013.

Dividend per share

Dividend per share is a useful ratio to calculate and is something in which investors are particularly interested; their primary concern is to get as much return as possible from their investment and this return is measured by the amount of dividend each investor receives.

Here's how it works:

$$\frac{\text{Total dividend paid to ordinary shareholders}}{\text{Number of issued ordinary shares}} = \text{Dividend per share}$$

Here's how to put this calculation into practice:

1. **Get hold of the amount of dividend paid to ordinary shareholders, from the profit and loss account (refer to Chapter 5) or in the detailed notes to the financial statements.**

2. **Look at the balance sheet (refer to Chapter 4) of the company (or the notes to the financial statements) and extract the number of issued ordinary shares that the company has issued.**

3. **Divide the dividend paid to ordinary shareholders by the number of ordinary shares the company has issued and the result is the dividend per share.**

In almost all cases the company is more than likely to pay a different amount of dividend each year, but one thing that shareholders don't want to see is their dividend per share decreasing – if anything they want to see it increasing!

Price to earnings ratio

Say that an investor has an idea of the value of a single share in a company but wants to know how the price of the share compares to its value. The first thing the investor needs to do is remember that the market, not the value of the company itself, determines the share price. Then the person can estimate whether the share is over- or underpriced by calculating the *price to earnings ratio* (P/E):

$$\frac{\text{Market price per ordinary share}}{\text{Earnings per share}} = \text{Price to earnings ratio}$$

Follow these steps to calculate the P/E:

1. **Check the stock market online at www.londonstockexchange.com, or ask your stockbroker what the market price per ordinary share is, and then calculate the EPS by following the steps we list in the earlier section 'Earnings per share'.**

2. **Divide the market price per ordinary share by the company's EPS to get the P/E ratio.**

When estimating the P/E, investors tend to look towards the future. The company hopes to continue making earnings over the course of several years, and the market price usually reflects that fact, being many times higher than the earnings of the company. As a result, you need to view the P/E in terms of what market investors think of the growth potential of the company. A high P/E compared to other companies in the same industry means that investors anticipate high growth, whereas a low P/E indicates anticipation of low growth or even negative growth. Sometimes, a company that isn't listed on the stock exchange but which operates in the same sector as a listed company will use a listed company's P/E ratio and adjust this to take into consideration the fact that the company adopting the P/E ratio isn't listed. This P/E ratio is referred to as a *proxy P/E*.

Of course, investors tend to be wrong . . . a lot . . . and so use caution when employing the P/E. Other ratios and calculations, particularly those related to the balance sheet, can help add more context to this measure.

Earnings yield

Earnings yield is a measure of the *potential* return that shareholders can expect to receive in exchange for purchasing a share in an organisation, and it's complementary to the price/earnings ratio in the preceding section.

Here's how it works:

$$\frac{\text{Earnings per share} \times 100}{\text{Market price of a share}} = \text{Earnings yield}$$

To put this method into practice, follow these steps:

1. **Work out the EPS, which you can find in the earlier section 'Earnings per share'.**

2. **Multiply the EPS figure by 100.**

3. **Obtain the share price from the stock market, or a stockbroker, and divide the result calculated in Step 2 by this price to find the earnings yield.**

Investors want to see earnings yield increase, but they do recognise that the earnings yield is only a *potential* one. The reality is that few companies pay every pound of profit out as a dividend – many firms tend to retain some profits to reinvest into the company.

Dividend payout ratio

As we mention in the preceding section, companies can choose to distribute earnings to its shareholders in the form of dividends. Investors calculate the percentage of earnings used for dividend payouts to ordinary shareholders as follows:

$$\frac{\text{Dividends per ordinary share}}{\text{Earnings per share}} = \text{Dividend payout ratio}$$

Here's how to use this equation:

1. **Find the dividends per ordinary share in the notes to the financial statements and follow the steps we list in the earlier section 'Earnings per share' to determine the EPS.**

2. **Divide the dividends per ordinary share by the EPS to get the dividend payout ratio.**

The number you get is the percentage of earnings that dividends comprise. The importance of this percentage is two-fold:

✔ Higher dividend payout ratios are an important part of the portfolio strategies of those investors who like to have a steady income from their investments.

✔ The ratio of earnings that companies pay out in dividends provides an indicator of the company's future plans for growth. Low dividend payout with no expansion may indicate trouble; the same is true for high dividend payout in a growing company. Generally speaking, large or stagnating companies tend to have higher dividend payout ratios, whereas small or growing companies tend to retain those earnings to reinvest in growth.

Dividend yield

What would you be willing to pay for the dividends that a company distributes? For investors concerned with the amount of income they generate from the dividends on shares they own, calculating the *dividend yield* is critical, because it tells them how much income they'll generate in the form of dividends for the price they pay on each share.

Comparing the dividend yield of different companies can help tell you whether you're getting a competitive level of dividend-based income for the price, as follows:

$$\frac{\text{Dividends per ordinary share}}{\text{Market price per ordinary share}} = \text{Dividend yield}$$

Here's how to put this equation to use:

1. **Find the dividends per ordinary share in the notes to the financial statements, and check the stock market or ask your stockbroker to find the market price per ordinary share.**

2. **Divide the dividends per ordinary share by the market price per ordinary share to calculate the dividend yield.**

The dividend yield determines what percentage of the price investors pay for their shares was issued in the last year in dividends. Keep in mind that the amount of dividends issued each year can change, meaning that the dividend yield can be an unreliable measure unless the company you're measuring has a history of maintaining a fairly consistent dividend payout each year.

Book value per share

Investors like to know the value of a share in a company after taking away all the earnings and investor speculation. In other words, if a company were to go bust and liquidate everything it owns, how much would each share in that company be worth? To find out, investors use, in part, the *book value per share:*

$$\frac{\text{Total shareholders' funds less preference shares}}{\text{Total ordinary shares}} = \text{Book value per share}$$

The following steps show you how to use this equation:

1. **Find the total shareholders' funds and preference shares at the bottom of the balance sheet (refer to Chapter 4) and the total issued ordinary shares on the balance sheet under the shareholders' funds section.**

2. **Subtract the preference shares from the total shareholders' funds; the difference is the total ordinary equity.**

3. **Divide the total ordinary equity by the total issued ordinary shares to get the book value per share.**

The answer you get reflects exactly how much value in assets each share is worth, based on the book value.

Book value is the amount that a company paid for its assets and is likely to be higher than the amount it can actually get during liquidation, which is called *market value* (or *fair value*). The book value per share can tell you what the company paid for everything, which would be the optimistic measure, but because the company must pay off all debt before the owners have any value at all, the book value per share shows what the company is worth to investors after all debt is paid off.

Dividend cover

One way to help determine the stability of a company's dividends is by esti-mating the company's ability to meet its dividend payouts using only cash flows that are generated purely from operating activities (*operating activities* are the day-to-day revenue-producing activities of the company). The use of cash flows from operating activities helps indicate whether a company's core operations are contributing to financial strength, which, in turn, helps inves-tors estimate whether related ratios are stable.

To determine how stable a company's dividends are, investors calculate the *dividend cover:*

$$\frac{\text{Operating cash flows}}{\text{Cash dividends}} = \text{Dividend cover}$$

Follow these steps to use this equation:

1. **Find the operating activities cash flows in the operating activities cash flows section of the cash flow statements (refer to Chapter 6) and the cash dividends paid in the notes to the financial statements.**

2. **Divide the operating activities cash flows by the cash dividends to find the dividend cover.**

This ratio can help those investors who prefer shares issuing dividends to determine whether a company is going to continue to have stable dividends. It also doubles as a way for other investors, as well as management, to calculate the competitive strength and financial efficiency of the company. After all, in a way, the cash dividend cover ratio represents the company's ability to generate earnings beyond what's required for the current rate of growth using only its core operations.

Generating Earnings from Interest: Ratios for Banks

Banks rely on a unique type of asset management to make money: they generate the majority of their earnings by charging interest on assets they lend out that were freely given to them in the form of deposits, on which they pay interest. In other words, banks make money by generating more interest income in loans than they pay to their depositors, which is called the *spread*. As a bank lends out a higher percentage of its total assets, it generates more income along with a much higher financial risk.

This unique set of core operations led to the development of the ratios and equations that we cover in the following sections; they're very powerful in terms of assessing liquidity, financial risk and effective asset management. That's not to say that banks' management necessarily use these calculations to make effective decisions, but the information is available to them just as it's available to analysts from any industry.

Earning assets to total assets ratio

Of all the assets that a company owns (referred to as *total assets*), analysts want to know what percentage of them are actually generating income. *Earning assets* usually includes any assets that are directly generating income, such as interest-bearing investments or income-generating rentals, but in some cases it can include other forms of assets that directly contribute to income, such as machinery, computers or anything directly involved in producing goods and services to be sold to customers.

You calculate the *earning assets to total assets ratio* by using this equation:

$$\frac{\text{Average earning assets}}{\text{Average total assets}} = \text{Earning assets to total assets ratio}$$

Follow these steps to get this equation working:

1. **Use the balance sheets (refer to Chapter 4) from the current year and previous year to find the average earning assets and the average total assets.**

   Add the earning assets from the current year and previous year and divide the answer by 2, to find the average earning assets.

   Add the total assets from the current year and previous year and divide the answer by 2, to find the average total assets.

2. **Divide the average earning assets by the average total assets to get the earning assets to total assets ratio.**

For companies that generate their income from loans and rentals, such as banks, a high ratio indicates a very efficient use of assets. A low ratio may indicate a poor use of assets and a need to decrease asset costs or improve volume. For all other companies, analysts can use this ratio to determine how effectively firms are generating earnings with their underused assets.

Companies in any industry can also include assets that are directly involved in the production of their products as an earning asset to evaluate their asset management.

Net interest margin

A good way to determine whether a company is using its earning assets effectively is to look at the proportion of income that's being generated for the value of the company's assets. In effect, you want to know whether the earning assets are making enough money to justify the interest expense or if the company would be better off paying off its debts to decrease the interest expense. To find out, you use the *net interest margin:*

$$\frac{\text{Interest income} - \text{Interest expense}}{\text{Average earning assets}} = \text{Net interest margin}$$

The following steps bring this equation to life:

1. **Find the interest income and interest expense in the profit and loss account (refer to Chapter 5).**

2. **Use the balance sheets (refer to Chapter 4) of the current year and previous year to calculate the average earning assets.**

   Add the earning assets from the current year and previous year and divide the answer by 2.

3. **Subtract the interest expense from the interest income.**

4. **Divide your answer from Step 3 by the answer from Step 2 to find the net interest margin.**

A negative ratio means that the company is paying more in interest than it's generating. For banks and rental companies, this situation means that the company would be better off using its assets to pay off its loans rather than attempting to loan them out. For these same companies, any positive ratio is better than a negative one, but a higher ratio represents a more effective use of assets.

For all other companies that don't generate a significant proportion of their income from interest, you can still use this ratio to supplement other asset management ratios. It isn't very effective on its own, however, because interest expenses are typically related to total earnings rather than just interest income.

Loan loss coverage ratio

Your 'rainy-day fund' is the money you set aside in case you lose your job and stop making money. Companies have rainy-day funds as well, which they measure by using the *loan loss coverage ratio:*

$$\frac{\text{Pre-tax profit} + \text{Provision for loan losses}}{\text{Bad debts expense}} = \text{Loan loss coverage ratio}$$

To use this equation, follow these steps:

1. **Find the pre-tax profit near the bottom of the profit and loss account (refer to Chapter 5), the provision for loan losses in the assets section of the balance sheet (refer to Chapter 4) and the bad debts expense in the expenses section of the profit and loss account.**

2. **Add the pre-tax profit and the provision for loan losses.**

3. **Divide the answer from Step 2 by the bad debts expense to get the loan loss coverage ratio.**

If a bank lends someone money and that person doesn't pay it back, the bank loses that money. Likewise, if a company sells a customer a product and the customer never pays the bill, the company loses that money. Companies need to know how much money to keep on hand to cover these losses. If a company has too much money on hand to cover losses, it isn't using its assets efficiently, but if it has too little on hand, it risks insolvency. Of course, decreasing the bad debts expense is the best option, but a company should always have potential losses covered, as well.

Equity to total assets ratio

Some companies are particularly interested in the proportion of their total assets that's comprised of equity ownership, because this ratio can decrease the amount that they have to borrow in order to generate the same amount of earnings. Maintaining a high ratio of equity to total assets provides a degree of protection against the risk that interest payments will exceed earnings, particularly for companies that generate their earnings from interest on loans or rentals.

You calculate the *equity to total assets ratio* with this equation:

$$\frac{\text{Average equity}}{\text{Average total assets}} = \text{Equity to total assets ratio}$$

Here's how to put it to use:

1. **Use the balance sheets (refer to Chapter 4) from the current year and previous year to calculate the average equity and average total assets.**

   Add the total equity of the current year and previous year and divide the answer by 2; this is your average equity.

   Add the total assets of the current year and previous year and divide the answer by 2; this is your average total assets.

2. Divide the average equity by the average total assets to get the equity to total assets ratio.

Investors like to calculate this ratio because it provides indications that are similar to the debt to equity ratio (which we describe in Chapter 7). A lower ratio may mean that the company is funding its assets inefficiently if it's paying a very high amount on interest expenses. A lower ratio can also mean that the company has very low net value for investors.

Deposits times capital

Deposits are the primary way in which a bank borrows money. A customer pays money into the bank, and the bank must pay that money back on request with interest. The primary difference between deposits and the loans taken by any other company is that deposits are loans that must be repaid on request and are often subject to cyclical fluctuations.

An effective way to determine the number of times over total equity that deposits cover is to calculate *deposits times capital:*

$$\frac{\text{Average deposits}}{\text{Average shareholders' funds}} = \text{Deposits times capital}$$

Use these steps to work through this equation:

1. **Use the profit and loss account (refer to Chapter 5) from the current year and previous year to calculate the average deposits.**

   Add the deposits from the current year and previous year and divide the answer by 2.

2. **Use the balance sheets (refer to Chapter 4) from the current year and previous year to calculate the average shareholders' funds.**

   Add the shareholders' funds from the current year and previous year and divide the answer by 2.

3. **Divide the average deposits by the average shareholders' funds to calculate the deposits times capital.**

This ratio is similar to the debt to equity ratio (check out Chapter 7) in that it can provide an idea of whether the bank's earnings may be volatile or the bank itself may be at risk of insolvency as a result of extremely high interest expense and account withdrawals.

Loans to deposits ratio

An important ratio for banks to calculate is their *loans to deposits ratio:*

$$\frac{\text{Average net loans}}{\text{Average deposits}} = \text{Loans to deposits ratio}$$

Follow these steps for this equation:

1. **Use the profit and loss account (refer to Chapter 5) of the current year and previous year to calculate the average net loans and average deposits.**

   Add the net loans of the current year and previous year and divide the answer by 2; this is the average net loans.

   Add the deposits of the current year and previous year and divide the answer by 2; this is the average deposits.

2. **Divide the average net loans by the average deposits to find the loans to deposits ratio.**

A high loans to deposits ratio means that the bank is issuing out more of its deposits in the form of interest-bearing loans, which in turn means that it generates more income. The problem, however, is that the bank's loans aren't always repaid. Plus, the bank has to repay deposits on request, and so having a ratio that's too high puts the bank at high risk. A very low ratio means that the bank is at low risk, but it also means that it isn't using its assets to generate income and may even end up losing money.

You need to use this ratio in conjunction with other banking ratios, particularly the loan loss coverage ratio (see the earlier section on this for details).

Using Ratios to Measure Operating Asset Management

The ratios in this section are of primary concern for people who manage, own or lend to companies with large capital investments - firms that need things that are very expensive to operate. These companies may be part of the manufacturing industry (which usually requires machines of some sort), the transportation industry (such as airlines, trains and buses) or utilities (such as electricity or water). These types of organisations tend to have an extremely high proportion of their assets held in extremely expensive pieces of capital that are directly related to their operations, called *operating assets.* For example, an aeroplane is an operating asset for an airline.

The big thing that these industries, as well as many others, have in common is that they're heavily dependent on *operating property* (all the large machines, plants or vehicles they need to carry out their business) and long-term debt. But even though the calculations we describe in this section deal first and foremost with these industries, you can also apply every single one of them to just about any organisation to provide a measure of the firm's asset management.

If you're analysing a company with lower levels of operating assets or long-term debt, don't forget to take that fact into consideration and use the ratios in context with other equations and information.

Operating ratio

The *operating ratio* measures the financial effectiveness of a company's core operations. You can use the following equation to calculate this ratio:

$$\frac{\text{Operating expenses}}{\text{Operating revenue}} = \text{Operating ratio}$$

Follow these steps:

1. **Find the operating expenses and revenues in the profit and loss account (refer to Chapter 5).**

2. **Divide the operating expenses by the operating revenues to determine the operating ratio.**

The answer is a measure of the ratio of assets that are taken up by expenses, all related to the company's core operations. For example, if the company is an airline, the operating revenues are ones generated from ticket sales and in-flight purchases, whereas the operating expenses are the cost of the planes, the cost of fuel, the wages for pilots and everything else related directly to the transportation service.

Percentage earned on operating property

After a company has bought its operating property, it likes to determine whether this equipment is capable of generating earnings. You measure the ability of a company's operating property to create income with the *percentage earned on operating property:*

$$\frac{\text{Net profit}}{\text{Operating property}} = \text{Percentage earned on operating property}$$

Here's how to put this equation to use:

1. **Find the net profit in the profit and loss account (refer to Chapter 5) and the operating property on the balance sheet (refer to Chapter 4).**

2. **Divide the net profit by the operating property.**

3. **Multiply the result by 100 to turn that number into a percentage.**

The answer is the percentage of operating assets that has generated income. For many companies, this ratio is the ultimate measure of whether they're investing effectively in their primary operations. A low ratio may indicate that the company isn't investing enough, is investing too much or is simply investing in the wrong assets. A high ratio may indicate that the company is generating a high level of income by using its available assets.

Determining which ratios are high and which ones are low depends greatly on the specific industry, and so for the percentage earned on operating property to be useful, companies have to compare with the competition and current trends.

Operating revenue to operating property ratio

Whether a company is able to make any money by using its operating property is something that managers, investors, lenders and pretty much everyone else want to know. Companies use operating property to generate operating revenues and therefore they calculate the *operating revenue to operating property ratio* as follows:

$$\frac{\text{Operating revenue}}{\text{Operating property}} = \text{Operating revenue to operating property ratio}$$

Work through these steps to use this equation:

1. **Find the operating revenue in the profit and loss account (refer to Chapter 5) and the operating property in the assets section of the balance sheet (refer to Chapter 4).**

2. **Divide the operating revenue by the operating property.**

Having an asset that doesn't do anything to generate earnings is a waste of money. Particularly for companies that have large purchases with long-term usage, determining whether or not those large purchases are generating enough revenue to make them worth the interest expense is a pretty big deal. The appropriate value of this ratio depends a lot on the specific industry in which the company works, and so for the ratio to be useful companies compare their ratio to those of their competitors, as well as watch for annual trends.

The operating revenue to operating property ratio should always be higher than the percentage earned on operating property (see the preceding section). If the percentage earned on operating property is very much lower than the operating revenue to operating property ratio, the company may be experiencing ineffective asset management in non-operating assets or other operational efficiencies.

Long-term debt to operating property ratio

Long-term debt is a critical concern for companies working in transportation or other industries that require a large degree of capital investment. To determine the degree of property that a company funds by using long-term debt, you use the *long-term debt to operating property ratio:*

$$\frac{\text{Long-term debt}}{\text{Operating property}} = \text{Long-term debt to operating property ratio}$$

Follow these steps to use this equation:

1. **Use the balance sheet (refer to Chapter 4) to find the long-term debt in the liabilities section and the operating property in the assets section.**

2. **Divide the long-term debt by the operating property to calculate the ratio of long-term debt to operating property.**

The appropriate level for this ratio depends greatly on the potential growth of the company. When a company makes purchases of large equipment, such as buses, planes or machines, the company increases the total capacity of its business. But these purchases are so expensive that all but the largest companies have to get loans to make them. So you can expect a high ratio for companies that are new or have even a moderate growth rate.

Part III
Placing Valuations on the Price Tags of Business

Five Macroeconomic Influences on the Performance, Value and Price of Stocks and Shares

- **GDP:** Gross domestic product is the total value of all production created in a nation. Increasing GDP is often taken as a sign that the economy is strong and that people should invest more in stocks and shares.

- **The business cycle:** Two or more consecutive *quarters* (a quarter being three-month periods) of negative GDP growth is the current definition of a recession, which is one of the four parts of the business cycle: the others being recovery, boom and slump. The rate of change in growth that an economy experiences changes stocks and share prices quite a bit.

- **Employment:** The ratio of people who have jobs compared to the total workforce. *Unemployment* is the ratio of people who don't have jobs compared to the total workforce. High unemployment tends to harm stocks and share prices.

- **Inflation:** A change in the purchasing power of a currency, meaning that you need more money to purchase an equal amount of goods. High inflation tends to slow stock market value growth.

- **Monetary policy:** Includes any policy regarding the quantity or price of money, such as altering interest rates, bank reserve requirements, the amount of money being printed or distributed, and other related policies. Expansionary monetary policy, such as lowering interest rates and reducing bank reserve requirements, tends to increase stock market prices. Increased interest rates and any policy that reduces the supply of money tends to lower stock market prices.

Companies can engage in tax planning to minimise the taxation effects of capital investments. To read more about this, check out the free online bonus article at www.dummies.com/cheatsheet/corporatefinanceuk.

In this part . . .

✔ Appreciate why the value of money alters over time, and under-stand the role that inflation and interest rates play in this.

✔ Apply a variety of capital budgeting factors to project management.

✔ Explore the different types of bond available and their various issuing institutions, and determine a company's potential for raising money through debt and whether a particular bond is an attractive investment for a portfolio.

✔ Incorporate shares successfully into an investing strategy or portfolio, through knowing a few simple things about how shares are traded, the different options available to you and what factors influence share prices.

✔ Discover how to limit risk, how to generate revenues and how to measure the value of the four most common types of derivatives.

Chapter 9

Determining Present and Future Values: Time Is Money

In This Chapter

▶ Understanding what influences the value of money

▶ Estimating future value

▶ Determining present value

*M*oney has a tendency to change in value over time. We don't mean the amount of money you have, but rather its *value*. In other words, a constant quantity of money tends to be worth less as you hold onto it for longer periods of time. The two primary causes for this decrease in value are inflation and interest rates. A number of variables influence these rates, indirectly affecting the changes in value over time, but these two forces are the most direct causes, and so they're the ones to which you need to pay most attention.

In their ability to change the value of money over time, inflation and interest rates play an extremely important role in how companies manage their liquid assets and their investments. Therefore, to have even a basic understanding of corporate finance, you need to understand what the time value of money is and how it influences companies. Fortunately, this chapter is here to help! We describe how and why money loses value over time, how this change in value impacts companies and how to measure and calculate changes in value over time.

Losing Value over Time

You can measure the value of money in two ways:

- ✔ **Nominal value:** Simply a measure of the number of units of currency you have – that is, the volume of money. For instance, £10 always has a nominal value of £10. Even if it's made of pure gold and is highly sought after by collectors for millions of pounds, a £1 coin still has a nominal value of just £1.

- ✔ **Real value:** Measures the ability of money to be exchanged in real terms for other things. Therefore, real value refers to the purchasing power of money, which includes nominal value plus inflation. (Check out the later section 'Increasing prices, decreasing value: Inflation' for more details.)

Time influences only the real value of money, not the nominal value. So £10 is still worth £10 next year, but it purchases less than it does this year. This distinction is vitally important, because the goal of companies is to ensure that their nominal value increases faster than the real value of each unit of currency decreases. In other words, they want to make more money faster than the money they have loses value.

The following sections take a look at the two main factors that cause money to change real value over time: inflation and interest rates.

Increasing prices, decreasing value: Inflation

Inflation is when a currency's ability to purchase goods (its purchasing power) is diminished – when its purchasing power decreases, causing people to spend more units of currency to acquire an equal quantity of goods.

For the purposes of this book, you don't need to worry about what causes inflation (phew!); instead, you focus on the impact that inflation has on finances after it has already occurred. In essence, inflation is quite simple: you know how things are more expensive than they used to be? Remember how the price of food (a Curly Wurly chocolate bar for 2½ pence anyone?), petrol (at £1 a gallon?) and many other consumer goods used to be lower than now? That's inflation.

Imagine that inflation is 2 per cent per year on average. That means that every single year, you need 2 per cent more money to purchase goods than you did the year before. If people make 2 per cent more money in wages than they did the year before, people are earning and spending more money to maintain the same quality of life.

Here's another example: if inflation is 2 per cent per year and you put £100 under the bed, over the course of 10 years that £100 loses 20 per cent of its value as measured by its ability to purchase goods.

Inflation can also work in reverse. *Deflation* occurs when money increases in value, meaning that it's able to purchase more goods for an equivalent price. Being able to buy more for your money sounds like a no-brainer; however, low levels of inflation are needed to ensure that enough money is going around the system for growth.

Maintaining your curiosity: Interest rates

The *interest rate* is the rate of return you make on an interest-bearing asset or the rate you pay when you borrow money. So when you have a bank account that generates 1 per cent interest per year, you'll have 1 per cent more money in that account next year than you have this year, assuming that you keep your fingers off the bank account during that period. If interest rates are increasing the amount of money you have at exactly the same rate that inflation is decreasing the value of each pound, you can continually purchase the same amount of goods using the money in that bank account.

Interest rates decrease the value of assets in a rather more abstract way than inflation (see the preceding section) and it has to do with the opportunity cost of holding an asset. *Opportunity costs* measure the loss of forgoing the next best option. For example, the opportunity cost of making an investment that earns 2 per cent interest may be the 1 per cent return of the next best investment.

Opportunity cost becomes a problem when the next best investment is better than the one you choose. For instance, if you buy an investment that makes a fixed 2 per cent per year and then the next day the interest rate on that investment increases to 3 per cent, you're generating less nominal value on your investment than the market is offering to investors taking it out now. In other words, you're losing 1 per cent per year by having the wrong type of investment, because you're earning less interest than what's being offered to other investors.

Predicting Future Value

In this section we show you how to predict the future! (If books came with eerie noises and smoke effects, they'd be in full swing right now.) But we're not talking about fortune tellers with a deck of cards, we mean future value.

The *future value* of an asset refers to the value that you estimate something is going to have at a point in the future. If you want to know what a machine will be worth after five years or how much will be in your bank account in six months, you can measure both things using future value.

The vast majority of future value calculations are functions of just three things:

- ✔ Present value (see the later section 'Calculating the Present Value')
- ✔ Rate
- ✔ Time

All future value calculations are simply a matter of determining how much revenue an investment is going to generate over a period of time at the interest rate offered by that particular investment. Two of the most commonly used future value equations in corporate finance involve interest rates – simple and compound interest – and we explain them in the following sections. You use the same calculations to determine the cost of debt for a company.

Making simple interest easy

Take a look at this equation:

$$FV = PV(1 + rt)$$

It shows that for any asset earning a fixed rate of interest, the future value *(FV)* of the asset is worth the present value *(PV)* multiplied by the function of interest rate *(r)* and time duration *(t)* plus 1.

Here's a quick example to show you how this equation works: say that you buy an investment for £100 that yields 1 per cent interest per year and you plan to hold it for 10 years. To calculate the future value of that investment, simply plug these numbers into the simple interest equation as follows:

$$FV = £100(1 + 0.01 \times 10)$$
$$FV = £100(1.1)$$
$$FV = £110$$

When you multiply rate and time in this equation, you get 0.1, and when you multiply that by the *PV* of £100, you get £10. That's the total amount of increase in nominal value that the interest earns over 10 years. Although that's good to know, you need to include the total amount you put into the account in the first place (the *PV*) in order to arrive at the future value of the investment as a whole. So you just add 1 to the 0.1, and multiply that by the original £100, resulting in a future value of £110.

Building an understanding of compound interest

Compound interest is similar to simple interest (see the preceding section) except that investments earning compound interest generate interest on the interest earned rather than just on the principal (sometimes called the *capital*) balance. Although this difference adds some complexity to the equation you use to calculate the future value of an investment that earns compound interest, the basic components are still the same, as you can see here:

$$FV = PV[(1 + r)^t]$$

For example, say that you buy an investment for £100 that pays 10 per cent interest each year and you plan on holding the investment for five years. To work out the compound interest, you start off with the interest factor:

$$(1 + r)^t = 1.1^5 = 1.61051$$

From there, you work out the future value, like so:

$$£100 \times 1.61051 = £161.05$$

Ten per cent interest on the £100 in each year is £10. Over five years this becomes £50 (£10 x 5 years). The extra £11.05 (£61.05 – £50) is interest on interest (compound interest).

For more on simple versus compounding interest, refer to Chapter 3.

Calculating the Present Value

Just as you can calculate the future nominal and real value of a company's cash and investments (as we explain in the earlier section 'Predicting Future Value'), you can also calculate the current nominal and real value of future cash and investments not yet *realised* (which means not yet turned into cash).

The ability to estimate the value of something today that's going to change value over time is essential not only when buying and selling assets, but also as a critical element of tracking the progress and efficiency of capital assets within an organisation. When you purchase a capital item such as a machine you may have estimates of the value that it will create for your business, and you may even have projections about the returns on investment it's going to generate, but you can't just sit back and assume that your estimates are correct. By tracking the amount of value it actually produces at specific intervals of time, you can check to see how accurate you were and make tweaks to your estimates along the way.

This approach becomes especially important if you plan to sell that item of capital, when you're buying used capital or if you deal with any sort of other investments such as bonds or derivatives (which we discuss in Chapters 11 and 13, respectively).

To help you better understand what present value is, consider a lottery win. If you take the whole £1 million that you won right away and put it in investments generating 1 per cent interest, that £1 million will be worth more in 10 years than if you accept annual £100,000 payments for 10 years. In the former of the two options, you earn an extra £1,000 in interest over 10 years. In the latter option, you earn less interest, and so the future payments are worth less than the current payments.

Although this example is helpful for lottery winners, it doesn't really explain how most people use present value calculations, particularly in corporate finance. That's where the following sections come into play.

Taking a closer look at earnings

When you calculate present value, in essence you're looking more closely at earnings or cash flows that you or your company will make in the future. For example, you can apply present value to bond investments in which investors know exactly how much money they're going to earn nominally and when (the exact date) they'll receive that money. In cases like this, where you know all this information upfront, you can determine how much of the total future value you've already accumulated at any given point by using the following equation:

$$PV = FV \div (1 + rt)$$

Here's what the variables in this equation mean:

- PV = Present value
- FV = Future value (plug in whatever future value we give you in this section; we discuss finding future value in the earlier section 'Predicting Future Value')
- r = Rate
- t = Time (in years)
- 1 = Percentage constant

To put this equation to use, consider an example in which the interest rate for a 1-year investment is 5 per cent and the future value is £100. To find the present value, simply plug these numbers into the equation:

$$PV = \pounds100 \div (1 + 0.05 \times 1)$$

$$PV = \pounds100 \div 1.05$$

$$PV = \pounds95.24$$

So the present value for this example is about £95. For an interest rate of only 4 per cent, the present value of a £100 future cash flow would be about £96 (£100 ÷ 1.04). The present value is higher in this case, because the difference between the present value and the future value is smaller given the lower interest rate.

If all these mathematical formulae are driving you to despair you can download present value tables free of charge; you can just simply type *present value tables* into a search engine and they'll be available for download. Some corporate finance text books also have these tables included at the front or back of them.

Another way of looking at present value is that the more interest you earn or pay on future cash flows, by way of higher interest or longer-term investments, the less the present value is going to be. In the case of higher interest, the present value increases at a much faster rate over time, whereas longer-term investments increase at the same rate but simply take longer to mature fully.

Being able to determine the present value of each potential investment, purchase or cash flow before committing to it helps you and your company to make the best possible decisions. For instance, in making a large purchase that may include several instalments, you can calculate whether your company would be better off paying for the item outright or making monthly payments with interest while keeping the remaining funds in an interest-bearing account of some sort. We look more at present value in Chapter 10 when we assess the value of capital assets and various financial investments.

Discussing discounted cash flows

Discount value is another term for present value and comes from the fact that you're taking a known future value and discounting it at the interest rate in question.

The reason for the distinction in terms is that *discount rate* and *discounted cash flows* are just a lot easier to say than *present value calculation rate* or *present value rate of future cash flows*. Beyond that, no difference exists in the meaning of the two terms. So although we use the term discounted cash flows, the only functional difference from present value is that we're talking specifically about exchanges in cash instead of simply value generated. In other words, we mean cash flows instead of value; but otherwise, present value and discounted value don't have a functional difference.

That said, *discounted cash flows* refers to the specific situation in which several cash flows appear in a single transaction. For example, when your company purchases a large item (say a vehicle on hire purchase), each cash payment the firm makes is considered a cash flow; when your company invests in a coupon bond (something we cover in Chapter 11), each payment it receives is a cash flow.

If your company purchases a machine for producing goods for resale, both the future costs of buying and operating that machine and the value of the goods created by that machine in the future are measured as discounted cash flows, with each individual cash flow discounted to its present value (sometimes referred to as the *present day value* or *today's value*). Even though each cash flow is likely to have the same interest rate, each one is going to have a different present value because each one is paid at a different point in time. So the present value of the most chronologically distant cash flows is the lowest.

Here's what the discounted cash flow equation looks like:

$$DCF = [CF_1 \div (1 + rt)_1] + [CF_n \div (1 + rt)_n]$$

The variables in this equation are fairly simple to define:

- DCF = Value of discounted cash flows
- CF_1 = Cash flow number 1
- r = Rate
- t = Time (in years)
- CF_n = Cash flow number n; whichever cash flow you want to measure (often, but not necessarily, treated as the last cash flow)
- 1 = Percentage constant

All this equation really means is that you add up all the present values of future cash flows to determine the value of discounted cash flows, also known as the *net present value* (NPV). In other words, NPV is the total value of all the discounted cash flows of a particular account, investment or loan. In the real world it can get a bit more complicated because the size of those cash flows will also be impacted by inflation so, in reality, companies often do a range of calculations showing what NPVs the outcome might range between.

We explore NPV in a little more detail in Chapter 10, but for now just bear in mind that if a particular asset is going to generate several future cash flows, each of those cash flows has its own present value. When you add up those present values, you get the net present value.

Chapter 10

Looking to the Future with Capital Budgeting

*W*hen you think of investments, you probably think of items such as stocks and shares. But they're part of only one class of investment, called *financial investments,* which are made in financial products. For most businesses, financial investments aren't even the primary form of investment – that honour goes to *capital investments.*

Capital investment is extremely important to every company, and fortunately capital budgeting is easy to perform. In this chapter we show you how capital budgeting happens, including calculating the rates of returns on capital, determining the value of cash flows and the residual value of equipment after it's no longer of use, calculating the payback period for the cost of capital and determining the current value of capital at any given point in time. We also explain how to track expected and present values, how to manage stocks efficiently and how to manage working capital and economic capital. Plus, we show how you can apply all the preceding factors to project management.

Understanding Capital Budgeting

Just about everything on which companies spend money can be considered an investment. After all, companies manage other people's money and so nothing they spend that money on is supposed to be for personal gain or enjoyment; instead, it's supposed to be used to generate returns for the owners of the company (the shareholders). So, every pound a company spends should contribute to the increased value of the business in some way. But that's not always the case, because many companies are wasteful with their resources. Plus, you don't really need to measure the returns on every single pound. We honestly don't think anyone cares how much value a paper clip adds to the total output of an organisation.

You start to run into matters of potential returns and capital budgeting, however, with larger expenditures – for example, when a company is considering buying a building, a new item of plant or new machinery; offering a new line or product; or starting a new project. All these undertakings need to be analysed carefully from a financial standpoint to determine their potential returns and risk before any action is taken.

Capital budgeting is the process by which you evaluate the financial potential for each of one or more possible capital investments. In those cases where several options are available but the company has enough resources to pursue only one, each option has to be compared against the others in order to determine which one may yield the greatest returns.

(To be honest, the term 'capital budgeting' is a little misleading, because the process has more to do with evaluating the potential of capital investments than budgeting. But the process was originally used to budget resource allocations, which is how it received its title.)

The implications of the evaluation go beyond simply making allocation decisions. The information that you derive from these financial valuations plays a big role in the financial projections for the entire company, its resource budgeting, its liquidity and asset management, and almost every other aspect of the company's finances and operations. The exact nature of the company's capital investments determines what production volume the business is capable of handling, how profitable and financially efficient it's going to be, and even how it sets its pricing strategies. The operational and cost efficiencies that the entire company experiences are largely influenced by its capital budgeting decisions.

Rating Your Returns

Say that you're preparing to invest in a new piece of capital – a machine that paints cars blue – but before you shell out over £1 million for this 'business venture', you want to know whether it's going to be profitable. In essence, therefore, you want to calculate the *rate of return* on the machine. This rate is the ratio of revenues to costs associated with purchasing something. If it's positive, you're making more money than you're spending. You may have noticed that companies like money, and so that's a good thing. If the rate of return is negative, you're losing money. Companies don't like to lose money.

The rate of return is usually measured in terms of years, though any duration of time is possible: months, weeks, days, hours . . . it depends on the life of the investment and the amount of work you feel like doing.

We like to make things easy, and so when we're carrying out capital budgeting, the first thing we do is determine the rate of return on a potential investment. This approach allows us to eliminate very easily any potential investments that won't be profitable or will be significantly less profitable than other options.

For example, if an investment can hope to generate only 1 per cent annual returns per year, but a local credit union pays 3 per cent per year on a savings account, you're better off putting the money in the savings account. So, you want to work out exactly what kind of potential each project has before you do anything else with your information, because that helps you avoid a lot of extra unnecessary work. Sound good? We thought you'd like that.

The first thing you need in order to calculate the rate of return is data. For any potential project, you need to know the following items:

✔ Investment costs

✔ Lifespan

✔ Operating costs

✔ Output volume

✔ Pricing and financing costs

✔ Revenues

✔ Scrap value

Together, that's just five things you need in order to do all the calculations we discuss in this chapter. For this particular section, your only concern is the rate of return, but you can take satisfaction in knowing that you don't need anything more for the rest of the chapter.

Looking at costs

A new capital item is likely to be expensive to buy and maintain. So, you have three separate costs to consider:

✔ Purchase cost

✔ Interest rate you pay on the loan you take out to buy the asset

✔ Cost of keeping/maintaining the asset

In reality, the cost of the purchase is also likely to include a tax expense, but we're aiming to keep the equations simple here.

Reckoning your revenue

After you calculate your costs, you need to work out your revenue – you're not going to pay all that money unless you can generate some revenues as a result, right? For the purposes of this book, you need to be concerned with only two major types of revenue:

✔ Sales of any product the asset makes

✔ Residual value when you come to get rid of the asset

In the real world, you also have tax savings in the form of capital allowances – Her Majesty's Revenue and Customs' (HMRC's) version of *depreciation:* the systematic allocation of the depreciable amount of an asset over its estimated useful life. Plus, you probably need more than one machine to create a single finished product, and so the revenues generated by that machine account for only a proportion of the total sales revenues, based on the amount of value that machine contributes to the final product. More capital simply means repeating the calculations, however, and we cover depreciation in Chapters 4 and 5, so although these two considerations add a bit more work, we don't go into more detail here.

Calculating the accounting rate of return

The simplest rate of return to calculate is the accounting rate of return (ARR), a fundamental calculation to determine how much value an investment generates for the company and its owners (the shareholders). The ARR requires only two pieces of information: the amount of earnings before interest and taxes (EBIT) generated by the project and the cost of the investment. When you know those two things, the calculation goes as follows:

ARR = EBIT attributed to project ÷ Net investment

So you calculate the ARR by dividing the amount of EBIT generated by the project by the net investment of the project. This calculation tells you the proportion of net earnings before taxes that you're generating for the investment cost; you usually do it on a year-on-year basis.

This equation doesn't take multi-period variables into consideration, and so you have to calculate it again for each period (usually a year). Say, for example, that in year 1 you calculate a –3 per cent rate of return. That sounds bad, but if you're talking about the investment on developing a whole new product line, you need to consider that sales are usually slow during the first year. By year 3, for example, perhaps you expect a 2 per cent rate of return.

You may be wondering how to determine the amount of EBIT to attribute to a given project. The answer isn't too difficult to work out. You simply go through the steps of developing a profit and loss account (or an income statement) as we describe in Chapter 5, but only for the new project. Find out how many sales this new line or product is generating, and then subtract the costs of operating the project. That's simple, right? Fine. Now we add just a little bit more complexity to show you how to do this for a single machine rather than a whole new project.

When your capital investment is only a single step in the production process, determining how much value is being added by that step takes a little more work. You have to break down the entire production process into its individual contributing steps. The total production process is 100 per cent of the final product.

You can determine what percentage of the production process a single step constitutes in a couple ways. One approach is simply to use a proportion of the total cost of production. This method is easy, but you have a better option, called transfer pricing.

Transfer pricing estimates the market value of each step in the process by doing some research to find out the cost of hiring some other company to perform that step. This method assists you in two ways:

✔ Transfer pricing helps you do your capital budgeting by determining the amount of added value for that single step and the amount of EBIT you can attribute to that step, to make sure that the investment really is going to generate a positive return on investment.

✔ Transfer pricing determines the fair market value of performing that step to see whether your company is being financially efficient. If some other company can perform that step better or more cheaply, you should probably outsource that step to the other company.

If you know the lifespan of the project or machine, you can forecast the rate of return you experience each year. Whether you're successful at this forecast or not depends entirely on how closely your forecasts match the actual rate of returns, of course, but you can still do these forecasts. The total rate of return on the investment is the total EBIT generated by that investment divided by the cost of the investment. The revenues used to calculate EBIT include all the revenues that the investment generates over its entire life, plus the final revenue generated using its residual or scrap value. The final revenue generated by any project is its scrap or residual value.

We talk about how to calculate residual value in Chapter 4. Here, we apply that calculation as our forecast for the final revenues generated by any capital investment.

Making the most of the internal rate of return through modification

The accounting rate of return in the preceding section is helpful, but it's so simple that it's extremely limited in its ability to provide you with useful information in your attempt to manage assets, investments and projects. (It's limited because it doesn't take into account the time value of money.) For that goal, you can use something called the modified internal rate of return (MIRR). 'Why modified?', you ask. Well, the internal rate of return (IRR) is a good equation, but it has some faults that are easily rectified, and so no-one really uses it anymore.

In this section and those following it, we talk a lot about the time value of money, and so if you haven't read Chapter 9 yet, we recommend you do so now.

The IRR is a calculation that attempts to take the net future cash flows of a project (all its positive and negative cash flows) and the discount rate at which the present value of the net cash flows is zero. Think of it as follows: a project is worth £0 at the beginning because it hasn't produced anything. So in order to determine the IRR, you attempt to calculate the rate at which the net present value of future cash flows is zero (we discuss net present value in the next section 'Netting Present Values'). That rate is the IRR.

As we said, however, the IRR has a couple of problems:

- ✔ It assumes automatically that all cash flows from the project are reinvested at the IRR rate, which isn't realistic in most cases.
- ✔ It has difficulty comparing projects that have differing durations and cash flows.

Otherwise, you can use the IRR to evaluate a single project or single cash flow.

The MIRR tends to be more accurate in its costs and profitability of projects, however, and because the MIRR is a more robust equation with wider applications, we jump to that now and forget about the IRR.

You use the following equation to calculate the MIRR:

$$MIRR = \sqrt[n]{\frac{FV\left(\text{Positive Cash Flows, Reinvestment}\right)}{PV\left(\text{Cost, Rate}\right)}} - 1$$

where:

> n = Number of periods
>
> FV = Future value
>
> PV = Present value
>
> Positive Cash Flows = Revenues/value contributions to revenues from the project
>
> Reinvestment = Rate generated from reinvesting future cash flows
>
> Cost = Investment cost
>
> Rate = Rate of financing the investment
>
> 1 = A number

Most of the time, the reinvestment rate of MIRR is set at the company's cost of capital. Of course, that depends a lot on how efficient the company is in its financial management, and so we tend to keep it an *open variable* (meaning that it's sort of unknown) based more on evaluations of the company's financial performance. The following quick example shows you how to calculate the MIRR of a project.

Imagine that a project lasting only two years, with an initial investment cost of £2,000 and a cost of capital of 10 per cent, will return £2,000 in year 1 and £3,000 in year 2. Reinvested at a 10 per cent rate of return, you calculate the future value of the positive cash flows as follows:

> £2,000(1.10) + £3,000 = £5,200 at the end of the project's lifespan of two years

Note that the '(1.10)' is one year's interest at 10 per cent, hence £2,000 x 1.10 + £3,000 = £5,200.

Now you divide the future value of the cash flows by the present value of the initial cost, which is £2,000, to find the geometric return for two periods:

$$\sqrt{\left(£5,200 \div 2,000\right)} - 1 = 0.61245 \times 100 = 61.25\%$$

This calculation doesn't take a financing cost into account. That's not an issue, though, because most companies can afford £2,000 with no problem, and we're trying to keep the example simple. Also note that if we had used the IRR instead of the MIRR, the rate of return would have been substantially higher, but also substantially less accurate.

Netting Present Values

One of the core calculations used in capital budgeting is net present value (NPV), which you calculate using the following equation:

$$NPV = \sum_{T=1}^{T} \frac{C_t}{(1-r)^t} - C_0$$

where:

T = Cash flow period

C = Cash flow

r = Discount rate

This equation says that you add up all the present values of all future cash inflows (money coming in) and then subtract the sum of the present value of all future cash outflows (money going out). In other words, you take the present value of all future cash flows, positive and negative, and then add and subtract as appropriate. If the equation looks more complicated than the description, that's because of how equations are built. The big 'E'-looking symbol is called a *sigma,* and it simply means to add things together – in this case, the present value of future cash flows.

In the case of capital investments, the cash flows come in the form of revenues and costs. In fact, that's true with all cash flows, but these are a little different because they're operating revenues and costs, rather than financing cash flows, investing cash flows or even 'other' types of cash flows. In other words, these cash flows influence directly the primary operations of the company. So the positive cash flows come from the sale of goods and services, as well as the rate of return generated through the reinvestment of the positive cash flows.

If the investment is part of a larger process, as we discuss in the earlier section 'Calculating the accounting rate of return', you attribute only those revenues that compose an equal proportion of the total value that this particular investment contributed to the final product. The costs of each present value include the financing costs, costs of maintenance and operations, and the interest paid for financing the investment. All cash flows are assumed, of course, to be discounted at the anticipated inflation rate.

Totting up NPV over time

What makes NPV special to capital budgeting isn't projecting the total value of a potential capital investment (we talk about that and use similar calculations in the earlier section 'Making the most of the internal rate of return through modification'); it's that you can continue to calculate NPV over time. Over the duration of a project's life, the project's NPV decreases over time. It has less life and fewer unrealised cash flows because it has already generated revenues in the past.

Performing these calculations allows you to do several things regarding earned value management (which we define in the next section 'Managing the project's value'):

- ✔ You can determine the value of an investment over the course of its life. That's great for evaluating corporate value and future operating potential.

- ✔ You can estimate the market value of an investment at any given point for use as collateral or to determine its liquidation value. Yes, that's a grim scenario, but you need to be aware of it – especially in challenging economic times.

- ✔ You can find vital information about the reinvestment of the net cash flows up until that point.

Managing the project's value

When you take the NPV of a project at time t (which is any year during the project), you can add the actual returns generated up until that point and more closely manage the project's value. Forecasts are always estimates, some more accurate than others, and so when the period for a forecast is over or is in the process of passing, you want to check and see how close you were to the forecast. Then the company can adjust its financial outlook accordingly.

The net cash flows generated so far are called *earned value* (or *enterprise value*) (EV). You calculate earned value as follows:

$$EV = \sum_{\text{Start}}^{\text{Current}} PV(\text{Completed})$$

Musing on amortisation

The calculation in this section assumes, of course, that you make the initial investment all at once. You don't have to handle things this way, though. For very large investments, you can take the future value of amortising (*amortisation* is the process of spreading out the payments of a cost, and is also seen in financial accounting for spreading the cost of an intangible fixed asset over its estimated useful life) and use that as your initial investment. In other words, if you have an investment that's so large

you need to finance it and repay the investment over the course of many years, you just add up all the negative cash flows.

Calculating the payback period for an amortised investment works only with fixed interest rates, however, where the nominal amount you repay isn't going to change over time. With variable rate loans, the calculation becomes a little trickier mathematically and is beyond the scope of this book.

Essentially, this equation says that you take all the present values (PV) you've completed and add them together. That big thing that looks kind of like a drunk 'E' is called a sigma (a capital sigma, not to be confused with a lowercase sigma, which we describe later in the book). It means you add things together. The 'start' on the bottom means that you begin with the start of the project. The 'current' on top means you end with the current period, without going further. Therefore, you add together cash flows from the beginning until 'now' (whenever 'now' is) and that's your earned value – and it's not necessarily going to be what you expect.

Maybe you're generating higher rates of returns than you expect from your MIRR calculations; in this case, your earned value is higher than your planned value at some point in time. If your earned value is lower than planned, you're generating lower returns than projected.

In both cases, you want to find out what the percentage of difference is and why it occurred. Even if you're getting higher returns than planned, you want to know why so that you can try for a repeat performance. Trust us on this.

Tracking the NPV of a given project allows you to manage the project more effectively, manage finances and resources more efficiently, and plan better for the future. These tasks form the fundamentals of project management, which we discuss briefly in the later section 'Looking at a Piece of Project Management'.

Determining the Payback Period

This short-and-sweet section is about the *payback period,* which is the number of periods needed to pay back the initial investment on a piece of capital. In other words, it's the number of years for a company to break even on its new capital investment.

The payback period is a crucial calculation not only for projecting the cash flows, interest payments and other value management techniques for the investment, but also for projecting the influence of the project on the entire company's asset management and profitability. You calculate it as follows:

Payback period = Initial investment ÷ Net annual cash flows

Start with your initial investment and then divide it by your average net cash flows. For example, say that you spend £10,000 on a piece of capital. This piece of capital is expected to generate, on average, an extra £1,000 in EBIT to your company and has a lifespan of 20 years (but bear in mind that what's worth £1,000 now won't be worth £1,000 in 20 years). The calculation to arrive at your payback period on this piece of equipment is 10,000 ÷ 1,000 = 10 years. You require ten years to repay the investment on capital. Those net cash flows generated from the remaining ten years of the life of the investment are pure profit. Nicely done!

Managing Capital Allocations

In the preceding sections of this chapter, you discover a lot of calculations relevant to determining the value and profitability of a capital investment at any given point in time. But how, you may be wondering, does all that information come together to help you make useful decisions regarding capital allocations and comparing different potential investments? Every investment has an opportunity cost – the loss of the next best option – and so companies need to make certain that they're opting for the best option, and that includes, potentially, making no capital investment at all.

Assessing the equivalent annual cost

The best place to start is by calculating the equivalent annual cost of each potential investment. You calculate this figure as follows:

$EAC = NPV \div [1 - (1 + \text{Discount rate})^{-n}]$

The equation allows you to compare the annual costs of potential investments with differing duration periods and cash flows in an apples-to-apples approach. (Don't confuse this EAC (equivalent annual cost) with 'estimated at completion', which we describe a little further on.)

The real test of whether or not any of the potential investments is going to be successful, however, depends greatly on the ability of the company to derive value from the project. Just because it has the capacity to create something, doesn't mean that it can create the demand or make it work. To discover that, you need to incorporate a calculation for capital efficiency (CE):

CE = Output ÷ Expenditures

When you have an idea of the amount of actual output being generated by an actual project, you can understand a few additional bits of information. To start, you can determine the amount of cash flows at a given rate of efficiency, and the degree to which that efficiency must increase in order to increase the NPV of the project. The percentage of deviation between current performance value and planned NPV is equivalent to the amount of increased efficiency that the company must derive from the investment.

You then use the estimate at completion (EAC; check out the later section 'Carrying out the budget calculations' for more on this) value to determine which one of several potential investments is going to generate the greatest returns for the company. Thanks to the equivalency of the analysis, whichever option has the highest EAC is the best one. Go with it. Unless, of course, they're all low or even negative.

If they're all negative, you'd lose money on them all and you shouldn't invest in any of the options. If they're all low enough that you'd be better off putting those investments into some sort of financial investment or bank account, that's probably the way to go.

Considering liquid assets

Liquid asset management is the frequent analysis of whether a firm is better off allocating resources towards liquid assets, with low returns but low risk, or to long-term assets, which usually have higher returns but higher risk.

Of course, if your long-term potential assets have low returns, don't take on the additional risk: just go with the liquid investments.

Allocating resources and assets into capital investments is about more than just long-term assets. Although these assets tend to get the most attention, because of their high cost and higher risk, you also need to evaluate liquid assets for their performance and returns. Whether you put money into a long-term asset or a liquid account is determined, in large part, by the amount of liquidity risk the company is facing as well as its estimated future cash flows.

Economic capital

All companies, of course, want to generate the highest rate of returns that they can from every single penny they own. Of course, this goal is impossible given the timing of their costs and expenditures, and so they need to maintain a type of extremely short-term liquid assets: economic capital. Basically, *economic capital* is all the money that's kept in banks, cash or anything else that you can use immediately to pay for daily cash requirements.

Any money kept in economic capital is money that isn't put into investments. Therefore, carefully assessing liquidity risk, cash requirements and future cash flows is an important part of efficiently using your assets to generate returns. (Certainly, keeping enough economic capital is a major focus for UK banks at the time of writing.) You may be awfully tempted to invest more money than is operationally wise into investments in order to maximise the rate of returns, but that's a temptation you need to avoid.

Stock

The other form of liquid asset you need to consider for the purposes of this chapter is called stock (sometimes referred to as inventory). *Stock* includes all the assets that are going to be sales, including finished products, work-in-progress and raw materials. These assets not only keep a company from investing, but also cost money to keep in storage. That's why many companies are now paying very careful attention to and innovating in the field of stock management. The ultimate goal is JIT (just-in-time) stock management.

To provide some perspective on what JIT means, the following list contains some descriptions of the various stages of production. Each phase has its own costs and valuations. JIT works to reduce the costs associated with each step as much as possible, ensuring that the final outlet for the sale receives its stock just as it runs out (ideally, in extremely small quantities delivered frequently):

- ✔ **Finished products:** Products that are ready to be sold. They're completely finished, and storing them until they're bought costs money. Direct sales tend to be cheaper because the costs of storage and distribution are lower without retailers, particularly for made-to-order products.

- ✔ **Work-in-progress:** Products that have been started but aren't yet complete. Decreasing the amount of time in-progress can cut costs and increase rates of return.

- ✔ **Raw materials:** Materials that haven't yet begun to be processed. The majority of stock management is focused here, ensuring that materials don't arrive before they're really needed.

The cost of stock comes primarily from storage. Just like any other capital investment, the increased expenditures required for space to store and maintain stock, known as the *cost of stock,* can reduce the rate of returns generated by selling this form of stock as capital. JIT attempts to manage the supply chain by ensuring that stock in its various forms arrives immediately when it's needed but not a moment sooner. This strategy ensures that stock remains available while reducing the costs associated with stock.

Applying NPV to stock management allows you to see that JIT can dramatically increase the rate of returns on capital. By shortening the duration of capital in stock, the NPV of stock increases almost instantly. The results are two-fold:

- ✔ Companies can generate returns on the money that otherwise would've been allocated to stock in the meantime.
- ✔ Companies can reduce the opportunity costs associated with short-term liquid assets.

Looking at a Piece of Project Management

Project management is a highly complex topic that involves a wide range of specialisms in management. For the purposes of this book, the only aspect you need to be concerned with is the evaluation and control of the project's finances, which are calculated using information about earned value management (EVM). *EVM* allows you to calculate, quite accurately, the amount of value being contributed to, or derived from, an investment project. The goals of this section are understanding the nature of this evaluation and ensuring that everything remains on schedule, under budget and, most of all, efficiently profitable.

Doing the value schedule calculations

As we explain in Chapter 9, time is money. So a problem arises whenever you have a deviation in the schedule regarding when a project will be completed or when it's going to reach certain milestones in earned value. Not only do you have a problem if you're falling behind, which is especially bad, but you also have a problem if the project is generating value ahead of schedule to the extent that the company's assets could've been managed more efficiently.

Schedule variation

The difference between earned value (EV) at time t and planned value (PV) for time t is called the *schedule variation* (SV), and you calculate it using the following equation:

$$SV = EV - PV$$

This equation says that the schedule variation is equal to the earned value less the planned value. If the earned value that you generate at any given point in time is equal to the value that you planned to generate at that point in time, the schedule variation is zero. Being above zero is also a good thing, but it still warrants an explanation so that you can figure out how to improve projections or repeat successes in the future. If the schedule variation is less than zero, people probably start shouting at you, which is never pleasant.

A negative SV can arise for two reasons:

- ✔ **The project may not be generating as much value as anticipated.** You can discover this scenario fairly easily by closely looking at each of the cash flows from the investment to determine why cash flows are deviating from their planned net value, and whether that trend is going to continue or influence the total rate of returns for the life of the investment.

- ✔ **Earned value is taking longer to realise.** A possibility is that the operating cycle is longer than expected. Merely being behind schedule, as opposed to an under-planned value, is certainly the less harmful scenario, although neither situation is good.

Schedule performance

Another way to look at the variance between EV and PV is through a ratio calculation called *schedule performance* (SP), which you calculate as follows:

$$SP = EV \div PV$$

This equation essentially states that SP equals earned value (EV) divided by planned value (PV). You can measure SP using time increments or pound-denominated value increments. For example, if a project is taking longer than expected, that would be a deviation in SP_t, whereas a deviation in pound value would be measured in $SP_\pounds$ (or whatever other currency you're using):

- ✔ **SP of 1:** The investment is generating value exactly as planned.

- ✔ **SP less than 1:** The project is coming in behind schedule or under value.

- ✔ **SP more than 1:** The project is coming in ahead of schedule or over value.

In the latter two cases, the company isn't using its assets as effectively as possible. Even if the investment is generating more value than anticipated, the company has no plan in place to reinvest that surplus income to optimise returns. Perhaps it could have pursued another investment with it, or more effectively managed its economic capital.

In any case, the performance of EVM is usually based on performance ratios at given time milestones. The value and time performance of a project ends up at 1 no matter how you measure it, and so these measurements are taken at intervals chosen before the investment is made. A common approach is to measure the investment's performance at, for example, 10 per cent repayment period, 50 per cent repayment period, 50 per cent asset lifespan or any other intervals, usually measuring multiple times over a given duration.

Carrying out the budget calculations

In this section, we go full-circle and return to the subject of budgeting (which we introduce in the earlier section 'Understanding Capital Budgeting'). When allocating resources to an investment to generate value from it (you can't just buy a machine without allocating resources to the operation, maintenance and financing of that machine), the company must develop a budget for that investment.

Ensuring that the investment is adhering to its budget is a big part of how successful executive management are going to consider the investment to be, we guarantee it; after all, large amounts of money and resources are being spent to generate a return on investment. Of course, the performance of an investment also comes through in the updated calculations of the MIRR over time (check out the earlier section 'Making the most of the internal rate of return through modification'), but some additional calculations are frequently performed in EVM that are concerned specifically with budgetary issues, in order to identify why deviations in the MIRR over time may occur.

Cost variance

The amount of value that a company can generate from an investment at a given cost is a large concern for an organisation: no-one likes to throw cash repeatedly into a 'black hole'. So reaching the anticipated 100 per cent value from your investment on-budget is preferred. Here's the calculation if some variation exists:

$$CV = EV - AC$$

where the cost variance (CV) is equal to the earned value (EV) less the actual cost (AC).

Spending more money to generate value at given milestones throughout a project is a bad thing. You may have to re-evaluate whether continuing to pursue the investment's value is worth the additional costs. If the actual cost is lower for a given point in earned value, you need to start planning how to use the surplus budgetary funding.

Cost performance

As with time-schedule calculations (see 'Doing the value schedule calculations' earlier in this chapter), another way to look at cost measurements is through a ratio. This time it's called the *cost performance (CP) ratio* and it's measured like this:

$$CP = EV \div AC$$

This ratio measures the earned value at a given point to the actual cost (AC) at that point.

Estimate at completion

You can measure the total cost of the capital investment at its completion with a simple equation called *estimate at completion* (EAC):

$$EAC = BAC \div CP$$

where BAC = Budget at completion and CP = Cost performance.

So, the planned budget for the entire project is divided by the cost performance of the investment when the calculation is being done (in order to use the most recent data available). By doing so, you get a monetary value answer that tells you how much the investment actually cost compared to how much you planned on it costing. Here's a quick example:

$$EAC = \$12,000 \div 1.2 = \$10,000; \text{ you're } \$2,000 \text{ under budget.}$$

That $2,000 is called the *estimate to complete* (ETC). Here's the formal calculation:

$$ETC = EAC - AC$$

You subtract the actual costs from the estimated cost at completion to see how much cost you have left to finish the project.

Whether or not the investment is worth pursuing after it has already begun to go over budget depends on whether the ETC is lower than the potential present value of future cash flows, calculated as:

$$\text{Efficacy of investment} = NPV - ETC$$

If the ETC exceeds the net present value (NPV) of future cash flows, you're just throwing money away by continuing the project.

To-complete performance

You calculate whether a company can improve the financial efficiency of an investment to make that investment worth pursuing by using the *to-complete performance* (TCP):

$$TCP = (BAC - EV) \div (BAC - AC)$$

You subtract the earned value (EV) from the budget at completion (BAC) and divide the result by the BAC less the actual cost (AC). This ratio tells the company by what percentage it needs to increase its performance efficiency. So, for example, if the TCP on a company's project is 1.10, it needs to improve efficiency by 10 per cent in order to get the project back on track to complete it on budget.

Chapter 11

Bringing on Your Best Bond Bets

In This Chapter

▶ Taking a look at various types of bonds

▶ Exploring fixed- and floating-rate bonds

▶ Understanding bond lingo

▶ Checking out some bond valuation equations

*B*onds are popular with companies and investors. Companies appreciate the fact that bonds don't dilute the value of equity in the way that issuing additional shares in an initial public offering (IPO) does. (Each time a company creates and issues brand new shares it's considered to be an IPO, as opposed to simply reselling *treasury shares,* which are shares that a company has repurchased from ex-shareholders; for more on treasury shares see Chapter 3.) Investors like bonds because they're less volatile than equity and guarantee nominal returns, although that doesn't mean that they have no risk whatsoever (for more on the subject of risk, check out Chapter 14). Still, most bonds have a fixed return, making them particularly attractive for investors seeking stability, such as people funding retirement accounts.

In this chapter, you explore the different types of bond available and their various issuing institutions and discover the differences between fixed- and floating-rate bonds. We show you how to research bonds and keep up to date on changes in bond valuations. In addition, our beginner's guide to estimating the valuation and pricing of bonds helps you determine your company's potential for raising money through debt and whether a particular bond is an attractive investment for your portfolio.

Exploring the Different Types of Bonds

A wide variety of different types of bond are available, each with several variables that make it unique. Different bonds have different traits depending on who issues them. Each issuer can also offer different options for additional features on those bonds, as well as using different underlying assets to generate the returns earned on the bonds or changing the methods by which repayments are made.

A number of different permutations can exist among bonds; for instance, a corporate bond may be a *zero-coupon* (meaning that it doesn't make payments of interest) convertible bond. Zero-coupon bonds are usually issued at a *deep discount,* meaning it is issued at a price well below its par value and the return to investors will be in the form of capital appreciation. Additionally, a number of features are unique to each type of bond. Bonds can't have more than one issuer, however, or have conflicting features (for example, a bond can't be both coupon and zero-coupon).

Although all this variety is great for companies and investors (when each is searching for just the right types of bonds for their own purposes), understanding the different options available takes a little more effort than, say, picking out a brand of washing-up liquid.

Considering corporate bonds

Corporate bonds are the ones that companies issue to raise capital with debt.

Pay extra special attention to corporate bonds, because they're particularly important for corporate finance purposes. Nothing is particularly special about these bonds except, perhaps, the performance ratios and calculations used to evaluate the risk associated with investing in this debt. Nevertheless, the role of these bonds is important from the perspective of investors (frequently organisations) and issuers (only companies issue corporate bonds).

Gauging government gilts

Governments are some of the biggest and most popular issuers of bonds in the world (in the UK and Ireland, government bonds are known as government *gilts*). Like all other organisations, governments issue gilts to incur debt that funds their spending. Every year the government budgets its revenues and expenditures, and when it spends more than it generates in revenues, the remainder has to be acquired by incurring debt through the selling of government gilts.

In some cases, gilts are issued to fund a specific project instead of making up for a general spending deficit. If a government wants to build, say, a power plant, as just one example, rather than attempting to budget for it out of its usual revenues, it may fund the entire project by selling gilts and paying them back from the profits generated by selling the energy.

The following sections take a quick look at some of the specific types of government gilts.

Conventional gilts

These gilts are the simplest form of government bond. A *conventional gilt* is a liability of the government that guarantees to pay the gilt holder a fixed cash payment (known as a *coupon*) every six months until the gilt matures. Upon maturity the gilt holder receives the final coupon payment plus the capital amount of the gilt (the term *capital amount* is also referred to as the *principal* amount of the gilt).

Conventional gilts are usually quoted in terms of £100 amounts, but can be traded in smaller units.

Index-linked gilts

Index-linked gilts are the largest part of the gilt portfolio after conventional gilts and the UK was one of the earliest developed economies to issue index-linked bonds for institutional investors (the first was issued back in 1981).

The coupon on an index-linked gilt reflects the borrowing rates available at the time of issue. Index-linked coupons reflect the *real borrowing rate* (which is an interest rate less adjustments for inflation) for the government, as opposed to the *nominal borrowing rate* (which is an interest rate before adjustments for inflation), and so a much smaller variation in real yields applies over time.

A notable difference between index-linked gilts and conventional gilts is that the half-yearly coupon payments and principal amount are adjusted in line with the UK Retail Prices Index (RPI). As a result, both the interest (or coupon) and the capital (or principal) amount paid on maturity are adjusted for the effects of inflation since the gilt was issued.

Three-month lag index-linked gilts

These gilts were first issued in 2005 and are issued on the basis of the *real clean price* (the price of a bond without any interest that has been accrued since it was issued or the most recent coupon payment) per £100 *nominal* (which means the stated value, so it remains permanent as opposed to its *market value* which fluctuates due to factors like inflation). Settlement proceeds (the amount by which the gilt is eventually settled) are worked out by multiplying the real clean price by the relevant index to arrive at an inflation-adjusted clean price and then adding the inflation-adjusted accrued interest to this figure. You can get the relevant index from the Office for National Statistics website (www.ons.gov.uk).

Double-dated conventional gilts

At the time of writing, only two remaining double-dated gilts are in issue, and they aren't issued any more. The government can choose to redeem these gilts in whole, or in part, on any day between the first and final maturity dates, but with a condition that the government gives no less than three months' notice in the *London Gazette* (the UK's Official Newspaper of Record, which you can access at www.london-gazette.co.uk).

Undated gilts

As at May 2013, eight undated gilts are in issue and they're the oldest remaining gilts (with some going back as far as the 19th century).

As with double-dated conventional gilts, the government can redeem these bonds at its discretion. One of the main reasons it hasn't done so yet is because they carry low coupons because of their age and so it wouldn't be cost effective, in the long run, for the government to redeem and refinance them. This is mainly because in 2009 and again in late 2011 (as well as at various times since then) the yield on these gilts (and in some cases the interest on them) has been higher than the actual redemption amount, so this implies that the stock market is pricing them on the basis that it thinks the government might redeem these gilts at some point.

Gilt strips

The term *strips* is an acronym for Separate Trading of Registered Interest and Principal Securities. The term *stripping* means taking a gilt and breaking it down into its individual cash flows that you can trade separately as zero-coupon gilts. So, a three-year gilt has seven individual cash flows consisting of six half-annual coupon payments and a principal repayment. These are only really suitable for certain investors, especially those who don't need ongoing income.

Receiving periodic interest with coupon bonds

The term *coupon bond* comes from the old days when bonds were physical pieces of paper. These bonds had a series of paper tickets attached to them, each maturing at a specific date in the future. Each coupon represented an interest payment, and accumulated interest was paid periodically in exchange for the attached coupons.

Bonds aren't usually physical pieces of paper anymore, but ones that periodically make interest payments are still considered coupon bonds. Investors just don't have to clip coupons!

Forgoing periodic payments with zero-coupon bonds

In contrast to coupon bonds, zero-coupon bonds don't make periodic interest payments: they have no coupons. They still generate income, but instead of making periodic payments, everything is paid out at maturity. Zero-coupon bonds are sold at a *deep discount* (which means they are sold for a price much lower than face value) and pay face value at maturity.

Figuring out deep discounted bonds

The term *deep discounted bonds* refers to a security that's issued at a price well below its face value (either more than 15 per cent in total or at a discount of more than 0.5 per cent per year).

As a consequence, a deep discounted bond has a low coupon rate. Investors who issue deep discount bonds receive much of, if not all, the return in the form of the repayment of the capital amount at redemption when the bond reaches maturity.

Sizing up asset-backed securities

Although not technically a bond, in the strictest sense, from a corporate finance perspective, asset-backed securities have not been short of controversy since the 2007 financial crisis. Advocates of such schemes certainly argue that they're unrelated to the types of asset that brought down Lehman Brothers at the height of the financial crisis.

Asset-backed securities are securities sold by a company in order to raise capital for an investment (such as issuing bonds) and then the securities are repaid using the revenues raised from that investment. For example, if a bank issues an asset-backed security, the money it raises from the sale can then be used to make a business loan to someone else. Whereas the asset-backed security may pay 5 per cent to the investor, the returns are repaid using part of the 6 per cent interest that the bank earns from the business loan.

In a typical business loan, if the business defaults on the loan the lender owns whatever assets it can take or sell from the business, provided that the bank has taken security over those assets. The security of an asset-backed security is repaid using the cash flows from the business loan, and so if the business defaults the assets of the business are sold and the profits used to repay the holders of the asset-backed securities first; only then does whatever's left over belong to the bank. However, it is important to emphasise that an asset-backed secured loan is not a typical business loan.

Having the best of two worlds with convertible bonds

Imagine for a moment that you're not sure whether you want to buy bonds or shares and you're weighing up the pros and cons of both. You know that the bonds are going to generate more returns if the company's share price drops, thus protecting your entire investment portfolio, but if the company does well the shares can easily outperform the bonds. Or perhaps your company really wants to sell shares but is afraid that issuing more shares will make investors believe that their own shares are overpriced. This perception may cause the investors to sell their shares, reducing the market price of all shares in issue and making the new shares worth less than you'd hoped. In both cases, you can find the answer to your problem in the use of convertible bonds.

Convertible bonds work just like normal corporate bonds (see the earlier section 'Considering corporate bonds'), except that purchasers have the right, at their discretion, to convert the bonds into a predetermined number of shares in the company. If you're the investor and the company starts doing very well, causing the share price to increase, you can convert your bonds to the more valuable shares. But if the share price drops, you're still guaranteed returns from your bond purchase – assuming that you're not foolish enough to exchange perfectly good bonds for falling share prices.

Spreading the risks to the unwary

Mortgage-backed securities are a special type of asset-backed security that's backed by (yes, you guessed it) mortgages. A bank issues these securities to raise money in order to fund mortgage lending. They're particularly noteworthy because, first, they're the most common of all asset-backed securities and, second (and more infamously), these mortgage-backed securities were a common way for US banks that were holding large amounts of troubled subprime mortgages likely to default to distribute their failure to investors and other banks. This technique wasn't always the case, but for a time leading up to 2007, it happened a lot.

These banks combined some of these subprime mortgages with normal mortgages to form a bundle of assets that, in turn, were used to form mortgage-backed securities. These securities were then sold, putting the risk of failure just as much in the hands of the holders of those securities as anyone else. When the mortgages started going into default, everyone who touched that mortgage or the securities derived from that mortgage began losing value and money. This practice caused a chain reaction of failure stemming from the reckless lack of proper risk management in a few very large banks, and it was this practice that was publicised quite heavily in the UK.

As a corporate finance manager, issuing convertible bonds allows you to raise equity without reducing investor confidence in the price of your shares. You're giving investors the option to exchange bonds for equity. Perhaps it's not the ideal situation for your capital structure, because in such instances selling equity is the most desirable option, but it provides the best option possible in some cases where a straight IPO would be harmful.

Using callable bonds to capitalise on interest rates

Issuing bonds can be extremely expensive for a company. For every bond sold, the company must pay back the principal as well as interest. If market interest rates drop below the rates that a company is paying on existing bonds, it would much prefer to stop paying the rate on those bonds and issue new bonds at the lower rate, right? Well, that's possible!

Callable bonds are bonds that are issued with a contractual clause that allows the issuing company to redeem the bonds before their maturity date at a price equal to the present value plus a premium. This premium, which is paid to the investor, acts like an early repayment penalty in order to reimburse the investor fairly for not extending the debt to its full maturity date.

Looking at the pros and cons of puttable bonds

If your company is buying bonds, it may want to protect itself from a change in interest rates.

Say that you're buying bonds at a 5 per cent interest rate and the rates go up to 10 per cent. *Puttable bonds* allow you to force the issuer to buy back your 5 per cent bonds so that you can use that money to buy 10 per cent bonds.

When your company buys puttable bonds and interest rates increase, you can insist on pre-maturity repayment of the principal, minus a penalty for early withdrawal. You can then use that money to buy higher-rate bonds.

For a company, however, using this strategy to attract investors can be particularly risky. If several of your investors exercise their 'put option' (check out Chapter 13), forcing your company to repay its debts, and your company doesn't have enough cash to repay them, it has to sell the capital it bought using that debt to make repayments. This scenario can lead to *insolvency,* where you simply don't have the money to pay your debts and are forced out of business. This form of potential repayment obligation isn't measured on the balance sheet, and so your company looks like it has more liquid assets than it really does.

Therefore, managers watching the company's liquidity need to use financial data that adjusts for these sorts of puttable bonds when determining the company's risk of insolvency or illiquidity.

Getting the gist of registered bonds

The vast majority of all bonds in existence around the world today are *registered bonds* (which means the owner's name and contact information is recorded and kept on file with the company who has taken out the bond), including the majority of bonds that fall into the categories we describe in this chapter.

Registered bonds don't exist as physical entities. Instead, they're electronically registered to individuals, and serial numbers connect those bonds to those individuals as a means of tracking ownership. Sometimes a certificate representing ownership is issued, but even that's not the norm, and exchanging it doesn't change ownership. Nearly all bonds are exchanged electronically now.

Counting on forgiveness with catastrophe bonds

These bonds are extremely rare but still worth noting because they play an interesting role as a method for raising capital and for diversifying operational risk.

Catastrophe bonds are bonds that raise capital for companies to limit the risk of an event occurring. The company issues bonds to raise capital with the stipulation that if a specific event occurs, bondholders must forgive repayment of the interest and/or principal. Any company can issue catastrophe bonds; they're an alternative to buying insurance to limit the risk of a potential disaster.

For example, an insurance company may issue catastrophe bonds to raise money in case of an earthquake. If an earthquake doesn't occur by the maturity date, the company pays the investors the principal with interest. The funds received from the sale of the bonds are usually reinvested by the insurance company to generate interest, which is then used for the bonds' repayment. If an earthquake occurs, however, the insurance company instead uses the money from selling bonds to help pay the huge number of claims that result, and the investors give up their claims to any future cash flows on the investment. The bottom line is that if the disaster happens, the investment is voided.

Looking at Bond Rates

Most of the bonds we discuss in the preceding sections, except index-linked gilts, are frequently fixed-rate bonds. You can also, however, find them in variable-rate forms.

Fixed-rate bonds are pretty simple. If the bond says that it pays 1 per cent interest plus principal, that's precisely what you're going to earn: no changes, no fluctuations, no nothing. The nominal cash flows of a fixed-rate bond are exactly as advertised: repayment of the principal with an added interest payment equal to the percentage rate.

A variable-rate bond, on the other hand, is one where the interest rate or the principal payments is variable. So, the amount of money you make by investing in variable-rate bonds changes over the life of the bond. You may make 1 per cent one year, 100 per cent the next year and then 2 per cent the year after that, depending on what the bond is pegged to. That's how the returns on these bonds are determined: they're tied to some other measure.

Here are a few common types of variable-rate bonds:

✔ **Floating Interest Rate bonds:** This type is easily the most common form of variable-rate bond. The interest rate on these bonds floats with the market interest rate. If the interest rate offered on bonds for sale on the open market increases, the bond pays more, matching the market interest rate. On the other hand, if the market rate decreases, so do the returns on your floating-rate bond.

These bonds are good options for attracting investors speculating on interest rate increases, but benefiting issuing companies when market interest rates decrease.

✔ **Inverse Floating Interest Rate bonds:** This type offers returns that are the opposite of the market interest rate. These bonds work just like standard interest rate bonds, except that they go in the opposite direction. When the market rate goes down, the rate on these bonds goes up, and vice versa. Investors like these bonds when interest rates are projected to decrease, and issuing companies like them when interest rates are projected to go up.

These bonds are also helpful for portfolio risk management, because they allow bond investors to buy equal amounts of opposite-direction floating-rate bonds (interest floats and inverse interest floats) to protect against all interest rate changes and help stabilise interest rate returns.

Many investors feel that this approach minimises returns, however, because a strategy of using your money to buy only the best investments, instead of using a portion for risk management, decreases potential. In Chapter 14 we provide a detailed discussion of the relationship between risk and reward.

✔ **Indexed bonds:** This type of variable-rate bond has its interest rate pegged to any of the many available indexes. For example, if you buy or sell a bond pegged to the FTSE 100 and this index increases by 10 per cent, your interest rate also increases by 10 per cent.

Be careful in the way you interpret these increases. If your FTSE 100-pegged bond starts out paying 1 per cent and the FTSE 100 increases by 10 per cent, your bond doesn't increase to 11 per cent returns; it increases to 1.1 per cent returns. A 10 per cent increase on 1 per cent is an additional 0.1 per cent.

Reading Bond Information

Look in the finance portion of any newspaper (for example, *The Financial Times*) or the finance page of any major website (such as CNNMoney's page at `www.money.cnn.com/data/bonds/`) and you can access information about the bond market. This data about specific bonds is designed to help buyers and sellers make effective decisions regarding the potential to invest in bonds or issue their own. The exact information provided depends a lot on the types of bonds being described.

The following is a list of common information about bonds that may improve your vocabulary and make sure that you know how to read bonds in the language of corporate finance:

- ✔ **Ask (sometimes referred to as the *offer*):** The price at which the seller is attempting to sell the bond. If this amount is above the bid price, no sale can be made until the buyer and seller give in and accept the price of the other party; the difference is called the *spread*.

- ✔ **Bid:** The price at which the buyer is attempting to buy a particular bond. If below the ask price, no sale is made until the buyer and seller agree on a compromise; again, the difference is called the spread.

- ✔ **Coupon/Rate:** These terms refer to the interest rate generated on a bond. This interest rate is expressed as a percentage with up to three decimal places.

- ✔ **Credit quality ratings:** Performed by a credit rating agency on a bond and then provided to the public in order to help prospective buyers assess the risk of the issuing corporation defaulting. When bonds are issued, the issuers are asking others to loan them money through the purchase of the bond. As a result, companies issuing bonds must undergo a credit check just like an individual getting a mortgage or credit card.

  Standard & Poor's (S&P) and Moody's are the two primary rating agencies. Each uses a slightly different rating system, but their purpose is generally the same. Table 11-1 lists their ratings from highest to lowest and explains what they mean.

Table 11-1		Bond Credit Ratings
S&P	**Moody's**	**Interpretation**
AAA	Aaa	Highest rated; lowest risk
AA	Aa	Very good; low risk
A	A	Somewhat good; low risk
BBB	Baa	Moderately rated; low risk but susceptible to troubles; may not be able to withstand economic or market fluctuations
BB	Ba	Susceptible to troubles; stable only as long as the market or economy remains stable; bad
B	B	Moderately high risk; bad
CCC	Caa	High risk; bad
CC	Ca	Very high risk; bad
C	C	No interest income bonds
D	D	Already in default

- **Face value/Par value:** The amount of the principal repayment on the bond.

  Before taking any action, however, be sure to confirm the value, because variations do exist and range a great deal.

- **Issuer:** The organisation issuing the bond.

- **Maturity/Maturity date:** Can be listed in one of two ways:

  - As a duration of time (for example, one year, ten years, and so on). The bond matures in an exact duration of time after the purchase date.

  - As a date (for example, November 2013, 15 February 2019, and so on). The bond matures on the date listed.

- **Price:** People often get confused with bonds when they start talking about price, yield and the relationship between them.

  Price isn't just listed as the nominal face value of the bond; it's listed as a percentage of the face value. So, if a bond is listed at 100.00, it's selling at the exact face value of the bond. If the bond is selling below face value, say at 99.95, it's selling at 99.95 per cent of the face value. If the price is 101.01, it's selling at 101.01 per cent of the face value.

  A bond that sells for under face value is selling at a discount, whereas a bond selling above face value is selling at a premium. At the end, the principal repayment is still going to be the face value of the bond, but the bond itself can sell for higher or lower than the principal repayment. Why do people do this? Interest payments! Even if the interest on a bond is well below market rates, a bond can still be attractive if it's sold at a heavy discount. If a bond is sold at a premium price, it can still be attractive if it has high interest rates.

  Bond pricing can also be considered in terms of dirty or clean prices:

  - *Dirty* is the bond price including accrued interest.

  - *Clean* accounts for just the price and not any accrued interest.

  The prices listed in most major outlets are clean prices.

- **Price change:** Refers only to the amount the price has changed since the last period, which can be anywhere from one day to one year, depending on where you're getting your information from. It can be expressed in two ways:

  - In nominal terms, the price change is expressed in terms of the sterling increase or decrease.

  - In ratio terms, the price change is expressed as a percentage of the previously reported price.

✔ **Volume:** Describes the total value of all bonds of a particular type being sold (as opposed to providing information about the value of any particular bond). So if someone issues and sells successfully ten bonds worth £10 each, the volume is £100 during that time period. In the next period, if only one person who bought that bond resells the bond, the volume drops to £10.

✔ **Yield:** The amount of returns that a bond generates at a given price. Yield is one of the most important terms in the financial markets because the yield is what you actually get back for what you've paid out. That's why yield is related to price – because the amount of returns on a particular bond that an investor generates depends on the relationship between price and yield. If a one-year bond yields £100 per year and the market price of the bond was £100, the yield is £0 or 0 per cent. On the other hand, if the price was only £50, the yield is £50 or 100 per cent. Yield, also known as *current yield,* refers specifically to the annual amount of interest paid divided by the market price of the bond (which is then multiplied by 100 to make it a percentage). This annual yield differs from yield to maturity, which is the total amount of returns generated by holding the bond to maturity rather than over the course of a single year.

✔ **Yield change:** Refers only to the amount the yield has changed since the last period, which can be anywhere from one day to one year, depending on where you're getting your information from. Like price change it can be expressed in two ways:

- In nominal terms, the yield change is expressed in terms of the sterling increase or decrease.

- In ratio terms, the yield change is expressed as a percentage of the previously reported price.

✔ **Yield to maturity (YTM):** The value of the returns on a bond if it's held until its maturity date, given the current price. Of course, if the price is higher, the yield is lower, because the percentage return on the investment is a lower proportion of the price. Conversely, the yield is higher if the price is lower. YTM assumes not only that the bond is held to maturity, but also that no coupons are collected, which allows all coupons to continue accruing interest until the maturity date.

Understanding Bond Valuation

The valuation of bonds refers to the process by which people determine a bond's value. This information is then used, in conjunction with your personal estimates of what you're willing to pay or your other options, to determine what's considered a fair price. These valuation methods allow:

- ✔ Investors to work out what they're willing to pay, what they can expect in returns and what their investment portfolio is worth at any given point in time.
- ✔ Issuing organisations to determine how much capital they can raise using debt, and the interest rates they need to offer in order to attract investors.

You value bonds with the following maths:

$$\text{Bond value} = \sum_{t=1}^{T} \frac{Coupon}{(1+r)^t} + \left[\frac{Face\,Value}{(1+r)^t} \right]$$

where r stands for the annual interest rate and t is the number of years that the single cash flow has until maturity. Therefore, this equation says that to find the total present value of the bond you need to add up the present values of all the coupons and then add the present value of the end principal payment. (If you're not familiar with present value, see Chapter 9.) That thing at the front that looks like a giant 'E' is called a *sigma*. All it means is that you're adding the values of different things together; in this case, the different present values of future coupon cash flows for each year.

The comforting part of understanding this equation is that even the more complicated equations are really just variations that build on this same theme, using additional variables and information to refine it and make it more accurate.

Zero-coupon bonds and other bonds that don't make periodic interest payments don't have this sort of calculation. Instead, because they generate all their cash flows at maturity, the bond value is equal to the present value of the single future cash flow after taking into account accumulated interest. Just look at them with the present value of its maturity date, instead of including any coupon payments.

If you're not holding a bond to maturity, or you want to calculate your percentage return on bond investment, you can do so by calculating the *holding period yield,* which is the amount of yield that a bond provides while a person is holding it. In essence this figure assumes that the person is selling the bond before maturity – though some people just really like doing maths:

Holding period yield = {[Coupon + (Net gain/Loss)] ÷ Purchase price} × 100

In this case, the net gain or loss is the price of selling the bond minus the price of purchasing the bond: in other words, the profits generated from buying and reselling the bond. You add any coupon payments you receive during the holding period to calculate what the bond is worth over a holding period rather than to maturity.

Of course, doing so assumes that you can estimate accurately the price you can sell the bond for, which is a pretty big assumption for some people. Take the value of that bond and divide it by your purchase price to show your return on investment as a proportion; multiply it by 100 to calculate it as a percentage.

Chapter 12

Being Savvy When Shopping for Shares

In This Chapter

▶ Understanding various types of share orders

▶ Looking at long and short stocks, chips, caps and sectors

▶ Determining whether you're dealing with a bull or a bear market

▶ Figuring out what a share is worth

S hopping for shares is a lot like going to a Black Friday sale every day of the year: a lot of otherwise rational people go completely out of their minds, pretend that they know what the value of everything in the shop is and start fighting with each other like lunatics over the right to buy or sell something that they don't understand and potentially have no use for. Yet people keep coming back to smoke from the pipe of *equities* (a term which you can use interchangeably with *shares*) that promises an easy fix in the form of quick payouts, but which far too often leaves them exposed and wondering where all their money went.

Things don't have to be this way, though. Share prices aren't random and you don't have to treat them as if they are. Just by knowing a few simple things about how shares are traded, the different options available to you and what influences share prices, you can incorporate shares successfully into your investing strategies and portfolios. This chapter alone can't do that for you, but it does help you understand what's going on in the stock market so that its workings don't look like complete and utter chaos.

We describe how shares are traded, the different types of purchases and sales you can make, the different categories of organisations and their respective shares, the different positions you can hold on any shares, and how to view and measure movements in the overall stock market. We also look briefly at each of the major influences on a share's price, reviewing many of the models used to determine whether a share is overpriced or underpriced compared to its value.

Exchanging Shares: Where to Buy and Sell

Exchanges (which means buying and selling, as opposed to swapping) in shares take place by different methods that facilitate the purchase and sale of equities between two or more people who otherwise have no other way of contacting each other. Exchanges are made through three primary methods, each considered to be a separate market for shares:

- ✔ **Stock exchanges:** The most commonly known market for the exchange of shares is, as you may guess, the stock exchange (such as the London Stock Exchange). These large, centralised exchanges are usually located in big rooms within buildings in major cities around the world, where brokers, dealers, broker-dealers and others involved in the exchange of shares congregate. The exchanges themselves offer a number of services, including the use of electronic communication networks (ECNs) to facilitate trades.

- ✔ **Electronic communication networks:** ECNs are computer networks that link traders, brokers, dealers and even stock exchanges in order to facilitate the trade of equities. ECNs have greatly increased in use over the past few decades and have made share trading much more accessible to non-professionals.

- ✔ **Over-the-counter (OTC) markets:** OTC markets are a less popular method of exchanging shares, but they often include access to shares that aren't available in any other way. Over-the-counter markets include any system other than stock exchanges or ECNs that facilitates the trade in equities. They're usually networks of brokers and dealers communicating outside exchanges. Over-the-counter shares include, obviously, those companies not listed on major exchanges. As a result, they experience far less volume and don't tend to attract as many investors.

If you're not familiar with the different types of shares, check out Chapter 3.

Looking at the Different Types of Orders

When you want to buy or sell shares, you have to decide on the type of buy or sell order you want to place, the price at which you want the transaction to take place and the timing of the transaction. You can control all these factors by managing your transaction *order* (or instruction).

Imagine that you want to buy 10 shares in the car manufacturer Ford for £10 per share, and you want the transaction to take place as soon as a seller of that many shares at that price becomes available. All you do is give that order to your broker or set it up online using your brokerage account. Whether your order is fulfilled or not depends on whether a seller can be found who's willing to sell 10 shares for £10 per share.

Which brings up the subject of the mechanism by which the price of equities is set. Pricing is performed in a sort of dual-auction system, where potential buyers and sellers negotiate back and forth on price until a price is established that allows a transaction to take place. This compromise is found through fluctuations in the *bid* and *ask* prices of the shares:

- ✔ **Ask price:** The price of a share for which the people who own the share are willing to sell it. When the owners of a share want to sell their shares, they must ask for a price that buyers are willing to pay, or else they're unable to sell their shares.

- ✔ **Bid price:** The price that buyers are willing to pay to purchase the shares. The buyers must pay a price that sellers are willing to sell their shares for, or else they're unable to buy those shares.

- ✔ **Spread:** The difference between the ask and bid prices.

The price of a share is established when two people find a compromise in the spread whereby the buyer is willing to pay a particular price and the seller is willing to accept that price. The price of a share increases when buyers are willing to compromise more, paying the ask price or even more. The price of a share decreases when the sellers are willing to compromise more, accepting the bid price or even less.

The different types of orders available are meant to manage the interaction between the bid price, the ask price and the spread. They do so by allowing the investor to determine when and at what price the transaction is going to take place, if at all. The following sections describe a few of these types of orders.

You have the option to do *fill-or-kill orders.* In this case, your order states that for the exchange to be executed, it must be for the entirety of your order, not just a portion of it. For those occasions when having your order filled in its entirety doesn't matter, you have the option to allow a transaction to fulfil a portion of your order while leaving the remaining portion to be fulfilled in another transaction, if at all.

Making market orders

The *market order* is the simplest type of order for the purchase or sale of equity. In a market order, the investor simply accepts the price set by the other side of the transaction. If the person setting the market order is a buyer, the price established automatically becomes the ask price and the exchange happens almost instantly, because the buyer isn't waiting for the seller to come down in price.

If the person setting the market order is the seller, the price automatically becomes the bid price, and that exchange, too, occurs almost instantly.

Controlling prices with stop and limit orders

The fact that stop and limit orders are even differentiated from each other is really rather silly, because the distinction has more to do with the motivation of the traders than the mechanism of the order. For now, we treat them as the same thing, but we do explain briefly the difference at the end of this section.

Stop and *limit* orders are used to manage the price at which a transaction takes place. For example, an investor may want to place an order whereby shares aren't purchased until prices drop below or rise above a certain level. When the trigger on which the order is dependent occurs, it automatically takes place, assuming that a partner to the exchange is available at a given price. The same can apply to selling shares: someone may place an order to sell a specified number of shares only if and when the price of the shares increases or decreases by a predetermined amount.

The motivation behind this strategy depends on the order and the price. Here are the four options:

- ✔ **Someone sets an order to sell shares when they drop below a certain price:** This person is probably attempting to limit her potential losses from the price going too low.

- ✔ **Someone wants to sell shares after the price increases:** This person probably has a strategy in mind that involves walking away with the revenues from the sale.

- ✔ **An investor wants to purchase shares after they drop below a specified price:** This person probably believes that the particular price is a good deal and that the price will go back in an upwards direction.

✔ **An investor wants to purchase shares after the price increases beyond a certain point:** This person may be waiting for the share price to have already started to creep up, to ensure that the company isn't simply performing poorly in the market.

The price that the order is set at isn't necessarily the price at which the transaction takes place. These types of orders are typically 'at price or higher' or 'at price or lower', and so market gaps can occur that cause the transaction to occur at a price that exceeds the milestone price. For example, say that someone owns shares priced at £15 per share and wants to sell those shares when they hit a price of £10 per share or lower in order to help limit risk. If suddenly no one is willing to pay even £10 per share, causing a gap in the spread, the order occurs at the next transaction price, even if that's below £10 per share.

If stop and limit orders are basically the same thing, why do we differentiate them? The answer is all about motivation:

✔ **Stop orders** are orders to sell shares when they drop below a certain price, stopping the amount of potential loss that may be experienced.

✔ **Limit orders** are orders to purchase shares when they drop below a certain price or to sell shares when they exceed the trigger price.

But stop and limit orders are really the same thing and are treated as such in computer-automated trading.

Pondering pegged orders

A *pegged order* is a bit like a stop or limit order (see the preceding section), in that the exchange doesn't take place until the trigger price is reached. But in a pegged order that trigger price changes along with the value of some other variable, such as an index or economic measure. When that variable reaches a particular value, the peg fluctuations stop and the order is set.

Counting on time-contingent orders

An order can be contingent on time. For example, some orders are delayed for a predetermined period of time before they're entered into the market. Other orders are cancelled if they're not fulfilled before a certain period of time. Day orders are time-contingent orders, because they're cancelled at the end of the trading day if they're not filled by then.

Comparing Long and Short Stocks

In the context of equities trading, the terms 'long' and 'short' tend to be a mystery for a large number of people. After all, shares always remain the same: whether you're buying long or selling short doesn't change the share itself, it just changes the nature of whether or not you're in possession of that share and for what periods of time.

In this section we set the record straight. We also discuss the use of *margin accounts,* which allow you to buy shares without being in possession of the funds to do so. Put simply, this approach is borrowing money to buy shares, though the mechanics of the transaction are similar to short-selling.

Buying long

When people think about buying shares, the majority of the time they're thinking about buying long.

Buying long means that you own the shares you're buying immediately after the transaction takes place, and you continue to own those shares until you sell them. People buy long with the intention of keeping the shares for at least a short period of time - perhaps for a few minutes or perhaps for as long as possible - before eventually reselling them. The exact length of time that you own the shares doesn't impact whether the position is considered short or long; the ownership is what matters. When people buy long, they believe that the value of the shares is going to increase while they're in their possession. So, they buy the shares, allow the value to appreciate (go up in value) and then sell them when the value is high enough. Buy, own, sell - pretty simple, right?

Buying long theoretically has limited loss potential but unlimited gain potential. When you buy shares for £10, the worst thing that can happen is the company goes bust and you lose the whole £10. On the other hand, that £10 may, in theory, increase in value by an unlimited amount. Of course, reality sets in when you realise that the chances of it increasing by even a moderate amount are volatile, leaving you with significant risk of loss. In other words, the gain potential exists, but the reality is often far less glamorous, usually somewhere well within the range of −10 per cent to +10 per cent annual change.

Selling long doesn't exist; after you sell the shares, they're no longer yours.

Using margin trading

Purchasing shares using *margin trading* means that you borrowed money to buy them. Most often this approach involves opening a margin account with your stockbroker, whereby the broker or an associated financial institution lends you money, usually with relatively low interest rates, in order to buy shares. Typically, buying on margin involves maintaining a minimum balance in the account (or a related account) as collateral in case you invest in a dead duck.

Investors are advised to be very, very careful when buying on margin:stock investing tends to yield volatile and risky returns anyway, whereas the interest you have to pay by borrowing on margin is a guaranteed cost. Buying on margin limits your potential gains while exacerbating any potential losses, because you have to pay interest on the borrowed funds.

Selling short

Just as no such thing as selling long exists (as we describe in the earlier section 'Buying long'), you also can't buy short. Instead, *selling short* (or *short-selling*) means that you're selling shares that aren't currently in your possession to someone else with the obligation to purchase those shares from that person at a later date. People sell short when they believe that the value of the shares is going to fall. They're able to make money when the share price performs poorly by short-selling.

Here's how short-selling works. The investor borrows a number of shares in a company from a broker and sells them to someone for the revenue. Usually this transaction is done using a margin account (check out the preceding section), where the investor has to maintain other assets as collateral for the loan. At some point in the future, the investor needs to purchase the same number of shares and return them to the broker.

If the share price goes down during the period that the investor shorted the shares, when she repurchases the shares she pays less than she earned from the sale. This scenario generates a profit. If the value of the shares rises during the shorted period, the investor must pay more to repurchase them than she generated in revenue from the sale, meaning that she loses money.

Short-selling is one method that investors use to generate income and returns even when investments are performing poorly. (Another is raising income by selling derivatives, as we discuss in Chapter 13.)

Short-selling can be extremely risky. When you sell shares and are obligated to rebuy them, the potential for financial loss is unlimited. Consider the following two examples involving a pet hamster trained to be a stock trader:

- ✔ Sergei the hamster short-sells 10 shares in ABC Ltd for £10 each. The company does very poorly and goes bust. Because the company no longer has shares to repurchase, Sergei gets to keep all £100 from the short sale and doesn't have to pay anyone to repurchase the shares. He uses the money to put an extension on his Habitrail home. Go Sergei!

- ✔ Sergei the hamster short-sells 10 shares of ABC Limited for £10 each. The company does amazingly well and the price of the shares increases to £10 million each, leaving him owing nearly £100 million. The difference between his initial £100 revenues (10 shares × £10 per share) and the £100 million it costs him to repurchase those shares (10 shares × £10 million per share) is £99,999,900. Sergei is found dead the next morning by the plumber unblocking the toilet. Poor Sergei!

Classifying Shares: Chips, Caps and Sectors

You may hear a lot of talk about different types of chips, caps and sectors when you're looking into investing in stocks and shares. These terms are all just different ways of classifying and lumping together different types of stocks and shares and their underlying companies:

- ✔ **Cap:** Refers to the size of the company in terms of its total value. A cap is also used in an agreement with a counterparty to set an upper limit for interest rates.

- ✔ **Chips:** Can mean a variety of things - company size, business or country - depending on the type of chip you're talking about.

- ✔ **Sector:** Refers to the type of industry in which a company operates.

A single company can be classified in several different ways. For example, British Airways is a blue chip company, a large cap company and operates within the travel and tourism sector. So each term represents a classification of different companies grouped together by similar traits.

Dipping into chips

This metaphor originally referred to the different coloured chips in a casino. Blue chips had the highest value, and so the term *blue chip* is used to refer to the highest value companies. Since then, other 'chips' have been introduced that have very different meanings, making the entire metaphor nonsense. Oh well, that's life.

No ideal way exists to summarise the chips anymore, and so we just dive into what each one means:

- **Blue chip:** Large, highly valued companies able easily to withstand market shocks and fluctuations; safe havens for investing with limited risk but also with limited growth potential.

- **Green chip:** Companies that work in green energy, sustainable products and services, or whose primary operations are otherwise associated with environmentalism and 'going green'.

- **Red chip:** Any Chinese company listed in an exchange outside China.

- **Purple chip:** Large, Chinese companies listed outside China (blue chip + red chip = purple chip); investors know their colour theory!

- **P chip:** Chinese companies listed in Hong Kong.

- **S chip:** Chinese companies listed on the Singapore Exchange.

Capitalising on market caps

A company's 'cap' refers to its *market capitalisation,* which is the total market value of all issued shares. Companies are categorised by their total value into five primary categories (though the actual criteria will all depend on the market concerned):

- **Large cap:** Total market capitalisation of £10 billion or more.

- **Mid cap:** Total market capitalisation between £2 billion and £10 billion.

- **Small cap:** Total market capitalisation of less than £2 billion.

- **Micro cap:** Total market capitalisation between £50 million and £200 million.

- **Nano cap:** Total market capitalisation of less than £50 million.

In for a penny...

Although you may hear people talk about *penny stock* as a sort of classification of market capitalisation, no single definition applies for one. Depending on who you talk to a penny stock can be an investment that sells for less than 1 penny per share, less than £1 per share or less than £5 per share. It can also mean any company in the micro or nano cap range or any shares that aren't traded on a major stock market.

Penny stocks do tend, however, to be the smallest, most volatile and riskiest of all investments.

They're very attractive to some people because penny stocks also have the most potential for growth, in those extremely rare instances when one succeeds. These investments also tend to be extremely volatile, changing in value by several hundred or thousand per cent in a single day, giving them some potential for people attempting to take advantage of interval trading (see Chapter 16 for more on this topic).

Market capitalisation is simple to calculate. All you do is multiply the number of shares issued by the market price per share. So if a company has 100 million shares in issue and each share sells for £20, the calculation looks like this: $100,000,000 \times £20 = £2$ billion. In this example, the company would be mid cap.

Investors watch the market capitalisation for companies very closely, because it's often used as a quick reference point for the amount of potential risk and return associated with an organisation. The larger a company's market capitalisation, the more likely it is to be viewed as a lower-risk company that will sustain its value and possibly pay dividends, although it's never going to be a fast-growing company. Smaller market cap companies tend to be higher risk and are less likely to pay dividends, but also have greater potential for fast growth.

Selecting by sectors

The sector in which a company operates refers to its *primary industry*. Different sectors respond differently to external economic conditions, seasonal trends and other variables, and so knowing which sector a company operates in, as well as the variables that influence the price and performance of the companies within that sector, can be helpful.

Here's a list of some of the most commonly cited sectors, with examples of the products or services available from that sector:

- **Automotive:** Vehicles.
- **Consumer discretionary:** Rock 'n' roll, fashion, booze, media and so on – essentially, spending on non-essentials.
- **Consumer goods:** Food, perfumery goods, cereals and so on.
- **Energy:** Petroleum, biofuels, wind power, solar power, nuclear power, coal and so on.
- **Financial:** All financial institutions.
- **Healthcare:** Doctors, hospitals, lab work and other medical services.
- **Hospitality:** Hotels, restaurants, tourism and so on.
- **Industrial:** Metal work, machining and other manufacturing.
- **Infrastructure:** Major construction work, such as roads, bridges, high-rise flats and so on.
- **Pharmaceutical:** Medicines and related products.
- **Technology:** Computers, robotics, engineering, research and so on.
- **Telecom:** Anything related to phones and Internet services.

Knowing Where the Market Stands: Bulls versus Bears

The bulls versus the bears? We can almost sense your intrigue as to how two animals fit into corporate finance. Well, they do as metaphors for what the stock market is doing at any given point in time. Exactly why the terms 'bear' and 'bull' were chosen has been lost in translation, but the usage of these terms in the context of stock markets dates back to at least 1714, according to the Oxford English Dictionary.

The terms each have several different usages and variations, but all have the same basic idea:

- **Bull market:** The stock market is *increasing* in value.
- **Bear market:** The stock market is *decreasing* in value.

No definitive criteria exist for how much the stock market must change in value, up or down, but the implication is that the change is significant enough to warrant that investors consider altering their investing strategy as a result. So that doesn't mean reacting to any temporary changes in value or market shocks that are going to rebound quickly.

Individual shares can also be a bull or a bear, meaning that the share is expected to increase or decrease, respectively, in value. The term can also apply to people. If we believe that a share or the stock market is going to increase in value, we're said to be *bullish*. If we believe that a fall in value is going to take place, we're *bearish*. More specifically, we may say that we're bullish on shares in companies that operate in the technological sector, which means that we believe that shares in such companies are going to increase in value. We can also say that 'we're bullish on technological companies, but Asus is a bear', which means that we think the value of shares in technological companies is going to increase in value except for Asus, which is going to decrease in value.

Blatant legal notice! We are *not* saying that share prices in Asus are going to increase or decrease. These statements are just examples of how the terminology is used. If you trade anything because of these examples, you shouldn't be allowed to touch your own money ever again!

Watching Stocks and Shares Indices

A *stock and share index* isn't a physical entity. Instead, an index is simply an average that's closely watched as investors attempt to use the information to get an idea of what's happening in the overall stock market. Each index is typically calculated using some form of *weighted average* (an average whereby each quantity is assigned a weighting depending on the relative importance of each quantity) that takes several different companies, weighs them using its preferred method and then takes the market value of the weighted average measured by the prices of the underlying stocks and shares. Each index uses its own method for calculating averages for different types of companies, different sizes of companies, different numbers of companies and so on.

Here are some well-known indices:

- ✔ **FTSE 100 Index:** A share index of the 100 companies listed on the London Stock Exchange with the highest market capitalisation.

- ✔ **Dow Jones Industrial Average (DJIA):** An average of 30 different companies in the industrial sector.

✔ **S&P 500:** A composite of 500 different companies chosen by Standard and Poor's.

✔ **NASDAQ:** Originally called the National Association of Securities Dealers Automated Quotations, it has 12 different indices, each focusing on a different sector or market capitalisation.

Lots of other stock and share indices measure the value of stocks and shares from different parts of the world: the Nikkei 225 is from Japan, the Hang Seng is from Hong Kong, plus many, many more.

No index includes all the stocks and shares from a particular nation. Instead, each attempts to provide an average idea of what the overall stock market is doing, as well as what individual categories of stocks and shares are doing (see the earlier section 'Classifying Shares: Chips, Caps and Sectors'), by taking a sample and determining the average change in value.

Calculating the Value of Stocks and Shares

Easily the most difficult part of investing in stocks and shares is working out what they're worth and projecting how their prices are going to change. A number of different factors influence the value and price of shares. You can measure the stocks and shares themselves using any of a number of equity valuation models.

Many people prefer to look at the individual company to assess its financial and competitive performance. Others look at the performance of entire sectors and then simply choose one or more companies from a sector that appears to be doing well given the current economic conditions. Many investors, particularly traders, watch for fluctuations in the total stock market, hoping to generate earnings by taking advantage of intervals in price over time.

Just about everyone, however, watches the national economy and the macroeconomic (see the later section 'Mulling over macroeconomics') indicators that can help you understand how the economy is performing and at what point in the business cycle a nation is currently standing.

Surveying equity valuation models

Far too many different valuation models are in use to be able to talk about each one here; many are becoming extremely involved due to the increased use of computers and financial engineering. But in essence, three primary categories of equity valuation models exist:

- **Absolute models:** Sometimes called *intrinsic models,* these look for the value of the company itself, seeking to find a measure that can capture the exact value of each company. These models include the following:

    - **Dividend discount model (*or dividend valuation model*):** Attempts to use the present discounted value of future dividends to value the price of a share.

    - **Liquidation value (or *net assets method*):** The total of the revenues achievable from selling all the company's assets after paying back liabilities; this is used as a price floor for total market capitalisation.

    - **Free cash flow method (or *present value of future cash flows method*):** Estimates cash flows to the firm and to equity, to estimate both fair price and growth rates.

- **Relative models:** Sometimes called *extrinsic models,* these intend to understand how the price or value of a company can be assessed by looking at variables that are influenced, at least in part, by things outside the organisation's control, such as share price, other companies in the sector and the performance of a company relative to economic and market performance ratios. Such ratios often include measures that involve comparisons to the sector, to the economy or to share price. Common values included in these models are earnings per share, the P/E (price to earnings) ratio and market responsiveness.

- **Hybrid models:** Tend to be more complex but only in the sense that they attempt to use methods employed by both absolute and relative models. Often they attempt to find differentials in the intrinsic and extrinsic values.

Checking out corporate analysis

Corporate analysis is one of the primary methods of determining the value of stocks and shares, because the value of the underlying company contributes strongly to the value of the shares.

Don't be confused; the actual price of the shares is different from its value, and whether you prefer to watch the value of the company or the price of the shares depends a lot on your investing strategy. High-frequency traders tend to watch share prices more than the value of the underlying companies, whereas value investors, as you can probably guess, tend to watch the value of the underlying company, because they're looking for stable long-term performance.

A number of different methods are used to analyse corporate performance. We include many of those methods in this book; check out Chapters 4 to 8 and 20. Despite advances in mathematics analyses, these methods are still among the most commonly used.

The great thing about corporate performance is that even though a share's price may fluctuate wildly up and down from an average, often these fluctuations are related more to the behaviours of the stock market than to anything inherent in the share or the company. So, by looking at the company rather than the shares, you can get an idea of whether it has quality and value, and whether the shares appear to be priced too high or too low compared to the value of the company. In the long term (over the course of years), the price of shares tends to float around the assessed value of the company, coming down eventually if it's too high or getting recognised eventually if it's a good bargain, driving prices back up again.

Evaluating industry performance

Each industry responds differently and at different times to different variables. Understanding how each sector responds to cycles and policies in the economy is very important for traders and investors alike. For example, during a recession companies that work in consumer goods (food, perfumery goods, cereals and so on) tend to see a boost in share prices, because demand for these things doesn't decrease greatly. People give up other, more discretionary goods in order to get the things they need.

This fact is particularly true for companies that offer cheap or discount consumer goods, such as Aldi supermarkets. As a result, you can begin to develop an understanding for how strongly each sector responds to changes in the economic cycle. When gross domestic product (GDP) growth slows, you can measure how much sector growth slows.

Another thing to consider is the timing of the response within the sector to changes in the economy, which happens because of the order of cash flows throughout the national economy. An injection of cash into the agricultural sector, for example, is likely to go next into agricultural supply companies, such as Associated British Foods, because farms and farmers tend to spend a large proportion of their revenues on the products these companies produce. When you understand how cash flows through the economy, you can begin to estimate the timing of the response that each sector will experience based on where the initial change in cash flows begins. This phenomenon is called *sector rotation*.

After you establish the relationship between a sector and other sectors in the economy, you can start to evaluate the sector itself. Here are some questions to consider when assessing a sector:

- How many competitors exist in this sector?

- What makes the successful firms more competitive?

- What are the risks of new entrants into the market or new technologies shaking things up?

- How is the industry as a whole changing over time?

- How is it doing compared to other industries?

Factoring in stock market fluctuations

The stock market is completely insane! The prices of stocks and shares can increase or decrease in response to something completely unrelated. Much of this subject is well outside the scope of this book, and moving into the territory of books specialising in investing in stocks and shares.

Chapter 22 on behavioural finance, however, does talk a little about these movements.

Mulling over macroeconomics

Macroeconomics is the study of large-scale, collective economic management. It's usually related to the national economy or other issues involving an aggregate of smaller economic entities. Macroeconomics is a very complex subject for specialised macroeconomics books, and so we talk just briefly about some of the macroeconomic influences on performance, value and price:

- **GDP:** Gross domestic product is the total value of all production created in a nation. Increasing GDP is often taken as a sign that the economy is strong and that people should invest more in stocks and shares.

- **The business cycle:** Two or more consecutive *quarters* (a quarter being three-month periods) of negative GDP growth is the current definition of a recession, which is one of the four parts of the business cycle: the others being recovery, boom and slump. The rate of change in growth that an economy experiences changes stocks and share prices quite a bit.

✔ **Employment:** The ratio of people who have jobs compared to the total workforce. *Unemployment* is the ratio of people who don't have jobs compared to the total workforce. High unemployment tends to harm stocks and share prices.

✔ **Inflation:** A change in the purchasing power of a currency, meaning that you need more money to purchase an equal amount of goods (check out Chapter 9 for more on inflation). High inflation tends to slow stock market value growth.

✔ **Monetary policy:** Includes any policy regarding the quantity or price of money, such as altering interest rates, bank reserve requirements, the amount of money being printed or distributed, and other related policies. Expansionary monetary policy, such as lowering interest rates and reducing bank reserve requirements, tends to increase stock market prices. Increased interest rates and any policy that reduces the supply of money tends to lower stock market prices.

✔ **Fiscal policy:** Refers to any issues related to taxation and government spending. The influence of these policies on stock and share prices depends greatly on the specifics of the policy. Increases in spending help those companies who receive the government funds. Even the impact of higher taxation depends greatly on who's being taxed, as well as on what the Treasury spends the tax receipts.

✔ **Leading indicators:** Include any measures of macroeconomic data that indicate what the health of the economy is going to look like in the immediate future: for example, new unemployment claims.

✔ **Coincident indicators:** Measures of macroeconomic data that indicate the health of the economy now: for example, new industrial production.

✔ **Lagging indicators:** Indicators that tend to confirm what the economy has already begun to do, such as duration of unemployment.

✔ **Sentiment indices:** Measures of how people feel about the economy. These measures aren't entirely accurate or always helpful, but they do help give an idea about how people feel about the economy, which tends to be tied to other hard data (such as facts and figures). Consumer sentiment, for example, tends to be down when employment is down or when people don't feel confident in their employment. These factors tend to influence stocks and shares nearly as much as other, more solid, indicators.

Chapter 13

Measuring Valuations of the May-Be: Derivatives

....

In This Chapter

▶ Getting an overview of the risks and benefits of options

▶ Understanding the difference between forwards and futures

▶ Switching things up with swaps

....

*F*or a financial tool that was originally designed to reduce the amount of risk associated with common corporate transactions, derivatives (named as such because they derive from another product; their price is derived from the price of an underlying asset) have become a veritable mine-field for many companies. Not only does a strong temptation exist to use derivatives to generate income, despite the high level of risk this approach can create, but also derivatives are frequently not represented properly in the financial statements of many companies that use them. Still, despite the common pitfalls, derivatives are quite simple to understand and use.

In this chapter, we focus on four of the most common type of derivatives: options, forwards, futures and swaps. We describe the three main aspects of each type: how to limit risk, how to generate revenues and, briefly, how to measure its value. Note that other types of derivatives are available and they all have multiple variations. We don't have the space to cover them all here, which is why we highlight just the most common ones.

Introducing the Derivatives Market

Derivatives are legal contracts that set the terms of a transaction that can be bought and sold as the current market price varies against the terms in the contract. Prices change a lot over time, which adds a degree of uncertainty and risk for those who produce or purchase large quantities of goods. Derivatives were originally all about bringing price stability to products that can be volatile in their pricing over short periods of time.

Say, for example, that a producer of wheat anticipates producing 10 tonnes but is afraid that prices are going to go down before it produces and sells all the wheat, putting the producer at risk of earning lower profits or even losing money on the sale (because it's incurring production costs as it produces the wheat). The producer calls its derivatives agent, who puts together whatever type of derivatives contract the producer wants and attempts to find a buyer to purchase the wheat at a later date, using the terms of the derivatives contract. The flip side of this situation is that a buyer of wheat knows that it wants to purchase 10 tonnes of wheat about four weeks before harvest but is afraid that prices are likely to increase by then. The buyer can also call an agent to create a derivatives contract for the purchase of wheat.

By speculating on the changes in future prices, companies have the opportunity to buy and sell many derivatives contracts at a profit simply because of other people's willingness to trade these contracts. As a result, derivatives have dramatically increased in popularity as a method of generating income.

You can purchase and then resell derivatives at a profit, but the whole process involves a great deal of many types of risk. Despite the pitfalls – and although derivatives have fallen under attack in recent years and been blamed, in part, for the economic crisis – when used responsibly, they can provide companies with a useful financial tool (and only a bad workman blames his tools). Indeed, they have become so popular that the global derivatives market is enormous, being worth as much as one quadrillion (that's a thousand million million) US dollars. That's the equivalent of ten times the entire production of goods in the history of the planet. So, you can see that we aren't talking small fry here!

We devote the rest of this chapter to talking about the four most common types of derivatives:

- ✔ Options
- ✔ Forwards
- ✔ Futures
- ✔ Swaps

Buying or Selling – Then Again, Maybe Not: Options

Options are contracts that give the buyer the right to buy or sell a fixed number of goods at a predetermined price, but they don't oblige the buyer to do so.

Here are the two primary types of options:

- **Put options:** When purchased, put options give the holder of the option the right to sell a predetermined unit quantity of some asset at a predetermined price, called the _strike price,_ before some predetermined future date, called the _expiry date._

- **Call options:** Call options work in a similar manner to put options, except that they give the buyer the option to purchase those goods rather than sell them.

When buyers decide to use the option to buy or sell goods, they _exercise_ their option; when they decide not to use the option, they either let the option expire or, if possible, try to resell it.

Managing risk

Companies can use put and call options as tools for managing risk – and let's face it, risk management is a pretty important thing for companies to ensure their survival. For example, when you buy a put option, your goal is to make sure that you can sell your goods for the best price possible. The put option may say, for instance, that you have 10 tonnes of wheat to sell at a strike price of £10,000. If the price goes down between the purchase of the put option and the expiry date, you exercise your option in order to sell the wheat for a higher price than the market is currently offering. If, on the other hand, the price goes up, you let the option expire, because you can sell the wheat for a higher price on the market.

Call options allow companies to purchase goods at the strike price. Continuing with the wheat example, to limit risk, an interested buyer may purchase the call option with a strike price of £10,000 for 10 tonnes of wheat in order to get the lowest price possible. If the price goes down before the expiry date, the buyer simply lets the contract expire and buys the wheat on the market for the lower price. If the price goes up, however, the buyer exercises the call option in order to buy the wheat more cheaply than the market is currently offering.

Generating revenue

In case you're wondering, options aren't sold for free. The seller of the option generates revenue equal to the sale price of the option (which also floats in a manner similar to shares based, in part, on investor sentiment and the belief of future potential), giving the seller incentive to sell the options; however, the seller must use them carefully because risk is involved. This risk applies to call *and* put options; they both generate sales revenues but also oblige the seller to a future transaction that may not be in the seller's best interest.

The seller of an option is planning to buy or sell the goods at the strike price anyway or betting that the buyer won't exercise the option due to price conditions that are unfavourable for the buyer. In the case where a seller sells options purely to generate revenue without any expectations of participating in an exchange at the strike price, that seller puts itself at a greater risk of losses or potential losses that aren't otherwise recorded on standard financial reports, which can cause concern for investors as well as the company itself.

Valuing

Experts have generated many mathematical models for estimating the value of an option. Most of these models involve maths that's too complex for the scope of this book, however, and so we focus on just one of the more popular valuation equations and show you how to apply it in an investing portfolio strategy.

To find the value of selling an option, simply use this equation:

$$P + X = \text{Value of selling an option}$$

P is the price of the option sold, giving the seller revenues, while X is the value of the exchange to the seller. You can assume that X is always negative; otherwise, the option holder wouldn't exercise the option in the first place, leaving X at 0, meaning that the seller generated only revenues and not a premium.

The equation for finding the value of buying an option is just as easy:

$$X - P = \text{Value of buying an option}$$

In this equation, you subtract the buying price (P) from the value of the exchange to the buyer (X). You can assume that X is always positive here; otherwise, the buyer wouldn't exercise the option, leaving P equal to 0, meaning that the buyer lost only the cost of buying the option in the first place.

The more complex and arguably more accurate valuation methods all incorporate two major elements:

- **Value over time:** The value of an option changes over time relative to increases in the risk-free rate and the underlying assets.

- **Probability of a particular outcome and the value placed on that probability:** The likelihood of the anticipated event is weighted by the influence that the event will have.

Option valuation holds a special place in the hearts of investors because it allows for some very effective portfolio strategies. After all, options allow investors to set parameters on the amount of loss or gain they can experience. For example if an investor is hoping to limit his potential losses, he purchases a put option only. If an investor is planning to sell his goods after the price goes up, he can sell call options at that price, generating income on the call options in addition to the revenue he makes from selling at the higher price. In turn, he can use the revenue generated from selling the call options to purchase the put options for mitigating loss, creating a strategy called a *straddle*.

Customising the Contract with Forwards

A *forward contract* (which from now on we call a *forward*) is an agreement between parties to perform a sale of a specific type of good in a predetermined quantity at a predetermined price and at a predetermined date in the future. Unlike an option (see the earlier section 'Buying or Selling – Then Again, Maybe Not: Options'), which gives the buyer or seller the right to participate in the transaction but doesn't oblige them, forward contracts are legal obligations to perform the transaction on or before a specific date. The good thing about forwards is that they're highly customisable and can include any details or additional terms as long as all the relevant parties agree to those terms.

Forward contracts aren't bought and sold in the same manner as many derivatives contracts. Instead, two or more parties develop a legal contract, sign into that contract and typically fulfil the contractual obligations themselves. So neither party purchases or sells the actual contract (unless you count the fees for having the contract drawn up).

Say that Amy, the purchasing director of a clothing manufacturer, wants to buy 200.5 pounds of wool. The industry standard is to sell wool only by the pound, not divisions of a pound. Amy is afraid that the price is going to increase before this season's *cuttings* (the wool term for *crop*), and so she talks to the farmer who produces the wool. Amy and the farmer agree to a forward contract, because the farmer is afraid that the price may drop. Here are the terms of their contract:

- ✔ **Product:** White lamb's wool, first cutting of the season, carded
- ✔ **Quantity:** 200.5 pounds
- ✔ **Delivery price:** £1,500
- ✔ **Delivery date:** 12 December 2013

Both parties in the contract must execute their part of the contract, and the contract itself is likely to include penalties for non-delivery. Note that in this example, the quantity agreed upon is 200.5 pounds, despite the industry standard of selling in increments of 1 pound. This high customisability is one of the primary benefits of a forward contract.

Managing risk

Companies and individuals enter into forward contracts to reduce the amount of price uncertainty and volatility, particularly seasonal volatility, involved with buying or selling goods. Forward contracts allow buyers and sellers to agree upon a price and quantity of goods to be exchanged, sometimes even before production begins:

- ✔ For buyers, this arrangement provides increased certainty that they get exactly the quantity they need, without competing with other buyers for the same pool of suppliers, and guarantees that the price doesn't increase by the time of the delivery date.
- ✔ For sellers, forward contracts ensure that they have a buyer for their products, instead of risking being left with a surplus, and also guarantees that the price doesn't drop suddenly before the delivery date.

On a national and a global scale, the use of derivatives for managing risk means price stability. Many goods around the world, particularly primary ones such as agricultural produce, experience seasonal fluctuations. During harvest season, the quantity of goods supplied increases quite a lot, whereas during the off-season, the quantity drops below demand. These fluctuations in supply cause serious seasonal price volatility. Derivatives in general help alleviate this volatility, and forwards are easily the best method for addressing the individual needs of both buyers and sellers.

Generating revenue

Generating revenues with forward contracts is more difficult than with most other forms of derivatives: forward contracts are so customisable that they aren't conducive to trading. After all, finding another buyer who wants the exact same contract you created to fit your needs and those of the other party can be nigh on impossible.

You can generate revenues from forward contracts in only one common way, but you need to be particularly confident in your assessment of the future price of goods. As a buyer, you can enter into a contract that has a price very low compared to your estimate of the future market price, get your stock of goods and then resell them at the market price. If you're a seller, you can simply enter into a contract that has a price much higher than your expected future market price.

Valuing

The value of a forward contract depends greatly on fluctuations in the market price of goods. You can use a number of different calculations to determine the value of a forward contract, but generally speaking, each calculation is built on the following two basic ideas:

✔ **The current price of a forward contract needs to be equal to the market price of goods at the delivery date, plus the opportunity cost associated with not pursuing the next best opportunity.**

For example, if you're an investor, the price of the forward contract today has to equal the market price at the date of delivery plus the market rate of compounding interest (for more about compound interest, flick to Chapter 9). Of course, you can't know exactly what the future market price is going to be (if you could, forward contracts wouldn't be much use), and that degree of uncertainty is where people attempt to generate income by speculating.

✔ **At the time of delivery, the value of the forward rate is equal to the delivery price minus the market price.**

This rather simple measurement uses hindsight to determine how effective you were at using forward contracts.

Adding Some Standardisation to the Contract with Futures

In theory, *futures contracts* are very similar to forward contracts (see the preceding section), except that futures contracts are highly standardised in a number of ways:

- ✔ Futures contracts must be for a similar *commodity* (a good or service) of a standardised type and quality (whereas forward contracts can be for just about anything).

- ✔ Each futures contract must be for a standardised quantity (whereas forward contracts can be for just about any quantity).

- ✔ Futures contracts must be in a single currency determined by the location of trade (whereas forward contracts can be in any currency or even in *barters,* meaning that goods or services are exchanged for other goods or services).

- ✔ Futures contracts must have a standardised delivery date (whereas forward contracts can be delivered at any date).

Basically, futures contracts of a single type must all be completely identical. This continuity allows futures contracts to be freely bought, sold and traded. The buyer of a futures contract is obliged by the terms of the contract until it's resold, but the buyer doesn't have to even read the contract (though we wouldn't recommend not reading any contract) to know what's on it because all futures contracts of that type are the same. As a result, unlike forward contracts, futures contracts are highly liquid; that is, they're sold in very high volume and very high frequency on markets (much like shares).

Managing risk

Although futures are less customisable than forwards, they're still extremely common (or perhaps even more common than forwards) as a form of risk management. After all, futures are extremely easy to buy and sell for companies that produce or purchase goods that are available for futures contracts for market trade. The initial contract sale by the producers, called the *primary market,* is quite easy to make, and then that contract is likely to change hands many, many times before the delivery date. It can be traded on the secondary market between investors and then, eventually, to the people who really want the underlying goods.

That said, the function of futures in risk management is essentially identical to that of forwards, except that the liquid nature of futures allows for more robust risk-management strategies that allow the investor to buy or sell many times before the delivery date.

Generating revenue

Futures are far more viable as a method of revenue generation than forwards, but buying and selling futures strictly to generate revenue can be very dangerous. Like shares, people purchase futures contracts with the expectation that the price is going to change dramatically, up or down, and then resell the contract to the seller or the buyer or perhaps even to other investors.

The aim is to sell these contracts before the delivery date for more than you paid for them or for less value than the delivery if you decide that you want the goods underlying the contract (which, in many cases, is cash, making that valuation particularly simple to calculate).

When you buy and sell futures solely to generate revenue, not only do you risk losing value through these trade exchanges as with shares, but also, in the case of commodities, the underlying goods to be delivered can be worth less than you paid for them. As with options (which we cover earlier in 'Buying or Selling – Then Again, Maybe Not: Options'), these risks cause deviations between the book value of a company's assets and the real value of asset obligations through futures contracts.

Valuing

The mechanics of a futures contract are the same as those of a forward contract, and so the valuation methods also tend to be the same. The basics of valuation for forwards that we discuss in the earlier section 'Customising the Contract with Forwards' still apply, and a number of variations have been applied to customise the calculations for the individual needs of the parties involved or to improve on the accuracy for investment purposes.

As noted earlier in this section, though, the increased liquidity in futures allows for additional strategies involving them that more closely resemble share investing strategies, instead of simply *hedging* (meaning, attempting to minimise) the risk of the exchange of the assets underlying the futures contract.

Exchanging This for That and Maybe This Again: Swaps

Of the four most common derivatives we cover in this chapter, the *swap* is easily the most confusing. Why? Because each swap involves two agreements rather than just one.

Swaps occur when companies agree to exchange something of value with the expectation of exchanging back at some future date.

Companies can apply swaps to a number of different things of value, usually currency or specific types of cash flows. Simply speaking, swaps allow companies to benefit from transactions that otherwise wouldn't be available to them in a timely or cost-effective manner. Swaps have become extremely popular as a method of managing risk and generating revenues, because they give companies the opportunity to shift the performance of their assets quickly and cheaply without exchanging ownership of those assets.

Swaps are typically done through a *swap broker,* a company that deals in swaps and makes money off the *bid–ask spread* (the difference between the bid price and ask price) on these exchanges.

Managing risk

Swaps are used to manage risk to ensure favourable cash flows, either through timing (as with the coupons on bonds) or through the types of assets being exchanged (as with foreign exchange swaps that ensure a company has the right type of currency). The exact nature of the risk being managed depends on the type of swap being used.

The easiest way to see how companies can use swaps to manage risks is to follow a simple example using interest-rate swaps, the most common form of swaps. The scenario is that Company A owns $1,000,000 in fixed rate bonds earning 5 per cent annually, which is $50,000 in cash flows each year. The company thinks that interest rates are going to rise to 10 per cent, which will yield $100,000 in annual cash flows ($50,000 more per year than their current bond holdings). But exchanging all $1,000,000 for bonds that yield the higher rate is too costly. Therefore:

1. **Company A goes to a swap broker and exchanges, not the bonds themselves, but the company's right to the future cash flows.** Company A agrees to give the swap broker the $50,000 in fixed rate annual cash

flows, and in return the swap broker gives the company the cash flows from variable rate bonds worth £1,000,000.

2. **Company A and the swap broker continue to exchange these cash flows over the life of the swap.** It expires at a date determined at the time the contract is signed.

In this example, swaps help Company A to manage its risk by making available to it the possibility of altering its investment portfolio without the costly, difficult and sometimes impossible process of rearranging asset ownership. As a result, Company A makes an additional £50,000 per year in bond returns.

Of course, as with many investments, the company can also lose money if interest rates decrease rather than increase. At the time of writing, UK banks had recently been lambasted for mis-selling interest-rate swaps, resulting in ordinary people ending up very much out of pocket and campaigning for compensation.

However, although swaps aren't always a win–win type of arrangement to get involved with (and you should always seek professional advice before entering into these arrangements), hopefully each side benefits from swaps. The swap broker's job is to help different companies that would benefit from swapping together to find each other. The swap broker earns money by charging a fee.

Generating revenue

When pursuing opportunities to generate revenue through swaps, the process is no different than in Company A's scenario in the preceding section, but the motivation behind the swap is to take advantage of differentials in the spot rate and anticipated future values related to the swap. To see how revenue generation works with swaps, consider the following example, which involves foreign-exchange swaps, a simpler (than interest-rate swaps, that is) but less common form of swap (in the example, GBP = UK pound):

1. **Company A has GBP 1,000 and believes that the Chinese Yuan (CNY) is set to increase in value compared to the GBP.**

2. **Company A gets in touch with Company B in China, which just happens to need GBP for a short time to fund a capital investment in computers coming from the UK.**

3. **The two companies agree to swap currency at the current market exchange rate, which for this example is GBP 1 = CNY 1.**

4. They swap GBP 1,000 for CNY 1,000, and the swap agreement states that they'll exchange currencies back in one year at the forward rate (also GBP 1 = CNY 1; the market is very stable in Example World!).

In the example, Company B needs the currency but doesn't want to pay the transaction fees, while Company A is speculating on the change in exchange rate. If the CNY exchange rate increases by 1 per cent compared to the GBP, Company A makes a profit on the swap. If the CNY exchange rate decreases in value by 1 per cent, Company A loses money on the swap.

This potential for loss is why using derivatives to generate income is called *speculating*. The term 'speculate' can mean 'to engage in the buying or selling of a commodity with an element of risk on the chance of profit', but it can also mean 'to guess'.

Valuing

The value of a swap isn't difficult to measure. Put simply, you start with the value of what you're receiving plus any added value that results from changes in rates or returns, and then you subtract the value of what you're giving away plus any increases in value associated with interest earned or changes in rates.

Of course, as with all known valuations, this is a hindsight calculation; it's easy when you know the numbers but can be a different prospect when you don't. When you're estimating future value, the calculations involve the time value of money and the probabilities of events occurring, both of which you need to treat in the same manner as estimating the value of futures (check out the earlier section 'Adding Some Standardisation to the Contract with Futures').

A swap is a combination of a spot rate exchange (which we define in Chapter 21) and a futures exchange in a single contract.

Part IV
Walking in a Risk Management Wonderland

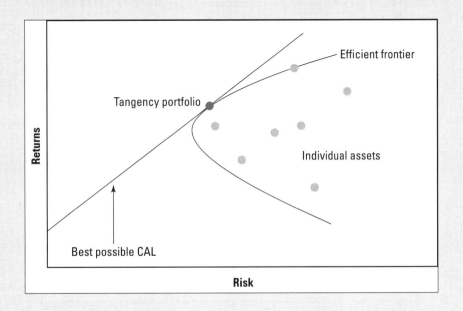

In this part . . .

✔ Peruse the more common forms of risk associated with corporate finance.

✔ Grasp the essentials of modern portfolio theory, understand why people use it and assess how it works.

✔ Assess investment methods and find new ones to gain an advantage, increase returns and customise products and, in doing so, become a master of financial engineering.

✔ Understand how to go about evaluating a company's capital structure.

Chapter 14

Managing the Risky Business of Corporate Finances

*B*usiness finance is filled with risk. Perhaps not the same kind of risk faced by soldiers or police officers (though witnesses to the trading floors of the London Stock Exchange say that it can resemble a war zone), but employees don't laugh when their jobs are threatened because someone messed up managing the risks associated with corporate finance.

This chapter discusses some of the more common forms of risk encountered in this area, including those associated with interest rates, inflation, credit and foreign exchanges.

Understanding that Risk Is Unavoidable

You may think that when managing corporate finances, you should avoid risk at all cost (pun intended!). But the reality is quite the opposite: risk is an inherent, and therefore unavoidable, part of every financial decision that a company makes.

The real goal of managing financial risk is to assess the degree of risk associated with each potential option for a given decision, mathematically calculate the probability of it occurring and determine whether the potential losses and probabilities associated with that risk exceed the potential returns.

On a broader level, you can think of risk as a form of cost. No business can avoid 100 per cent of risk all the time, and whenever something goes wrong the company loses money resolving the problem. The total amount of losses due to the risky nature of financial transactions influences how competitive your business is, the price you should charge for goods and services and your company's profitability. As far as possible, you need to manage costs that don't add any actual value to the product or the company (known as *non-value-added costs*) to minimise the risk while maximising returns.

In general, risk falls into the following categories, which we list in the order we describe them throughout this chapter:

- **Interest rate/inflation risk:** The risk that interest rates or inflation will exceed your returns.
- **Market risk:** The risk that the entire economy may do poorly.
- **Credit risk:** The risk that borrowers won't repay their loans.
- **Off-balance-sheet risk:** The risk that something not included on the balance sheet is influencing the value of the company (such as unrealised gains/losses from investments in derivatives).
- **Foreign exchange risk:** The risk of losing value through fluctuations in foreign exchange rates.
- **Operating risk:** Risks associated with corporate operations.
- **Liquidity risk:** The risk of not having enough money available when bills become due.

Investigating Interest Rate Risk and Inflation Risk

The vast majority of products available for investment that yield interest offer *fixed rate returns,* so that when you purchase, say, an investment that offers a 1 per cent annual interest rate, you're going to earn 1 per cent annually – no more, no less.

When you earn a fixed 1 per cent interest on an investment, no matter how high inflation rates go or whether interest rates go up or down during that period, you still earn only 1 per cent. This risk of losing value on assets, because the interest rates you earn have the potential to lag behind market interest rates or inflation rates, is called *interest rate risk.*

The interest rate can quite easily surpass the rate inherent in fixed rate investments. If you purchase a bond that pays 1 per cent per year in cash flows (in other words, every year the bond earns you another 1 per cent of the purchase price in coupon payments), but then the market interest rate increases to 2 per cent, the value of your future cash flows decreases by 50 per cent relative to the market rate. So, if you try to sell the bond or any part of it, it isn't worth nearly as much, and even if you continue to hold the bond, your future cash flows don't keep up with market returns.

The risk that inflation will surpass your assets is often categorised as a special type of interest rate risk called *inflationary risk*. This form of risk is fairly simple to understand: inflation means that the overall price level within a nation increases. Bread, eggs, fuel and so on used to be much cheaper than they are today because inflation reduces the amount of goods you can purchase with a single unit of currency. (We discuss inflation in more detail in Chapter 9.)

Therefore, if inflation increases by 1 per cent in a year, £1 purchases 1 per cent less next year than it does this year. If you have your money in an investment that's earning 0.5 per cent interest each year, you're losing 0.5 per cent of the purchasing power of the currency, reducing the real value of your investment even if the nominal value is increasing. This problem usually applies only with investments that are considered 'risk free', such as certificates of deposit, savings accounts and some low-yield bonds.

Minimising Market Risk

We're sure that your company is careful. It chooses only the best customers and best investments, uses derivatives only to mitigate potential losses, diversifies clients and investments, and does everything right to reduce the risk associated with every single penny. You have the safest and most stable company in the entire country . . . and then the entire national economy collapses.

No matter how successful you are at managing the risk of your company, the possibility is always present that the nation in which you're operating experiences total economic meltdown (called *market risk*).

The vast majority of company owners and managers have no idea how to recognise the warning signs of a very large recession in the near future; not that it would help them to know it's coming, mind you, because a single company can do nothing to stop it from happening. But a company *can* take steps to mitigate the amount of loss associated with market risk, such as implementing international diversification or the use of derivatives (check out Chapters 21 and 13, respectively).

The best way to decrease the amount of market risk your company experiences is to diversify internationally. That may sound like a much more problematic strategy than it really is. The big problem with market risk isn't necessarily the loss of value, but rather the loss of customers. Even simply exporting your goods or services internationally to nations not experiencing the same recession may help to stabilise your company's revenue streams to an extent, at least minimising the damage, though not eliminating it altogether. However, you do have to be careful about foreign exchange risk, which we look at in the later section 'Factoring in Foreign Exchange Risk'.

An advantage for companies of these recessionary periods is that the pool of potential employees all competing for a limited number of jobs increases. This competition allows your company to acquire labour at cheaper prices, helping to decrease costs during an otherwise difficult period.

Don't think for a single moment that your company is immune from market risk. National recessions are common (look at what's been happening around the world recently) and inevitable under the current methods of economic management. They can also be highly devastating for the companies in the nation experiencing the recession; many companies lose customers, file for bankruptcy or even go out of business entirely.

Evaluating the Risk of Extending Credit

Credit is a form of loan. Companies frequently provide their goods or services to customers *on credit,* which means that they expect to get paid at some later date (usually 30, 60, 90 or 120 days later, and sometimes even longer!). Extending credit is common for furniture stores, car dealerships, many businesses that sell to other businesses and just about any company that deals in goods that are considered expensive for customers to purchase.

Imagine that you use your credit card to pay for your weekly shopping at the local supermarket. That purchase is a risk for the company that issued you the credit card, because it pays the supermarket for your weekly shopping under the expectation that you're going to pay it back. On the company's balance sheet, this transaction is considered a debtor for the lender until it receives payment.

Offering credit sounds like a great idea for the company. More expensive items can be quite difficult to purchase all at once, and so allowing customers to make purchases on credit improves their ability to afford the company's products. This strategy also helps companies generate revenues by earning interest on those sales made on credit.

Being exposed to credit risk

Overexposure to credit risk was the first mistake that many banks made leading up to the 2007 financial collapse. Issuing mortgage and other loans to people who lacked the ability to make the payments, or otherwise had a history of defaulting on loans, increased the degree of credit risk that the banks experienced.

During the start of the recession, when banks exposed to high levels of credit risk stopped receiving deposits from their customers (who were becoming unemployed as the result of an economic slowdown and stopped making payments on the loans they'd taken out), they could no longer make the payments on the loans they'd taken out themselves. They fell victim to another type of risk that we discuss later in this chapter (flip to 'Looking at Liquidity Risk' for more).

A company has to be very careful, though, when attempting to benefit from extending credit to its customers, because the chance always exists that the company doesn't get paid back. So *credit risk* is the risk that people don't pay back their loans.

Credit risk is typically assessed on an individual basis, with customers being evaluated on the following criteria:

- ✓ **Book value:** Ensures that if they default, collateral is available to pay back the loan.

- ✓ **Cash flow:** Determines whether they have the cash to pay off the loan.

- ✓ **Payment history:** Checks how they paid back previous loans.

This credit risk assessment works a lot like a personal credit rating. Customers a company decides are too likely to default on the loan (in other words, are at high risk of not paying it back) don't get that loan (or at least shouldn't; as the major banks around the world have proved recently, stupidity knows no credit score).

When people don't pay back their loans, the company loses money. As with other forms of risk, because this loss of money doesn't add any value to the company, it's considered a non-value-added cost, which is a bad thing. In fact, if the department in charge of managing risk is bad at its job, the company may even lose more money due to credit risk than the potential increase in revenues generated by customers using credit. Such a loss is rarely the case, however.

Most companies determine the interest rate they charge based on the level of risk incurred. On average, a customer who's a higher credit risk incurs greater costs for the company, and so the company charges a higher interest rate to make up for the higher costs. This strategy is debatable, of course, because the higher interest rate increases the risk that the person defaults. Creditors continue extending credit to customers of higher and higher risk until the costs of extending that credit (in addition to the costs associated with repayment risk) exceed the amount of revenues generated for that person: in economics terms, the point where MR (Marginal Revenue) = MC (Marginal Cost).

Understanding Off-Balance-Sheet Risk

A number of financial activities and transactions don't influence the balance sheet (to which we introduce you in Chapter 4) as much as the actual trans-action may imply. These instances of *off-balance-sheet* activity are typically considered to be contingent assets and contingent liabilities, which are only realised if some future event takes place to trigger the transaction.

Although we discuss derivatives in Chapter 13, we don't really cover the influence of derivatives on the balance sheet: these derivatives are some of the most common forms of off-balance-sheet transactions. The sale of deriva-tives, such as options, commits a company to sell or purchase assets in the future, but that commitment is dependent upon whether the purchaser of the option decides to exercise her right to that option. As a result, this commit-ment to a transaction is recorded on the balance sheet only if the option is actually exercised.

Off-balance-sheet transactions cause a unique problem for the company in question as well as its investors and lenders, because many balance sheet ratios aren't able to take into account these contingent exchanges. This problem can cause financial mismanagement on the part of the company and misled investments on the part of investors. When doing balance-sheet analy-sis using ratios, always take into account any off-balance-sheet transactions, which you can find within the accompanying notes to the balance sheet or you can request.

Factoring in Foreign Exchange Risk

Different nations use different types of money. The United Kingdom uses ster-ling (Great British Pounds) and Mexico uses pesos, for example. These differ-ent types of money change value at different rates, and so the value of money in one nation can change compared to the value of another nation's currency.

For instance, you're probably familiar with the fact that exchange rates change. Well, that's one result of a change in the value of a currency. Another result when money changes value is a change in the value of everything measured using that currency. That change in value creates a special class of risks called *foreign exchange risk,* where a change in the value of money between nations causes a change in the value of exchanges or a change in the value of foreign-held assets.

Describing transaction risk

Between the time you sell a product and the time you receive payment, a chance exists that you end up making less money than you expected. The same can be said about the time between purchasing a product and receiving the goods: the goods may be worth less than you paid for them. These variations happen due to fluctuations in something over which a single company has absolutely no control: the exchange rate. These two situations are descriptions of something called *transaction risk:* the risk that a transaction loses value at some point before it's complete.

The following is a completely fictional example of transaction risk using companies whose names have been subtly (!) changed to protect the innocent. A UK car manufacturer, Vauxmall, purchases £10,000 worth of electronic components from Korean electronics company Samsong, but before Vauxmall pays for the parts the UK pound drops in value compared to the Korean won by 50 per cent. So when Samsong tries to exchange the pounds into its own currency, it receives only about half of what it originally expected.

A company can't do anything to stop exchange rates from changing, but it can employ strategies to make the best of such changes. In this example, Samsong can compensate for the change in the exchange rate in one of three ways:

✔ Samsong can improve the value of the UK currency by simply using it to purchase goods from the UK, returning the currency to its country of origin for something of greater value to the company.

✔ Samsong can hold onto the UK pounds in the hope that the exchange rate increases their value again.

✔ Samsong can account for the loss as a cost and learn how to avoid this mistake in the future – before it happens! A novel concept in risk management is the use of preventative measures such as those we discuss in Chapter 13.

Tackling translation risk

When you're managing assets across several nations (or at least several currencies), you don't even have to enter into a transaction to be subject to foreign exchange risk. That's right, the value of your assets can plummet while you're just sitting there daydreaming about winning the lottery on Saturday evening. This situation isn't a result of an actual decrease in the usefulness of the assets, a decrease in the quantity of assets or even necessarily a decrease in the nominal value of those assets in a single currency.

Translation risk is so named because of the translation of value from one currency to another, and it's the risk that a change in exchange rates makes your foreign-held assets worth less when exchanged into your home nation's currency.

Two distinct detrimental impacts can result from translation risk:

- ✔ If a company expects to repatriate its foreign cash assets by bringing them back to its home nation and then exchanging them into the home nation's currency, the company gets less currency than it expected prior to the change in the foreign exchange rate.

- ✔ A fluctuation in exchange rates can have a significant impact on the balance sheet of the company. Any assets denominated in a foreign currency cause a decrease in the book value of the company as a whole if that currency depreciates against the home currency. This depreciation has the potential to alter significantly the ability of a company to attract capital, because the proportion of debt to total assets increases when the total asset value decreases. As you can imagine, this proportionate change is a bad thing for investors as well as for an organisation that wants to attract new debt or equity.

On the other hand, if a company doesn't intend to move its assets or attract new investors, this change in asset value does little harm to the company. The assets maintain equivalent nominal value in the foreign currency and equivalent usefulness for the company except in exchange rate transactions.

The decrease in book value can even provide the company with an opportunity to purchase equity shares more cheaply as its share price drops in response to the decrease in book value. After all, the company's fundamental operating strength hasn't changed and exchange rate fluctuations tend to be cyclical over time, meaning that the company can resell those treasury shares for a profit later.

Considering other foreign exchange risks

Two more major forms of risk are associated with holding foreign assets, although they aren't related to the value of the assets themselves but, rather, the ability to use these assets:

- ✔ **Convertibility risk:** You may have a foreign currency on hand, but you may not be able to convert it into another currency. Some currencies can be extremely difficult or nigh on impossible to exchange for more common currencies simply because no one wants them.

  If you have operations in a nation whose currency is highly volatile or rarely used, you may have difficulty finding anyone willing to take that currency in exchange for a more common one.

- ✔ **Repatriation risk:** Usually considered a subcategory under the broader heading of political risk. But from a purely financial perspective, *repatriation risk* reflects the possibility that a foreign government may decide to cap or even prohibit any assets – financial or otherwise – from leaving the nation (a bit like Cyprus did when it re-opened its banks following a two-week closure due to serious economic downturns).

  This policy is usually adopted by nations with very small or otherwise volatile economies. In an attempt to bring growth and stabilisation, they require investors and local nationals to maintain assets within the country instead of attempting to repatriate them back to their home nation. The belief is that this action is going to stimulate additional trade and investment within the nation, because people are forced to spend their income and profits in the country rather than taking them outside of it.

  The result for businesses is the risk that they can't use their assets outside of that nation, making them useless unless they have an existing reason to use them there as part of a broader business strategy. The issue of how these overseas operations are taxed is another minefield that needs to be considered (but which is way beyond the scope of this book); anyone involved in corporate finance needs to keep the tax side of things in mind.

Identifying Operating Risk

Operating or *operational risk* is the risk of losses or costs associated with business operations. According to the Basel Accords on banking supervision (the widely used reference for the definition and parameters of operating risk), this category includes just about every possible non-value-added cost (those adding no value to product or company) that a company can experience – from fraud and theft through to negligence and stupidity, and accidental events such as the acquisition of faulty equipment or the occurrence of a natural disaster such as an earthquake.

For our purposes, operating risk is the probability of any non-value-added costs being incurred as a result of a company's internal operations, systematic or not. Here we give you two quick examples, including how to reduce the associated risk.

We are, by no means, experts on earthquakes and we don't know whether predicting them is possible, but we assume for illustrative purposes that earthquakes can't be predicted. That said, any company that sets up operations in an area known for having earthquakes is subject to the risk of losses and costs associated with earthquakes. That doesn't mean setting up in an earthquake zone is a bad thing; it just means that the company must assess the potential losses associated with earthquakes in that region and determine whether it can earn enough revenues to make up for those costs.

Financial management can't do much to mitigate the risk of earthquakes except, perhaps, purchase insurance. Financial analysis, however, can provide information about whether the benefits of locating a company in an earthquake zone compared to the next-best choice exceed the expected costs associated with purchasing insurance, repairing damage and potentially even rebuilding completely.

In our second example, financial management can help to identify the problem. Where a company isn't operating as efficiently as it should be, but no one can work out why, management can bring in the finance department to be detectives! Any financial analyst worth her salt can trace the internal cash flows, meaning that she can break down every function of the company and account for the costs incurred by each department compared to the movement of cash between departments.

The analyst may discover that money is being lost in the marketing department that isn't accounted for in its expenditures and that a computer has been hacked that's allowing an employee to siphon money from the marketing budget. Performing internal audits in this way helps companies to reduce losses from operating risk.

Looking at Liquidity Risk

Do you have money owed to you but not enough to pay your bills in the meantime? If so, you're a victim of *liquidity risk!* The most extreme form of liquidity risk, called *insolvency,* occurs when a company is completely incapable of paying the money it owes and must enter into administration (to restructure or eliminate debt), sell its operating assets to make the payments it owes or simply go out of business by way of *liquidation* (which means that an insolvency practitioner sells off the company's assets to pay creditors).

Insolvency doesn't necessarily happen when a company is doing poorly; quite the contrary, it can happen just as easily when a company is too successful (you see, sometimes you can't do right for doing wrong!).

Imagine for a moment that you own a company selling large manufacturing robotic equipment (a bit like that used in the manufacture of cars). Each one sells for £1 million. Now, £1 million isn't exactly cheap for a piece of kit, even for very large companies, and so the chances are that your customers pay for these robots on credit, making monthly payments over the course of several months or years. Say that this company of yours becomes wildly popular and starts making lots of sales with very high profits.

The problem comes when your firm starts spending more money to make the machines you're selling than it's receiving in monthly payments. In order to fulfil these sales orders and make the big profits you want, you still have to order supplies to build the machines you're selling. If you spend all your money on supplies but don't receive enough in monthly payments from previous customers to cover the cost, you're putting your company at liquidity risk.

This scenario isn't insolvency yet because you're still making payments, but liquidity risk can turn into insolvency if the problem isn't resolved quickly. Sometimes the act of selling more goods faster than you can bring in cash is called *over-trading* and can, in some cases, bring a company to its knees. Bear in mind the phrase 'cash is king' – cash is the lifeblood of a business. Companies can make huge amounts of profit, but unless they can turn that profit into cash to continue supplying goods those profits can be worthless.

That's not to say that liquidity risk can't be derived from simple poor financial management: it can. If a company generates too much of its capital from debt, it may find itself in a position where it can no longer afford to make the interest payments and needs to consider raising equity to decrease the interest payments. A lack of customers stemming from an inability to compete or generalised market risk can also cause insolvency.

When the banks involved in the 2007 financial collapse stopped generating revenues as a result of their poor management of credit risk, they became incapable of making payments on those loans they'd taken out themselves, including the interest owed on deposits and other bank products. This scenario led to many of even the largest banks becoming insolvent as a result of liquidity risk. Many banks went out of business, and some of the largest banks in the world required government assistance, most at the taxpayers' expense.

Chapter 15

Through the Looking Glass of Modern Portfolio Theory

*I*n his book *Through the Looking Glass,* the sequel to *Alice's Adventures in Wonderland,* Lewis Carroll describes a girl who walks through a mirror into a world of wonderful yet threatening nonsense. That pretty much sums up modern portfolio theory: the mathematical modelling of investing strategies is wonderful in its ability to make sense out of chaos, yet threatening in its current form because it attempts to use fantastical ideas and methods that are dangerous for the novice corporate financial analyst or investor.

Nevertheless, this high magic holds valuable lessons. Although the assumptions people use in modern portfolio theory are at the very boundaries of possibility to use in a functional way, they do provide an understanding of the way things work in theory, which in turn gives people a foundation upon which to develop their understanding of the real world.

In this chapter, we discuss the different components of modern portfolio theory, how it's used, why some believe that it's outdated, how it evolved from its original form and whether or not any of it really works. We talk a lot about risk, how variations in individual investments influence the rest of the portfolio and how you can measure your personal degree of risk aversion. All these factors are intricately inter-related.

Delving into Portfolio Practicalities

An investment portfolio isn't a physical thing or a single entity. An *investment portfolio* is a collection of different investments treated as a single combination, similar to the way cement is a collection of tiny rocks and minerals but is treated as a single substance. You can measure and analyse an investment portfolio as a single collection of different investments and do the same for each individual investment within a portfolio.

Surveying portfolio management strategies

Portfolio management is the buying, selling and trading of investments within a portfolio – optimising the returns of the portfolio by managing which investments the portfolio holds. But the portfolio itself remains constant despite the changes of its exact contents. The portfolio itself changes only when the underlying investment strategy changes.

That's why organisations often have many investment portfolios. Each portfolio is managed using a unique strategy based on the goals of the investors. For example, a company may have a stock investment portfolio that it uses to generate returns on petty cash, while also maintaining a capital investment portfolio that includes land, corporate acquisitions and subsidiaries, and other types of capital. Each of these portfolios has different contents and different purposes for existing, and the strategies involved in managing the contents are very different as well.

The following list looks briefly at three different portfolio management strategies:

- ✔ **Debt portfolio:** This type of investment portfolio invests exclusively in bonds of different types and with different maturity dates, usually with the intention of staggering maturity dates and coupon maturities in order to maintain regular cash flows.

- ✔ **Hedge portfolio:** Not to be confused with a hedge fund, a hedge portfolio is intended to *hedge* (take actions that limit risk or uncertainty) other forms of risk by managing derivatives and diversifying investments. A portfolio like this changes based on the types or amount of risk the company is accepting.

- ✔ **Slush fund/petty cash portfolio:** A company that maintains a cash account for irregular small payments that crop up from time to time can still generate a return on this cash by maintaining a portfolio of short-term, highly liquid investments, such as dividend-generating funds.

Throughout this chapter, we refer to stock investment portfolios, but we use the term 'stock' for the sake of consistency. You can include any type of investment – whether shares, bonds, capital or options – in an investment portfolio and analyse them using the methods we describe in this chapter.

Looking at modern portfolio theory

Modern portfolio theory isn't about how to value individual investments, but instead how to assess the potential combinations between several investments. The relationship between two or more assets can change the balance of a portfolio's total returns and the total risk involved. Modern portfolio theory uses a number of mathematical formulae and financial modelling in an attempt to formalise a method of improving your understanding of investing.

Of course, any successful method of standardising portfolio management is quickly adopted by a large population of investors as they rush to take advantage of the new strategy before others have the opportunity. This response changes the market balance of many types of investments, as investors make inherent changes in their approach to investing, and some of the front-runners then sell to the later-adopters as the prices of those equities heavily influenced by the new method jump in price. Partly because of the nearly instant response to market changes, and partly as a result of advances that improve upon the original methods of modern portfolio theory, this field is a study in the constant evolution of ideas. Nothing drives innovation like the promise of getting rich!

Understanding passive versus active management

When applying modern portfolio theory – or any theory of portfolio management for that matter – you can choose to take a passive or an active approach:

- ✔ **Passive portfolio management:** Refers to setting up a portfolio to match the entire stock market or some well-known index, such as the FTSE 100, as closely as possible. When established, these portfolios are simply left alone to fluctuate along with the indicator that the portfolio is set up to follow. Although this approach may seem lazy or negligent, in fact it avoids common human error and over-thinking. We talk more about the performance differences between managed portfolios and general market portfolios (the most common form of passive portfolio) later in this chapter in the section 'Optimising Portfolio Risk'.

✔ **Active portfolio management:** Involves regularly changing the contents of a portfolio. Every portfolio manager has his own strategies and methods for analysing and optimising returns, but the point is that the portfolio manager is buying, selling and trading actively the underlying investments. He may try to take advantage of short-term fluctuations in price: for example, making multiple trades every day.

Regardless of the precise approach you take, actively managing a portfolio is a full-time job. It entails constantly re-evaluating existing investments, searching for new investments to compare your existing investments against and assessing the degree of risk and the returns being generated by the portfolio as a whole. So as you've probably guessed, quite a bit's involved in managing a portfolio of investments!

Hypothesising an Efficient Market

Two economists are walking down the street when they see a £100 note lying on the ground. The first economist stops to pick it up when the other says, 'don't bother: if it were a real £100 note, someone would've picked it up already'.

This often cited analogy embodies effectively the nature of the efficient market hypothesis. The *efficient market* hypothesis states – incorrectly – that the market responds instantly to new information, ensuring that all investments and assets are valued at their fair market price. According to the hypothesis, if people all have the same information at the same time and have equal access to exchange markets, prices adjust instantly to their *economic equilibrium* (their natural point given the market levels of supply and demand). For example, if news comes out that a nation's gross domestic product (GDP) has dropped, all bonds and stocks influenced by this news immediately adjust to the perfect price level.

If the efficient market hypothesis were true, any opportunities to generate returns on investments are useless because all investments instantly change to their proper price whenever new information becomes available. Therefore, successful investing is either a matter of being lucky in choosing investments that are subject to good news, or a matter of adopting better methods of understanding the way investing works. If anything in this book were brand new, it would also be subject to the instant market response, because all readers would have the same information and be able to use that in their investing strategy. However, finding undervalued investments that increase in price quickly because of resale is a common strategy for traders in finance, and so the efficient market hypothesis simply isn't true.

No-one actually believes that the efficient market hypothesis is true. Assets are valued incorrectly all the time and investments fluctuate in value in response to . . . well, everything really. Sometimes the stock market seems to jump or fall simply because the wind blows the wrong way one day. Of course, measurable reasons lie behind market movements, but they're often completely unrelated to the real value of the asset or investment itself (for more information on this subject, check out Chapter 22).

After all, not everyone has the same information; some people know more than others and many receive information at different times and mentally process it in different ways. People don't have equal access to exchanges: professional investors often have custom-designed software programs that react to changes in the stock market in fractions of a second, whereas the average casual investor doesn't have this advantage.

The decisions that people make regarding investments vary as well, because investors react to news in different ways, have different strategies and measure the value of stocks differently. The market is efficient only in the long term. In the short term, frequent and intense levels of volatility can push the value of an asset, investment or even an entire company well away from its 'real' value.

Having said that, those short-term fluctuations tend to revolve around the real value of the asset. If the price of an investment is too high, or overvalued, it drops at some point in the future when people realise it's not worth the price. If an investment is undervalued, it increases in price when people notice the amazing bargain that's available. In the meantime, however, exactly how far and for how long the price deviates from the real value of the investment defines how inefficient the market really is.

Of course, like much of modern portfolio theory, the efficient market hypothesis isn't really meant to be applied as-is. Instead, it provides a starting point, a way to measure what the value of an investment or portfolio *should* be. From there, investors can build their understanding of markets and measure deviations from efficient response. Incorporating those deviations into their calculations makes them more accurate.

Risking Returns

Risk is an unavoidable part of corporate finance. If a company were to try to eliminate financial risk, all operations within the entire organisation would come to a complete standstill within a couple of weeks (if not sooner).

Instead of attempting to avoid risk – or even to make decisions that have the smallest of risks – companies tend to make choices that have the biggest differential between risk and financial returns. They measure the amount of returns they expect on a potential investment and determine the potential costs associated with the risks of that investment. Then they use mathematical modelling to determine their best investment option.

In portfolio management, you can minimise the level of total risk and still maximise financial returns by carefully measuring how different investments change in value compared to each other in multi-asset interactions. One way to do this is to look at the underlying principles that build your views of financial risk.

If you want to review the nature of risk, turn to Chapter 14 for a more general discussion.

Looking at the trade-off between risk and return

A central tenet of modern portfolio theory is that a trade-off exists between risk and return. All things being equal, if a particular investment incurs a higher risk of financial loss for prospective investors, those investors must be able to expect a higher return in order to be attracted to the higher risk.

Be very careful in your interpretation of the preceding paragraph, because perception can be misleading. Just because an investor believes that a higher-risk investment is going to generate higher returns doesn't necessarily make it true. Sometimes higher-risk investments become less risky over time, attracting more investors who then drive up the price/value of the investment by competitively outbidding each other. (A larger pool of investors tends to mean a higher price.) In the vast majority of cases, though, no promise of higher returns on risky assets is made, and so the higher risk tends to scare off potential investors, keeping the returns on a given investment low as investors will be put off by the high risk of financial loss. The only investments that can really try to promise higher returns for higher risk are bonds, and even then the higher returns aren't generated if the organisation issuing the bond defaults on the terms of the bond.

Whether or not a riskier investment does generate higher returns is up to the individual investor to decide. We talk more about how this decision is calculated in the later section 'Measuring risk', but for now, just note the following:

✔ Exactly how risk is assessed, and the amount of expected returns, changes depending on the individual investor.

✔ Investors will, in fact, invest in higher-risk opportunities if they feel that doing so is going to generate higher returns.

A company refuses to buy into a higher-risk investment if it doesn't think that the investment is going to generate extra returns. The fact that so many high-risk investments do attract investors obviously indicates some perception of higher expected returns (we discuss this topic more in the later section 'Measuring risk').

Here's an important but subtle difference: higher risk doesn't necessarily mean higher returns, but only those investments that are expected to provide higher returns attract investors. If the risk is too high without the expectation of additional returns, no-one buys the investment.

The preceding discussion is all about the amount of risk in an individual investment. You can minimise that risk by choosing the right combination of investments (read the next section for a heads-up on this strategy).

Diversifying to maximise returns and minimise risk

The risk of a single investment can't be totally eliminated, and so companies attempt to reduce the risk of a portfolio by picking investments that are likely to change in value in different ways or at different times. This process is called *diversification*.

Diversification means taking advantage of differences in risk among your investments and the fact that investments tend to change in value at different times and even in different directions. So if your portfolio consists of several different investments and only one of them loses value, the portfolio loses a smaller percentage of its value than a single investment does.

Here's a theoretical example with an extremely low probability of actually happening. Say that a company holds two investments, and these two investments change in value in exactly opposite ways. So if one decreases in value by 1 per cent, the other increases in value by 1 per cent. Between the two investments, any changes in value result in not only zero gain or loss but also zero risk.

The goal of diversification is to reduce risk by finding several investments that change in value at different times, in response to different events, by different percentages, or in completely different directions (as in the preceding example). In this way you reduce the severity of any losses that may occur in a portfolio from the risk associated with only one investment. You can measure the effectiveness of portfolio diversification mathematically, as we discuss in Chapter 20.

Now, you may be asking yourself 'why do companies not just invest all their money in only the best assets?' After all, if you diversify your portfolio by investing in a number of different assets, you're investing money in assets that aren't your first choice. The opportunity cost (the loss of forgoing the next best option) of purchasing an investment intended to diversify a portfolio is the returns generated by the best investments that you could've spent that money on instead.

Warren Buffet, CEO of the US company Berkshire Hathaway, Inc, (and one of the richest people in the world as a result of his investments) claims that diversification is used only when a company lacks confidence or ability, maintaining that diversification is a tool only for the incompetent (though he's a bit more tactful about it).

This criticism holds an important distinction: diversification simply for the sake of diversification isn't very helpful.

Yet even Warren Buffet's company (which buys ownership in other companies) holds investments in at least 54 companies, far more than your average investor. The point of diversification is to reduce the risk to your portfolio more than you reduce the returns.

Here's a quick example. Say that Investment A generates 10 per cent annual returns, Investment B generates 5 per cent annual returns and your portfolio has an equal split between Investments A and B. X is the amount of portfolio risk as a percentage of total value. For this example, 7.5 per cent is the amount of annual returns generated by the portfolio (10% + 5% = 15% ÷ 2 = 7.5%).

Here's what you can discover from this example:

- **If X = 7.5%:** Obviously Investment A generates 100 per cent more returns per year, but the actual importance of this act depends on the amount of risk. If Investment B reduces risk, the change in risk is the same as the difference in returns between A and B.

- **If X > 7.5%:** If diversifying risk means that the total risk of the portfolio stays above 7.5 per cent, the amount of returns generated decreases at a faster rate than diversifying risk. In other words, the portfolio is being diversified poorly, taking on more risk for the amount of returns being generated.

✔ **If X < 7.5%:** If the portfolio has less than 7.5 per cent risk through diversification, it's generating more returns for the amount of risk being incurred, because risk is decreasing at a faster rate than returns. This scenario is considered an effective use of diversification.

You want to look for the best investments you can find and then diversify by purchasing those investments that provide the highest returns but risk losing value under directly opposite conditions. For example, share prices tend to increase in value when interest rates decrease, whereas variable rate bonds decrease in value under the same conditions. Therefore, putting shares and bonds together in a portfolio is a good choice for reducing risk through diversification, assuming that both investments were good options individually as well.

Considering risk aversion

The risks that you can eliminate or greatly minimise through diversification (the technique we describe in the preceding section) are *specific risks:* those associated with an individual investment. Specific risks include default risk on a bond, liquidity risk on the company underlying a share and the risk of a building losing value in the property market.

But this strategy can't stop the entire economy as a whole from going down the pan. Sometimes, no matter how perfect an individual asset is, or how well a portfolio is diversified, a nation's economy essentially collapses and everything loses value. The risk of that happening is called *systematic risk.*

To minimise systematic risk, your options are to diversify internationally (national economies tend to change at different rates just like individual investments – see Chapter 21), become very good in economics or just hope to be very lucky.

You may well ask, however, 'what about risk-free investments such as bonds?' (which we discuss in Chapter 11). Well, yes, short-term, fixed-rate, highly liquid assets issued by organisations with great credit scores are considered to be risk-free. Basically that boils down to treasury bills, which mature in as little as a few weeks but no more than one year, are issued by the government (which has a very high credit score), have a fixed return and can be easily sold. The amount of risk associated with treasury bills is so small that they're considered risk-free.

The problem is that they also offer very, very low returns, on par with certificates of deposits or some savings accounts at credit unions. Still, you do get a financial return on these without incurring any risk, and risk-free assets are the assets against which all other investments, considered to be risky assets, are compared. The risk-free rate is the annual return on a risk-free asset, and so any investment that has more risk than the risk-free asset must also offer at least proportionally as much return. Otherwise, it's in the best interest of the investor to buy only risk-free investments.

How much risk a company takes depends on how risk averse the investment or treasury manager of that company is. Many people are willing to take on far more additional risk just for the chance of generating a little bit of extra return. Some barking-mad people take on extra risk even when they could generate just as much financial return from a lower-risk investment. Some onlookers think that those individuals are addicted to the risk, a bit like compulsive gamblers. We reserve judgement for the therapists on that one, though.

Often the amount of risk aversion that a company has depends on its timeline. Portfolios with short-term goals are usually more risk averse because they have less time to make up for any losses. Long-term portfolios can ride out any losses from systematic risk by waiting for the economy to regain strength.

Exactly how do you measure an investor's risk aversion? Well, simply asking investors doesn't work. Saying, for example, 'very averse' is subjective and so doesn't help you mathematically.

You can employ a number of ways to measure how risk averse a particular business or investor is. Insurance companies like to measure risk aversion in terms of how much insurance a person needs, often calculated as the total potential loss if the insured asset/person experiences a worst-case scenario. Many financial advisers measure risk aversion in terms that don't use a risk function and instead choose to use only their time horizon. They choose the lowest-risk investments available that are likely to generate the necessary returns within the time horizon. Those who simply seek to maximise returns for their client often take the average cyclical duration of investments into consideration; in order to avoid nearing the end of the portfolio time horizon during a recession, they gradually shift the focus of the portfolio towards less risky investments as the end gets closer.

Modern portfolio theory uses something called an aversion function. An *aversion function* is measured by determining how much additional return a company must think is possible to be willing to take on just one additional unit of risk. Risk is measured, in this exercise, as the probability of loss *(p)*, while $(1 - p)$ is the probability that no loss will be experienced. This measurement is true because $1 = 100$ per cent and p is any number between 0 and 1. So, if *p* is 0.4, a 40 per cent chance of loss exists as well as a 60 per cent chance (1 – 0.4) that no loss will be experienced. This strategy is completely hypothetical, however, as a method of measuring risk aversion.

In the extreme, a company that's completely neutral to risk – in other words, willing to take on any amount of risk for additional gain – has a risk aversion of 0, which is often true for extremely low-risk assets, such as the difference between a Treasury bill and a Treasury note. A risk aversion of less than 0 means taking on additional risk without the expectation of additional gain, which is nonsensical.

So, put simply, the aversion function is a curved line that measures how much additional return must be generated for a single unit of additional risk. The function changes depending on how much risk the company has already incurred, but is measured by dividing the percentage change in expected returns required by the company by a percentage change in risk.

Another way to measure risk aversion is in terms of the risk premium demanded by an investor. Mathematically, it looks like this:

$$A = [E(r_m) - r_f] \div \sigma_m$$

where:

   A = Risk aversion

   $E(r_m)$ = Expected returns on risky assets required to attract the investor

   r_f = Rate of return on risk-free assets

   σ_m = Amount of risk in risky assets (the actual measure of risk is highly debated, but we talk more about that in the next section, 'Measuring risk')

This method provides more of a singular measurement of risk aversion rather than the variable one provided in the previous method. Mathematically inclined investors combine the best of both methods, but we don't get into that complex subject here. Our goal is simply to help you understand the role of risk aversion: that investors who are more risk averse require higher returns to invest in riskier assets than investors with low risk aversion.

Measuring risk

Exactly how risk is measured is a complicated issue. The actual measurement of risk is a matter of significant disagreement, but this section looks at the two primary approaches to measuring risk: CAPM and APT.

In modern portfolio theory, before you can begin managing a portfolio you have to look at individual investments. Originally, this task was done using a calculation called the capital asset pricing model (CAPM). Today the CAPM is seen as an unrealistic view of investing, but it's still valid as a starting point of the purely rational and efficient upon which to build better and more practical models.

The CAPM leads to the use of the arbitrage pricing theory (APT), which is more flexible and has gained more credibility as a functional approach to quantifying portfolio management.

In both cases, the goal is to assess whether an investment is worth purchasing by determining the rate of returns and the risk compared to the risk-free rate of return.

Capital asset pricing model (CAPM)

Take a quick look at the following CAPM equation to help clear up CAPM and APT a bit:

$$r_s = r_f + \beta_a(r_m - r_f)$$

where:

> r_s = Rate of return demanded to invest in a specific asset
>
> r_f = Rate of return on risk-free assets
>
> β_a = Level of risk on a specific asset
>
> r_m = Rate of return on a market portfolio (an investment portfolio that perfectly matches the investment market)

By subtracting the risk-free rate from the market rate of return (which is best accomplished by investing in an index portfolio that matches something like the FTSE 100), you're determining what market premium is being offered for investing in risky assets. In other words, the market premium is the amount of financial return you can generate by managing a market portfolio of risky assets instead of only risk-free assets. By multiplying the risk of just a specific asset, you're calculating the risk premium being offered by a specific investment.

Of course, investors want a return premium that's higher than the risk-free rate, and so you add the risk-free rate back into the equation to get the rate of returns demanded by investors to entice them to purchase an investment under CAPM. Nice and easy, right? Well, not really. The following sections present a couple of considerations.

Beta

The risk symbol beta (β) isn't actually a measure of risk. Beta is actually a measure of volatility, which means that a particular investment can fluctuate far above normal market returns and still be considered high-risk, even though it's making huge gains compared to the market. Meanwhile, another investment can be consistently only 0.01 per cent under market returns and still be considered low-risk, even though it's losing value like there's no tomorrow compared to the market.

Beta is measured as follows:

$$\beta = [Cov(r_s, r_m)] \div \sigma^2_m$$

It measures the amount that the value of an individual asset changes in response to a change in market value. *Cov* is short for covariance and refers to any movement in one variable that's inherently linked to movement in another variable. Consider shares for a moment. If the stock market increases by 10 per cent and an individual share increases in value by 20 per cent in response to the change in value of the stock market, the beta of that particular stock is 2, or twice as volatile as the stock market itself.

So, beta doesn't measure risk of loss at all, it just measures volatility. Beta is still useful, however, but only when used properly, which doesn't include using it to measure risk.

What this equation does allow investors to do is to better understand the movements of an investment. Calculating the covariance alone tells you how much volatility in an investment is simply in response to market volatility, and how much of it is unique to that investment (the proportion of variance not accounted for by the covariance is unique to the investment). This knowledge allows you to predict volatility more accurately. When calculating beta, you can estimate the severity of the volatility that will occur. This factor can help companies that participate in active portfolio management to determine when to buy and resell investments by helping to project how high or low the price of the investment is going to go. This calculation is exclusively for active portfolio management, though, where losses and gains can occur as a result of fluctuations that otherwise have no impact on the underlying value of the asset.

Instead, measures of risk used by *value investors* (investors who focus on finding undervalued and overvalued assets) use primary measures that compare accounting values to market prices. For example, in shares, measures of risk include the balance sheet and a comparison of the book value to the current market price as well as the book value per share to the market price per share. When an investment's price is higher than its value, it's considered overpriced, making it more likely to lose value. When the investment's price is lower than its value, it's considered underpriced. This analysis is done in conjunction with assessments of the quality of the underlying asset of the investment, in order to ensure that the market truly is overpricing or underpricing rather than anticipating qualitative traits, such as amazing management.

The exact methods used to determine risk vary from investor to investor. Investors don't like to talk about their methods in case they give away a 'trade secret'. But in reality it's all just about value versus price; this book contains all the information used by top investors, except that they use it in proprietary ways.

Test some things out and see what works best for you. Measures of risk are used in far more than just CAPM, and so knowing this stuff is useful. You'll face a test at the end of this book – a test called life!

Assumptions of perfection

No one is claiming that CAPM is perfect, quite the opposite in fact: CAPM is imperfect because to be functionally useful it requires several assumptions of perfect data. Nobody has a perfect market portfolio. No one has perfect access to information, nor do all investments provide returns perfectly to a level of risk. CAPM ignores factors of behavioural finance, and it assumes that all returns above market returns will be lost in the long-run and that the distribution of returns in a market portfolio is statistically perfect (for those statistically inclined, CAPM assumes a normal distribution of returns). Basically, CAPM makes the assumption that everything in the world of corporate finance adheres to the lessons of first year statistics/finance classes. That's simply not how the world works, though.

But we have to talk about CAPM because it helps you understand reality. Nothing's wrong with assuming that everything in the world works perfectly and is easy to understand as long as you realise that you have to modify the model in order to make it useful. Discovering CAPM is a bit like putting stabilisers on your bike. They help you understand how riding a bike is supposed to work, but you really haven't learned to ride a bike until you can take the stabilisers off. All these assumptions we make that allow CAPM to work are your stabilisers, and the stabilisers are about to come off!

Arbitrage pricing theory

Arbitrage pricing theory (APT) is far more flexible and effective than CAPM. Instead of worrying about returns on a market portfolio, APT looks for differentials in the market price of a single investment and what the market price of the same investment actually should be. You can think of it in terms of volatility measures, similar to the way beta should be used (refer to the preceding section). The expected returns on an investment change in response to other factors and the sensitivity that the investment has to that factor.

When the price of an investment is lower than the price predicted by the model, you should purchase it because the prediction is that it's undervalued and is going to generate more value or increase in value in the future. If a price is higher than the price predicted by the model, the investment is considered overvalued and you should sell it. Use the proceeds of the sale to purchase an investment whose market-to-expected price differential is negative (meaning that the market price is below the expected price) or to purchase risk-free investments until you find such an opportunity.

The APT model itself is very easy to understand and just as easy to customise, which is useful. Take a look at a sample model:

$$r_s = r_f + \beta_1 r_1 + \beta_2 r_2 + \dots \beta_n r_n + \varepsilon$$

where:

r_s = Return on a specific investment

r_f = Return on risk-free investments

β = Change in returns in response to a change in a variable

r = Variable that influences returns on an investment

ε = Error variable that accounts for temporary market deviations and shocks

In CAPM, beta measures the amount of change in value that an investment experiences in response to a change in the market. In APT, beta measures something similar: the amount of change in returns caused in response to a change of a particular variable. That variable can be interest rates, the cost of oil, GDP, annual sales, changes in market value or anything else that influences the returns on an investment. It's a little bit like guesswork. You try out different factors to determine whether changes in that factor correlate with changes in the value of the returns in an investment. If an investment's price is low compared to the price estimated by the model, it's a good investment to make.

The APT model doesn't really take risk into consideration at all, because it's not using measures of probability to determine the value of the investment. Instead, it's looking for differentials in value of the current market price and the price that the investment should have. Therefore, the only risk to be concerned with is market risk; the state of being over- or undervalued has already been established rather than relying on probabilities of risk.

The variable ε is sort of a catch-all variable, which is meant to account for short-term variations in the value of an investment caused by unrelated or temporary influences. If you're able to pick out the type of variables that have an influence and the amount of influence they have, good for you. But doing so is practically impossible. So ε is really a variable that accounts for all deviations in price that aren't accounted for elsewhere. Until you have a much more advanced understanding of statistics and finance, consider ε to be 0 and work to maximise the amount of value being accounted for by known variables.

Overall, APT isn't so different from CAPM. They both rely heavily on changes in value in response to a specific variable, both use the beta function (though in different ways) and both expect returns over the risk-free rate. In contrast to each other, APT doesn't have the same shortcomings of relying on impossible assumptions, but it also doesn't illustrate the variable of risk. Risk, in the context of investing, does exist. Of course, APT is flexible enough to include such a variable.

Optimising Portfolio Risk

Collections of individual assets interact together to influence the overall portfolio. So when several investments are lumped together in a portfolio, every single investment has an influence on the portfolio.

Consider this analogy: a ring is held up by several rubber bands tied to it. Each rubber band acts like a single investment, so that the location of the ring in the middle is determined by the length of each rubber band. Now, if you pull on one of those rubber bands, the ring doesn't move as much as the rubber band because the ring is still being held somewhat in place by the other rubber bands. That's a bit like how individual investments influence a ring . . . we mean, portfolio.

Figure 15-1 illustrates something called the *efficient frontier:* the maximum amount of returns that can be generated for a given level of risk in a portfolio. The straight line labelled 'Best possible CAL' illustrates the best potential proportion of returns to risk. CAL stands for *capital allocation line,* which means that any optimised portfolio falls on that line.

The contradiction is that the individual assets don't fall on that line, and so you have to use diversification of your portfolio to make that happen. Because investments that change value in opposite directions reduce risk below the risk of any individual asset through diversification, you can decrease the total risk of a portfolio, shifting it to the left, at any given rate of return. The portfolio is optimised at the point of tangency, where the efficient frontier intersects the best possible CAL using a given investment portfolio. The dot where the lines intersect in Figure 15-1 shows the point of an optimised portfolio generated using the individual investments illustrated by the other dots.

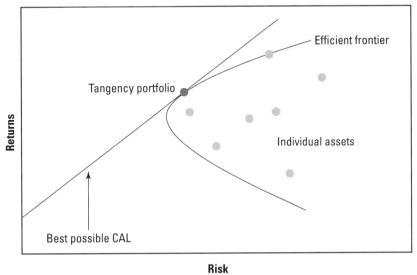

Figure 15-1:
Efficient
frontier
showing
every com-
bination of
risky assets.

To ensure that you're maximising the opportunity of getting the highest expected return for a given level of risk, and to measure the influences that individual investments have on the risk and return of the whole portfolio, you use maths!

According to CAPM, you measure the returns of a portfolio as follows:

$$r_m = \sum_{k=1}^{n} w_k r_k$$

This equation says that the returns on a portfolio are the sum of the returns of the individual investments weighted by the proportion of their contribution to the portfolio. Here's a quick example to illustrate. Assume the following facts about Investments A, B and C:

- ✔ **Investment A:** 10% returns, 50% portfolio.
- ✔ **Investment B:** 5% returns, 25% portfolio.
- ✔ **Investment C:** 0% returns, 25% portfolio.

You calculate the returns on the portfolio like this:

$$10\%(0.5) + 5\%(0.25) + 0\%(0.25) = 5\% + 2.5\% + 0\% = 7.5\%$$

According to CAPM, you measure risk (remember that risk is defined by CAPM as volatility rather than actual risk; refer to the earlier section 'Capital asset pricing model (CAPM)') as follows:

$$\sum_{k=1}^{n} w_k \, \mathrm{cov}\left(r_k, r_s\right)$$

This equation works just like the portfolio returns under CAPM, except that it uses the weighted sum of covariances of the individual investments. In contrast, the portfolio variability under APT is calculated as follows:

$$\Sigma w_i \beta_i$$

Again you use the sum of weighted variability, but this time you measure the variability of the individual factors influencing the individual investments. Doing this calculation allows you to input the value into another equation that measures the portfolio returns under APT:

$$r_p = E(r_p) + \beta_p + \varepsilon_p$$

Here, the returns on the portfolio are the expected portfolio returns while also accounting for the portfolio variability and any short-term market shocks influencing price.

Yes, we know, it's a lot of mathematical exercises. The question becomes whether or not all this maths is worth the effort or whether you should simply invest in a passively-managed index portfolio that matches an asset index (indices of shares, bonds, derivative investments and all sorts of stuff). The truth is that the vast majority of portfolios consistently generate fewer returns in the long run than index-matched portfolios. If anyone were to develop and announce a better method of portfolio management than the efficient market hypothesis, the rest of the market would adopt the new method, eliminating the ability of the inventor of the new method to continue making money using that method. So, it's no surprise that if anyone does have a better method, they're not going to tell you about it.

A big part of professional portfolio management that allows some investors to generate returns over and above usual returns comes from technology. Asset trades are now measured in milliseconds, and so the person with the fastest automated transactions is able to generate the most returns by simply making a purchase before the price is driven up by other investors or selling before the price is driven down. Although effective, this advantage speaks more about these investors' expertise in technology than in finance.

Another observation about these above-normal returns in a portfolio is that many of the successful portfolios lose their gains during an economic downturn, such as in a recession. Investing is easy when the economy is growing, because just about everything is doing well. Portfolio managers take on extra risk to gain those extra returns, but when the economy starts to shrink, all those gains disappear.

You can mitigate this drawback by carefully watching the national economy and taking the following precautions when indicators start pointing towards a downturn:

- ✔ Start buying options
- ✔ Start selling some of your portfolio
- ✔ Transition to lower-risk investments
- ✔ Continue to take risk by short-selling assets

All you can do is cross your fingers and hope to avoid the loss that high-risk portfolios bring during a recession in contrast to the gains they make during an economic boom. But you need to take precautions and develop a keen mind for macroeconomics (which as we explain in Chapter 12 is the study of large-scale economic management).

New innovations for portfolio management crop up all the time: new calculations, new models, new advances in mathematics and statistics, and new technologies. Plus, new and better ways to measure risk, find combinations of factors that influence APT calculations and identify more accessible markets arise as well.

The overriding goal is to better use the connections between assets to maximise the returns that corporate investments yield while limiting the amount of risk to which they're exposed. When you start talking about a company's money (which is exactly what we're talking about), huge amounts of energy and resources go into finding new innovations to generate better returns on investment, regardless of the type of assets in which the company is investing.

Chapter 16

Entering the Science Lab: Financial Engineering

*P*eople are serious about their money and go to great lengths to revolutionise the world in their efforts to make more. Financial engineering is the practice of continuously assessing current investment methods and finding new ones in order to gain an advantage, increase returns and customise products.

Financial engineering isn't something to take lightly: it can become insanely complex very quickly. It's becoming increasingly prevalent in corporate and personal finance, allowing you to improve your financial understanding and ability to manage finances and increasing the number of financial tools available. It's capable of creating an amazing array of products, services and investment options and is already within the reach of average consumers. This increase in complexity, however, inevitably requires an increased understanding of what's becoming available – and many investors have been financially ruined because they didn't fully understand what they were doing.

In this chapter, we talk about the propensity for turning everything into a security investment, for merging financial products to make hybrids, for combining and splitting investments and cash flows for different purposes, for developing new, exotic and specialised investment tools, for the mathematical development of portfolio strategy, and for the incorporation of new computer technologies and the ability to drive technological progress.

Creating New Tools through Financial Engineering

Financial engineering is nothing more than the creation of new and interesting financial tools, often accomplished through the use of mathematic modelling and computer engineering. It's a bit like the science lab of the world of corporate finance, where new ideas are developed and tested.

Financial engineering is where the majority of innovation is occurring in the field of finance. These innovations include new ways of interpreting information, investments, debt, transactions methods, strategies and accounts, and brand new ways for organisations to improve their financial efficiency and overall financial wellbeing – assuming, of course, that they know how to make effective use of the tools available to them.

In order to explain this field of financial engineering with all its broad, new and often experimental activities, we break it down into some of the most common, recent and successful trends to arise in the last few decades.

The bottom line is to be careful with unique and exotic financial tools and products. If you're not certain about what you're doing, ask an expert (which doesn't include the person trying to sell you something).

Making Securities from Just about Anything

When people talk about securities, usually they're referring to equity securities, also known as shares. Equity securities aren't even close to being the only type of available security, though.

Securities include any financial investment that derives its value from an underlying asset. So although shares are a type of security whose value is derived from the ownership in a company that's also changing in value, bonds derive their value from underlying assets, as do mutual funds and derivatives. With that in mind, people can make securities out of almost anything.

Securitisation is the creation of new forms of securities, or new classifications of an existing security, based on some asset that currently has value or future value but in which no one is yet investing. The goal is to raise funds (usually on international markets) and distribute risk to a group of people seeking risk. You can do securitisation with just about anything that has a value and it's a common trend in financial engineering. Raising money in this way, rather than through traditional bank loans, has become popular in banking markets in recent years.

Consider the role of *commodities trading* (the buying and selling of physical or virtual goods; a *commodity* can be anything from coffee and wheat to gold and oil). Although it isn't considered a form of financial engineering, commodities trading helps illustrate the nature of securitisation. In commodities trading, brokers act as intermediaries between producers and processors or retailers, usually for agricultural goods and natural resources, though a number of other things are also included, such as gold, diamonds and industrial metals.

For example, say that coffee growers want to lock in a price: they want to sell 20 tonnes of coffee for £X per tonne, and so they get in touch with their broker, who writes up 20 derivatives contracts (usually as options or futures; we look at derivatives in more detail in Chapter 13). Each of these contracts now has the value of 1 tonne of coffee, the sterling value of which changes depending on how the market price of coffee changes. The contract can be bought and resold multiple times until its delivery date, at which point the holder of the contract has to purchase the coffee definitively for the price listed in the contract.

The contract itself is the security, whereas the coffee is the underlying asset.

Realising that you can securitise everything

People don't just securitise items such as coffee, gold and businesses, they securitise everything (for example car loans and credit card debts). One of the trends in financial engineering is to find assets that have value and securitise them, developing securities that derive their value from that asset.

Probably the most successful development in securitisation, as measured by the popularity of its use, is the mortgage-backed security (MBS). An MBS starts out with the banks; they issue mortgages just like any normal bank. The future cash flows on these mortgage loans are considered an asset now, because the bank receives repayments from the borrower for the principal (sometimes called the *capital*) balance as well as the interest payments. The banks then sell securities that use those future cash flows as the underlying asset. They sell the securities for cash to investors, and then repay the investors using the future cash flows on the mortgages. The investors generate a return on investment, and the banks use the capital raised from selling the securities to reinvest and increase the current value of future cash flows from the increased number of mortgages issued.

Alternatively, MBSs are a way for banks, particularly smaller ones, to limit their exposure to risk by issuing loans. A mortgage that goes into default doesn't continue to generate cash flows, and so the holder of the MBS is the one who loses value on the investment if a mortgage defaults, not the bank. By selling mortgage loans to the investment market in the form of MBSs and thereby distributing the risk among a larger group of people, banks can reduce their own risk exposure on these loans.

Sounds great, but with new financial products often come new risks. This distribution of risk in the form of MBSs helped to distribute the risk of subprime mortgages to a larger variety of banks, with the result that the mistakes of a small number of banks harmed a wider range of other banks and investors. The damage done was much worse and far more widespread than it otherwise would have been because through this form of lending, banks had rejigged their balance sheets to release more capital to make profit that they might not have made if they hadn't rejigged their balance sheets.

Imagine, for a moment, the possibilities for securitisation. What things do you come into contact with that have some sort of future value or sustained current value? What about a manufacturing firm? Instead of issuing debt to purchase a machine, the firm can sell securities on the future cash flows generated by selling the products that the machine makes and repay investors using the profits. If the company goes bust, the products are sub-standard or the machine breaks, the risk is distributed to the investment market in the same manner as MBSs.

Slicing securities into tranches

Financial engineering has taken securitisation even further, allowing individual securities to be divided into classes, called *tranches,* of investments that have varying repayment periods. This strategy varies the amount of interest-rate risk associated with each tranche and attracts a wider range of investors to a single security.

With MBSs, for example, this division is a special class called *collateralised mortgage obligations,* and the tranches are classified by class: A, B and C. Investors in each class receive their portion of the interest payments for as long as their portion of the principal isn't yet paid off. Regarding the principal, Class A shares receive their repayment first, followed by B and finally C. So although Class C shareholders receive more interest payment in the long run, they're also accepting a higher degree of risk that interest rates will exceed the payments they're currently receiving. The Class A tranche has the lowest risk but receives repayment over a shorter period of time. The class that investors choose depends greatly on their level of risk avoidance as well as their current portfolio strategy needs. *Credit rating agencies* (agencies that decide how much of a credit risk a company or an individual is) are also involved in this whole process too, which demonstrates how attractive these products are to investors.

Looking at Hybrid Finances

A *hybrid* is anything made by combining two or more things. Hybrid cars, for instance, are cars that run some of the time on an electric engine and some of the time on a standard combustion engine (in other words, they're part electric car and part normal car). A hybrid breed of dog is created by breeding two types of dogs together: breeding a Labrador retriever and a poodle results in a labradoodle. Ancient cultures loved hybrid creatures, often including within their mythology creatures that combined the physical traits of humans and any of a variety of other animals, or even multiple different animals. Unicorns, for example, appear to be a cross between a horse and a *narwhal* (a medium-sized tooth whale that lives in the Arctic and has a long tusk), though we shudder to think how that may occur in nature.

You may be wondering what on earth strange animals have to do with finance. The answer is simple: financial professionals are strange, too! Besides that, they also create hybrids, taking two financial products and mashing them together into a single product. Some work more effectively together than others; sometimes the traits of each component of the hybrid function separately, creating no benefit other than having two financial products rather than one.

The more successful hybrids are those where the traits of each component complement each other in some way.

The following three sections take a look at some examples of hybrid financial products.

Meeting the mixed-interest class of hybrids

Whether you're talking about investments (for example, bonds, money markets, annuities or any other income-generating investment) or loans (such as mortgages, business loans, credit cards and so on), *mixed-interest hybrids* combine aspects of fixed-rate and variable-rate financial products.

A mixed-rate bond (or hybrid bond), for example, guarantees a minimum rate of return that also matches interest rates if they go over a certain level, giving you the best of a variable- and fixed-rate bond. A typical mixed-rate bond may include, say, a minimum guaranteed fixed 3 per cent interest rate with the potential to increase above 3 per cent if interest rates rise above that level. This sort of hybrid interest rate is partially pegged to some other indicator, such as interest rates or some index.

Another type of mixed-rate product is time-dependent. Many mixed-rate mortgages include *teaser rates,* where the interest on a mortgage remains fixed for a period of time (often referred to as a *fixed rate* mortgage for the time the interest rate remains fixed) before switching to a variable rate. These types of mortgages have come under fire recently as a form of *bait-and-switch* arrangement (customers are 'baited' by low rates only to find that they're not available and are then sold another mortgage with higher rates of interest). Such facts are sometimes hidden in a mountain of legal and financial jargon. Mixed-rate loans can be quite beneficial in the right circumstances, but the reality is that these circumstances can be extremely difficult for even professionals to predict, and even more so for someone who's less in-the-know about financial modelling and forecasting.

For example, if you expect interest rates to fall in the future you may benefit from considering a time-dependent mixed-rate loan. So a market does exist for these types of loans, even if it's smaller than many lenders like to believe.

Circling around single asset class hybrids

Some hybrids combine different types of a single asset class. *Convertible debt,* for example, are loans that have the option to be converted into a fixed number or value of shares. *Convertible preference shares* also have the option to be converted into a fixed number or value of ordinary shares. This form of hybrid doesn't provide the same sort of simultaneous benefits of each component as other forms of hybrids do, but the option to choose which traits you have available to you in your investing is still a valuable benefit for strategic and portfolio investing.

Furthermore, a number of hybrids combine completely different types of asset classes. Packaging different types of investments together with call or put options (which we cover in Chapter 13) is a particularly popular option. In cases of equity, debt and even money-market investments, hybrid investments are now available that include, by default, put options that allow you to sell your investment at a given rate or price. Contracts are available to purchase an asset with a call option to purchase more on or before a certain date at a given price. These vehicles can be particularly useful for people managing strategic investment portfolios, which often supplement with risk-hedging strategies. They're also quite handy as standalone investments for companies that are more risk averse than the underlying investment alone can accommodate.

Becoming a financial Frankenstein: Index-backed CDs

One hybrid investment uses several of the hybrids we discuss in the two preceding sections to create a sort of *chimera;* something that has been combined with so many different things that it barely resembles its original form anymore. This investment is the *index-backed CD* with a put-option hybrid.

To create this monstrosity, you start with a standard certificate of deposit (CD), which is a timed deposit that works like a savings account, except that it includes an obligation to maintain the principal balance for a minimum period of time. You combine that with a variable-rate security that's pegged to an equity index, so that the interest rate floats with the index. Now, you tack on a put option that allows the investor to sell her stake in the CD for a set return that's usually based on the present value.

We describe this particular investment to show that the development of new forms of hybrid financial tools is just starting; brand new types of transactions that no longer resemble anything in existence today may easily evolve from these innovations.

Bundling Assets

Not all combinations of investments are hybrids (see the preceding section). Grouping together several of a single type of asset, or sometimes several different types of assets, and selling them collectively as a single security is called *bundling*.

Bundling has come to have a unique role in corporate finance since the start of the 21st century. The act of bundling involves taking several different assets and lumping them together in something called an *asset pool* with a nominal value equivalent to the sum of the values of the individual assets included. The issuer takes the total value of the assets or their future cash flows and sells equity backed by this value, whereby ownership in the asset itself or its cash flows generates returns. The source of derived value is similar to that of a share or a bond, respectively.

The aspect that makes bundling significantly different from standard securitisation is the matter of risk: the risk-adjusted value is higher than the sum of the individual assets. By its very nature bundling creates a certain amount of inherent diversification within the security (if one of the assets in the pool fails, others are still valid), and so the risk of the bundle has to be measured as a unique set in itself. This assessment is done by classifying each individual asset by its risk level, and then taking the weighted average of the different classifications present within the bundle.

Making a bundle with multi-asset bundles

One form of bundling includes grouping together multiple different types of assets. Mutual funds are a common example of this type of bundling, because they frequently group together different types of equities, bonds and other forms of assets into a single pool. Investors then purchase shares of ownership in the mutual fund itself.

As opposed to a hedge fund, where people give their money to someone who then manages their cash as a pool, *mutual funds* are pools of assets in which people invest.

The risk of these multi-asset bundles is measured a bit differently compared to single-asset bundling, because the risk of each individual asset isn't measured in the same way and each asset often doesn't have the same type of risk.

In fact, these bundles are similar to investment portfolios; in a way, they're investment portfolios that have been securitised. As a result, the most effective method to assess the risk of these bundles is to measure them in the same way you would an investment portfolio.

Unbundling securities

Another innovation related to bundling comes into play when a single security is broken into several different securities, in a process called *unbundling*. This term usually refers to the process by which the cash flows from a single security, such as a bond, are broken apart and each is sold as a different security.

For example, a coupon bond that makes interest coupon payments as well as principal repayment at maturity can be broken into several different types of securities. The issuer can bundle the individual coupon payments into a single security to be sold on its own, while the principal repayment at maturity is sold separately. Each security is treated as a separate investment with its own valuation, pricing, cash flows and ability to be sold and resold, but both securities derive their value from the same underlying asset – a single bond or pool of cash flows from coupons or principal repayments.

This form of unbundling is lagging behind in popularity compared to bundling, although it holds just as much potential for being applied to any sort of investment that generates cash flows over time. The cash flows from a single mortgage can be unbundled, not only by the types of cash flows, as with unbundled bonds, but also with regard to their repayment periods. This process makes several new types of investments from a single mortgage, each with a differing level of risk not only from credit risk, but also from interest-rate risk: the longer the repayment period on the security, the higher the interest-rate risk.

Appealing to a Large Market with Exotic Finances

Exotic financial products aren't entirely new; in fact, they're new and/or rare variations of existing products. The word *exotic* is used in finance to mean that something is attractive simply because it's out of the ordinary. On the flip side, 'ordinary' products are popular because they appeal to a larger market. The exotic products being developed through financial engineering are rare and extraordinary in large part because they appeal only to a small market of people who have much more experience in financial management and unique needs.

Exotic doesn't necessarily mean useful. Just because an asset or investment is available doesn't mean that you need it. The attraction that people have to something that's novel – even if they won't benefit from having it or don't have a particular use for it – is one of those bizarre behaviours in the world of finance that causes otherwise rational, and sometimes quite experienced, people to act like excited and inexperienced beginners.

Still, these great products fulfil a number of roles in the financial world, and even if they're designed to fill only one role, they may inspire others to model new products off the back of them to meet other requirements.

The following sections touch on some of the strange and exotic financial wildlife that exists in the financial engineering laboratory.

Owning options

The derivatives market, which is based almost entirely on contracts that can be customised as long as a legal agreement is in place between the issuer and the holder, has been rife with the development of exotic financial tools. A number of unusual *options* (the right to buy or sell equities, bonds, foreign exchange contracts and such like at a future date but at a price that is agreed now – see Chapter 13 for more on options), for example, have been developed.

Options are available that are dependent on some milestone occurring before the option expires but after it's issued. Some options become valid only if the price of the underlying asset drops below a certain level, whereas others become invalid if they drop below that level. The same can be said for some options that become valid or invalid when they rise above a certain level. The value of some options depends not on the final stock or share price on the expiry date, but on the maximum or minimum price achieved while the option was 'in play'. The value of some options varies depending on different macroeconomic indicators, such as unemployment levels, the balance of trade or any of a number of indicators, such as the gross domestic product (GDP).

Seeking out swaps contracts

Swaps contracts are derivatives whose value varies not with the value of the underlying asset or even in response to variations in some indicator, but in response to the level of variation itself. Here are three examples:

- **Variance swaps:** Derive their value from the amount of volatility experienced, called a *variance strike*.

- **Forward contracts:** Customised by their very nature (in contrast to futures, which are standardised; check out Chapter 13 for more on this topic). As a result, forward contracts can become unique to the point where you may see a particular variation only once, depending on what the two parties to the contract agree upon.

- **Indexed-principal swaps:** Have their principal value (instead of – or in addition to – their interest payments) vary with some index, usually inflation or interest rates.

Other unique swaps include foreign exchange swaps, but they've come under fire recently because some banks have been sued for making misleading claims.

Living with exotic loans

The development of exotic financial products isn't limited only to derivatives. A number of loans are becoming more exotic as well.

Some lenders promote *interest-only loans,* which have extremely low initial repayment rates because borrowers are only paying back the interest without chipping away at the principal balance. Repayment of the principal comes after a certain length of time, at which point payments increase dramatically.

To illustrate using a real-life scenario, you may have an interest-only mortgage where you simply pay the interest to the bank but at the end of the term you're expected to have put enough cash away in order to pay the capital element of the mortgage. The Financial Conduct Authority (who replaced the Financial Services Authority) estimated recently that just under half of borrowers whose interest-only mortgages end in 2020 are facing the prospect of not being able to pay off their mortgages in full; worryingly, a third of those borrowers need to find more than £50,000.

Although these types of loans are attractive, because they attract lower payments, don't be fooled! You still need to cough up the cash to repay the principal at the end of the term.

Another type of loan, called a *negative-amortisation loan,* requires borrowers to pay less than their interest payments at first, deferring those payments back into the principal loan and thereby increasing the amount they must pay back in the long run when repayment costs jump.

Engineering Your Portfolio to the Max

Portfolio engineering and investing strategy go hand-in-hand and are easily the most mathematically complicated subject in all financial engineering. As Isaac Newton pointed out, modelling the madness of men is more difficult than modelling the movement of the planets. Portfolio engineering is an extreme example of just how true this is. As a result, we don't talk about any of the maths used, and restrict our discussion to how the experts use the calculations when they're done to arrange portfolios according to different strategies.

Getting fancy with maths

Financial engineering often involves highly advanced probability and calculus, but here are a few things you may like to know:

✔ These algorithms are widely varied and highly customisable for the people implementing them. A huge number of algorithms and other models are available, each with varying degrees of success and intended for different purposes.

✔ These algorithms are used primarily by active portfolio managers to take advantage of very fast and very small variations in pricing (we discuss passive versus active management in Chapter 15). They're used to generate revenues by quickly buying and reselling assets. As such, they're more related to market and human behaviours as opposed to the actual value of the assets.

✔ These algorithms don't consider the price or value of an asset as much as the interval of variation that occurs in the price of assets. For instance, one algorithm may prescribe buying any asset that experiences

a 5 per cent price drop within any period of time less than 1 minute. The value of the asset or what the price is doesn't matter, just that this time-dependent price interval indicates, according to the algorithm, that the price will increase by some interval range in the future.

✔ Many of these algorithms are adaptive or evolutionary. In other words, they automatically adapt to new trends and become increasingly complex over time. This adaptation is possible because as more data becomes available over time, it's continuously added to the equation in order to incorporate additional patterns, trends and other data and increase its responsiveness to future changes and its ability to predict movements.

Again, unless you're a maths genius, don't even begin to worry about how all the maths works. You have an easier time doing the calculations related to space travel than financial modelling. Even Isaac Newton saw that one coming.

Examining the fundamentals of portfolio engineering

Portfolio engineering is all about developing models and strategies that use combinations of assets to maintain a certain percentage return on investment. A wide variety of investments are typically used – including equities and debt, bundled and hybrid investments – but they're almost always derivatives of some sort. The intention is to ensure a certain amount of return on investment. Some of the early portfolio strategies include options with colourful names such as *covered call, protective put, straddle, iron condor, collar, strangle* and *ironfly.* Many futures strategies focus greatly on generating revenue *off the*

spread, which is the difference between the ask price and the bid price (for more about ask and bid prices, flick back to Chapter 12).

More and more companies are beginning to move away from these simple strategies, however, and towards the use of *algorithms* (step-by-step procedures used for calculations, data-processing automated reasoning) to determine financial transactions and strategies for the development of portfolios. These algorithms are often based in *stochastic calculus,* which, when applied to mathematical finance, sets out to estimate and predict time intervals of asset prices by treating them as a random variable. (Check out the nearby sidebar 'Getting fancy with maths' for more on algorithms.)

Finding out about flash crashes

Modern portfolio management is done, in very large part, automatically: managers preset computer algorithms that are designed to take specific actions if specific milestones are reached. For example, they may automatically buy or sell a certain amount of shares that change in value to meet specific criteria, depending on the current value of other assets already in the portfolio at that moment in time. Again, this strategy is all determined using mathematical models.

On 6 May 2010, the stock market experienced something called a *flash crash,* where the Dow Jones Industrial Average (DJIA) stock index lost nearly 10 per cent of its entire value almost instantly and then regained that value in just minutes. It was caused by the use of automated algorithms as a form of portfolio management.

When one algorithm triggered a sell-off of a particular quantity and type of asset, that action triggered other algorithms also to sell certain things, and the entire thing became a chain reaction, similar to a row of dominos falling. As prices dropped so low, those managers aware of what was occurring took the opportunity to buy up the undervalued assets and at some point the algorithms eventually triggered a repurchase, driving up the price again.

This example neatly illustrates two trends in financial engineering:

✔ The flash crash was primarily caused by the use of automated mathematical modelling, making it an issue of concern for portfolio engineering.

✔ The crash couldn't have happened without the use of advanced computer engineering, which allows high-frequency trading and automated responses to occur.

Moving into Computational Finance

The most significant trend in the manner in which financial transactions take place and the financial implications of this change comes from an overlap between financial engineering and computer engineering, called *computational finance*. Portfolio engineering and computerisation have become intrinsically interconnected. As the calculations related to financial decision-making become more and more complex, doing them manually is no longer efficient (or even possible in some cases). Instead, the process is automated. The financial management is more related to computer programming, and pre-setting action triggers is more connected to the portfolio strategy than to actual trading.

That's only one aspect of computerisation, however. In addition to portfolio management, computerisation has also changed significantly the dynamics of trading as a whole, altering how transactions take place. With this change in the manner of transactions comes a change in the methods used to gain an advantage. Those methods are now focused on the nature of computing.

The success of financial managers is increasingly intrinsically connected to their computer skills. Every company needs to link its finance and IT departments, regardless of the range and scope of its financial functions. More than anything, this aspect of financial engineering has completely reshaped the world of finance, and this trend is sure to continue to have implications for all companies around the world. Those who don't evolve are destined to suffer at the hands of their competitors who do recognise the changing world of finance and adapt to such changes.

Changing the face of trading

With regard to corporate investments, nearly every aspect except capital investments and the setting of strategies is done by computers now. The stereotypical image of the trading floor of a stock exchange is ancient history, because those floors are now set up with rows or circles of computers where all exchanges take place. The screaming and shouting between traders are rare and becoming extinct.

This shift to e-trading has opened the door for amateurs, casual traders, the previously retired and just about anyone else to become nearly as effective as the professionals. Not only do they have access to fast transactions using some of the same networks, or at least similar ones, but these transactions are extremely cheap. Discount brokers often charge less than £10 per transaction, and people no longer have to go through a professional for these transactions to take place; it's all done on the computer.

The spread of fibre-optic broadband

Computerisation and the speed of transactions is extremely lucrative. British Telecom now offers 300 megabits per second (mbps), fibre-optic broadband connections. That's three times the maximum of 100 mbps that the company previously offered. BT is spending £2.5 billion on fibre-optic and says that by December 2014, two-thirds of the country will have access to 'ultra-fast' fibre-optic broadband if they want it.

In addition, the UK Government says that it wants 90 per cent of UK businesses to be connected to ultra-fast broadband by 2015. This advantage will benefit financial market traders, with the speed of financial transactions increasing to less than 1 second.

Computerisation has hugely changed what makes one trader competitive compared to others. Traders and portfolio managers are becoming more competitive based on the effectiveness of their automated algorithms and the speed of their computer network. The speed of orders and trades is measured in milliseconds as traders attempt to ensure that they're the first to get their orders through, before other automated systems have a chance to drive up or down the price of a particular asset. The fastest can take advantage of this ability by instantaneously reselling at the higher or lower price, making extremely high volume trades within seconds of each other and generating revenue by repeating this process countless times throughout each day.

Offering online banking

The scope of computerisation extends beyond corporate investing. Almost all banks and building societies offer online banking, transfers and bill-payment facilities, making banking much faster and also cheaper.

One of the services that's available as a result of computerisation is automated bill-payments and invoicing – but this service is one in which many companies wouldn't want to participate when paying bills. Consider a company that makes thousands of purchases each month, or even just a few very expensive purchases consistently. It can pay the bill immediately, as automated bank payments sometimes require, or it can wait until the very last moment to pay the bill in order to keep the money in an account that generates interest.

Now reverse this scenario. A company is owed money, and the sooner it gets its payment, the sooner it can begin to generate interest. Of course a conflict of interest exists and no supplier can force its customers to pay before the due date. The supplier can, however, benefit by offering automated bill-payment facilities to its customers as a convenience, while not automating the bill payment facility itself, or ensuring that its automatic bill payment facility is timed to make the transaction after a specified time period. The firm can even employ services that provide intermediary automation, which generates interest off the spread between interest rates paid and received in short-term repayments.

Looking at logic programming

Logic programming isn't a new concept; all computer programming is based on logic to some extent. Over time, however, the programs have become far more mathematical, and now they're starting to be used for such things as tax management and even executive management. Automated systems that track directly a company's financial activities, or interact with other financial computer systems, make decisions based on tax legislation or other more advanced algorithms related to business-decision management.

As with most jobs, computerisation and computer engineering is being applied to corporate finance at the functional level as well. Computers are supplementing or replacing multiple financial roles within organisations.

Here's a list of some of the more common financial software packages:

- ✔ **ERP Financials:** Comprehensive financial management
- ✔ **Hyperion:** Financial management
- ✔ **JD Edwards:** Several financial software packages
- ✔ **Peachtree:** Basic financial recording and reporting
- ✔ **Quicken:** Basic functions of recording, reporting and invoicing
- ✔ **SAS:** Modelling and analysis
- ✔ **SPSS:** Statistical analytics
- ✔ **STATA:** Modelling and analysis

Computerisation is easily the most dynamic, comprehensive and fast-changing aspect of financial engineering, and so these software packages are prone to becoming outdated at any point. Still, most of them are well integrated into the financial community and have been around, in one form or another, for quite a while. For example, SPSS changed its name to PASW for a period of time, before changing it back when IBM bought it. This particular area of financial innovation changes at a fast pace and companies must review it continuously to remain competitive.

Chapter 17

Assessing Capital Structure

*F*or companies, an understanding of debt and equity has, at its heart, the goal of managing the cost of capital. Raising capital isn't cheap, and if a business wants to make money (and, let's face it, who doesn't?), it has to ensure that any prospective projects or operations generate more value and therefore more revenues than the company needs to pay as repayment for that raised capital.

In this chapter, we give you the lowdown on how to assess *capital structure* – which is the way a company finances its assets through a combination of debt or equity, or a mixture of both – including investigating the cost of capital and deciding on the proper capital structure.

Making More Money than You Borrow

When you borrow money, you want to make sure that you bring in more money than the interest you're paying on that loan (a subject we introduce in Chapter 3). In other words, if the repayment of loans and equity is higher than the revenues generated, 'you're doing it wrong'.

You can apply capital structure evaluations in two ways, both of which act in a similar manner:

- ✔ **Overall corporate capital structure:** The total amount of assets in the company and how efficiently the company is managing them as a whole. This approach helps the company determine how to manage the structure of its overall capital and address important questions. How much of the required capital should the firm fund using debt (such as taking out loans and other sources of finance) and how much with equity (such as selling additional company shares)? What types of debt and equity should the company use? The answers to these questions can strongly influence how successful a company will be, and ideally you want to answer them before a company even begins operations.

- ✔ **Project capital structure management:** This approach is a little more focused than overall corporate capital structure. Before deciding whether to take on a new project, you need to determine the project's cost and weigh the costs associated with raising those funds against the projected future cash flows that the project is going to generate for the company. Between the total cash outflows and inflows associated with a project, you can calculate the net present value (NPV) of the project, allowing your company to determine the best of several possible projects available (flip to Chapter 10 for more on NPV).

Calculating the Cost of Capital

The best way to measure the costs associated with raising capital is to calculate the cost of capital. You can calculate these costs in a number of different ways, and if you're mathematically inclined you can easily play with the particular calculations to make adjustments as needed to meet personal preferences. We don't go into the fine detail of these variations, but we do talk about the fundamental calculations of the cost of capital as well as how to apply the information in useful ways throughout this chapter.

To start, here's a simple calculation to work out the cost of capital:

Cost of capital = Cost of equity + Cost of debt

The cost of debt comes primarily in the form of interest payments, which is simple to measure and calculate. The cost of equity, meanwhile, comes from several different sources and is a little harder to define. Part of the cost of equity comes down to dividend policy (particularly for preference shares), part of it is the increased tax costs, and the risk of equity also plays a role.

We discuss dividend policy in more depth in the later section 'Discussing dividend policy'.

Calculating the cost of capital allows people not only to determine how much they're spending through their financing activities, but also where the cost is coming from (equity or debt), the required minimum returns necessary to stay profitable and even how to manage the capital structure of the company to minimise the cost of capital.

Measuring cost of capital the WACC way

The most common method of measuring the cost of capital that you see in financial management textbooks is called WACC (pronounced 'whack'), which stands for *weighted average cost of capital.* (Weighted average cost of capital is the average rate of return determined from all sources of finances employed by a company, which can be used as a discount rate for investment appraisal decisions.) This particular equation takes the basic cost of capital equation that we supply in the preceding section (Cost of capital = Cost of equity + Cost of debt) and contributes the proportions of total corporate value that each source of capital composes.

The following equation makes WACC a little bit more clear:

$$WACC = \left(\frac{E}{V} \times C_E\right) + \left(\frac{D}{V} \times C_D\right)$$

You can do a number of additional things to this equation to account for variations in cash inflows, interest rate differentials, inflation, tax rates and so on. We don't talk about all that, though, because we're on a mission to discuss something else. For the time being, the important thing is that you look at how this equation works and why it's important:

E = Market value of equity

D = Market value of debt

V = Company value (*book value* (the value in the financial statements) of debt plus book value of equity)

C = Cost of equity (E) or debt (D)

In essence, you're looking at the Cost of capital = Cost of equity + Cost of debt equation, but with a twist. The (E ÷V) and (D ÷V) are simply weighted proportions. The market value of equity is divided by the total corporate value to determine how much of the company's value is funded by equity, and you do the same calculation for debt.

When calculating this equation, you're really calculating the cost of capital in the proportions of the sources of capital – a little like taking the debt-to-equity ratio (from Chapter 7) and splitting it up among the cost of capital. Doing so assists you in determining the proper capital structure for a company; it helps to identify disproportionately high costs and find out how to maximise returns by pursuing the sources of capital that optimise the financial balance between debt and equity.

Factoring in the cost of debt

Calculating the cost of debt is pretty simple, and so we don't spend a huge amount of time on it. Debt includes any long- or short-term debt that's used to finance the operations of a business.

The biggest influence on the cost of debt is simply the interest rate on debt incurred, measured by using the present value of future cash flows to repay the loans (as we describe in Chapter 9). Well, in this chapter, you're looking at the same thing from the perspective of corporate costs of debt instead of investor potential for debt. Still, if the time value of money was the only influence, you'd simply use the yield to maturity on all the company's debt to determine the cost of debt; however, it's not.

You need to consider the following issues:

- ✔ **Default risk** isn't a direct cost, but a company must anticipate that as the amount and proportion of debt it takes on increases, so too does the rate of return it must promise to attract investors. A company with large amounts of debt or a high debt-to-equity ratio is at greater default risk, and so to attract more investors looking for debt it needs to offer higher rates. As a result, debt becomes increasingly more expensive as the company relies on it more heavily.

- ✔ **Debt expenses** are frequently *tax-deductible* (which means that you can take the expenses into account when determining the amount of profit on which a company pays tax), decreasing the relative cost of debt. To calculate the after-tax rate applicable for debt capital, you simply multiply the pre-tax rate by (1 minus the marginal tax rate), to get the after-tax rate, which is obviously lower by an amount equal to the proportion deducted for tax purposes.

Looking at the cost of equity

The cost of equity is a little less straightforward than the cost of debt. *Equity* is any funding raised through the selling of company shares. Different people have different ways of measuring equity.

Some people prefer simply to use the capital asset pricing model (CAPM) or some other form of arbitrage pricing theory (APT) (we explain both in Chapter 15), estimating the cost of equity as an amount equivalent to the risk premium on returns paid by the company to its investors. In this manner, any returns generated in excess of the risk-free rate are deemed to be the cost of equity.

This calculation is simple to use, but it also takes into account fluctuations in the value of shares on the secondary market, which really has no cost to the business. We aren't fans of this method, but some people argue for its benefits.

Another slightly different method is to include all dividend payments made by the company (because the risk-free rate still costs the company money). To that amount you then add the influence of share value *dilution* (which means an individual shareholders' holding becomes less due to additional shares being issued to new shareholders) on treasury shares (which we define in Chapter 3), either at the time of selling treasury shares or at the time of issuing an additional initial public offering. This method takes into account all cash outflows and all depreciated book value on the company resulting from the decision to push extra shares into the marketplace. At that point, investors can decide for themselves whether the returns they're generating are sufficiently above the risk-free rate.

Discussing dividend policy

The cost of equity is heavily influenced by the company's dividend policy. When a company makes a profit, that profit technically belongs to the owners of the company, who are the shareholders. So companies have two options regarding what they can do with those profits:

- ✔ Distribute them to the shareholders in equal payments per share as dividends.
- ✔ Reinvest them into the company as profit and loss reserves.

In either case, those dividends are going to increase the value for the shareholders, and so for investors, in theory, it shouldn't matter what the company's dividend policy is. Either the profits available for distribution as a dividend go to increase the book value of the company or they increase the income of the shareholders, both in equal values.

This idea that dividend policy shouldn't influence investor preference, and yet does, is called the *dividend puzzle,* which evolved from the *Modigliani–Miller Theorem.* This theorem states that, in an efficient market, a company's capital structure doesn't influence firm value. This idea applies only in theory, though, because the choice of dividend policy does change the costs associated with capital structure, as well as the marginal returns associated with using those profit and loss reserves to grow the company.

Increasing book value by retaining earnings doesn't necessarily translate into an increased share price. Profit and loss reserves don't represent a fixed value and don't necessarily generate additional income or value over time. Companies don't always have a use for profit and loss reserves, and so the value of dividends depends on the context of share price (for the investor) as well as the company's total book value (for the company deciding on its dividend policy).

That's where the study of dividend policy comes from – deciding what approach to dividends is going to optimise corporate capital structure and maximise shareholder wealth.

When deciding on dividend policy, companies have a few options available to them:

- **Preferred cumulative dividends:** Companies have no option but to pay these dividends eventually, and so the influence of cumulative preference shares must be anticipated even before issuing those shares. After the dividends are issued, the company only has the choice of whether to pay them now or delay payment and pay them using earnings later. Even if the company doesn't report a profit one year, cumulative dividends are guaranteed and must be paid later. Delayed dividend payments are considered dividends in arrears until they're paid, but they must always be paid eventually (unless the company goes bust and uses all the funds generated from liquidation to pay its debts). These dividends always take priority, right after making all debt payments.

- **Preferred noncumulative dividends:** These dividends are paid after the cumulative shareholders get all their money first. Noncumulative preferred dividends are paid in a similar manner as cumulative dividends and are 'guaranteed' in the sense that they're paid anytime the company makes profits. If the company operates at a loss one year, however, these dividends aren't necessarily paid. If these dividends aren't *declared* (which means the official allocation of profits to pay a dividend, even though the dividend hasn't yet been paid), they're forfeited. In other words, use it or lose it. Like cumulative shares, these dividends have a guaranteed cost of capital assuming that the company is successful.

✔ **Ordinary dividends:** These dividends paid on ordinary shares have no guarantee. If any money remains after a company pays all its debt payments, the preference shareholders get their dividends, the company determines its requirements for retained earnings and then the ordinary shareholders get the leftovers as ordinary dividends. The role of these dividends within the capital structure of a company varies depending on how these dividends are managed.

These dividends are easily the most flexible of dividends because they're not guaranteed, which gives management the ability to determine most effectively whether to use profits to fund future projects and so lower the costs of capital from equity. Using ordinary dividends in this way can even increase equity capital funding in the future by attracting investors via increased total company value compared to the total number of shares outstanding for which investors may receive dividends, thereby providing higher dividends per share.

✔ **Retained earnings (profit and loss reserves):** These earnings, or profits, that the company retains are the funds kept by the business to fund operations and growth. These earnings are generated after all preference shareholders get their dividends and the tax office has been given its share of the cake. The company takes its share of retained earnings, and then the rest is given to the ordinary shareholders. Retained earnings is a very popular method of funding growth and operations because it doesn't increase debt costs or devalue existing value as would the issuance of more equity.

Retained earnings aren't always sufficient, however. In those cases, companies fund projects as much as possible with retained earnings and then pursue other forms of capital sourcing for the remainder. Still, growth simply for the sake of growth isn't healthy, either, and so unless the company has a use for its retained earnings, it shouldn't incur the extra costs of growth without anticipated increases in revenues, obliging it to declare dividends on earnings.

Here are a couple of important things to note regarding dividend policy:

✔ Dividends on ordinary shares aren't required to be paid, but if the company doesn't intend to incur the extra costs associated with using retained earnings to expand the company, any unused earnings must be paid as dividends. (In the final analysis, those profits have to go somewhere.)

✔ Even on preference shares, dividends are guaranteed only on cumulative preference shares: the shares that accumulate dividend payments over time if they're not paid during the time promised, generating something called *dividends in arrears.* On noncumulative preference shares, these dividends in arrears are dropped from the dividends creditor if they're not declared. Most preference shares are cumulative, however.

Getting Warren Buffett's take

The US investor Warren Buffett explains dividend policy as assessing whether the company or the shareholder can generate greater returns using the same amount of money. In other words, because the company doesn't own the profits that it generates (the shareholders do), it should look at profits as a source of capital funding similar to equity.

When deciding how to fund a future project, corporate growth or operations, companies need to assess the future cash flows generated from retaining those earnings (total value generated by reinvesting those earnings minus the costs associated with pursuing a new project or corporate growth) against the average returns generated in market investments. If the business can generate more value for its investors by pursuing projects funded by retained earnings than the investors are likely to generate by reinvesting dividends back into the market (or by reinvesting at the risk-free rate, depending on who you're talking to), the company should retain the earnings; otherwise, it should pay the

dividend. This dividend attracts more investors, and so maximises the translation of value on profits to share price.

Buffet's view is supported by a theory of dividend policy called *Walter's Model*, in which companies that can generate returns using retained earnings greater than the cost of capital in funding operations should retain those earnings to give the shareholders greater value. This view is also supported by *Gordon's Model*, which takes into account the risk associated with longer-term investments, where dividend payments generate a realisation of cash flows in the short term, decreasing the increased risk returns realised only in the long term as with retained earnings, thereby attracting more investors. In other words, Gordon's Model takes a 'bird in the hand' approach, where known dividends paid are worth more than potential equity gains from retained earnings. But in our opinion Gordon's Model tends to place too much weight on risk.

Choosing the Proper Capital Structure

From the company's perspective, investing, debt and equity all come back to the original question of how to fund its operations and how properly to balance the amount of debt or equity that's being used to raise capital. In other words, all this information is being used to manage the company's capital structure.

When setting the company's policies regarding capital structure, the goal is to minimise the costs associated with raising capital – which means, when applicable, choosing the cheapest option for capital funding. If interest rates on debt are going to be too high, issuing equity may be the cheaper method. If issuing more equity is going to generate more tax burden (or decrease the tax advantages of incurring debt, for the business or even for the shareholders, in a manner that would cause the market value of shares to drop), generate greater dividend payments or too greatly influence existing shares in a negative manner, issuing more bonds may be the better option.

Of course, a business takes and measures this decision within the appropriate context of the present value of the future cash flows anticipated in both options. Another consideration, though of minimal consequence compared to others, is the agency costs associated with each option. Issuing a new initial public offering tends to be more expensive than taking out a business loan, for example, and the company needs to take this aspect into account when deciding which method is best to raise capital. The increased number of shares can also dilute the value of each existing share, because total company value is distributed across all shares in issue.

A wide number of variations on the basic calculations and variables are used for each of the equations that we discuss throughout this chapter. Some include the costs of potential liquidation when debt can't be repaid. Others take into account the increased short-term liquidity requirements during the debt repayment period, and the influence that such reserve requirements have on lost potential revenues possible from reinvesting that cash into longer-term assets. The Modigliani–Miller Theorem from the preceding section, for example, suggests that capital structure has no bearing on company value, though this model is widely considered to be purely theoretical, established as a foundation upon which more useful models can grow.

The reality, though, is that legislation governing corporate finance and the benefits packages of company executives are such that, in the majority of cases, decisions regarding capital structure are going to be those that maximise the value of shares. This requirement means making decisions that increase earnings per share as much as possible and, in some cases, taking on excessive amounts of risk through higher amounts of debt, plus accepting the greater risk of loss in specific initiatives in order to preserve share value and place a maximum amount of risk on debt.

This attitude towards capital structure has been cultivated by a combination of the *shareholder wealth maximisation* model of corporate governance (which requires companies to do whatever they can to increase the value of the company's shares), but also by executive incentive packages that include a large proportion of share options as well as income based on the performance of the company's share value.

Part V
Understanding Financial Management

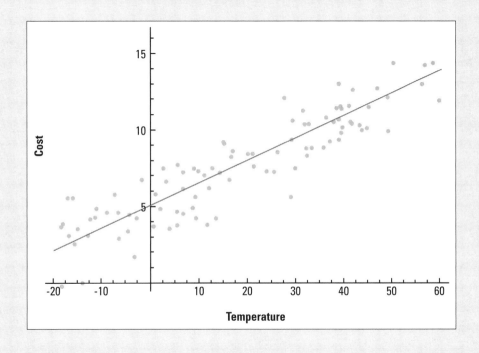

In this part . . .

✔ Find out how to assess whether a particular company manages its finances effectively (or not) and whether that company's performance is improving over time – or getting worse.

✔ Wade into a world of company, industry and wider economic statistics to predict the future financial performance of a business.

✔ Uncover the mysteries of mergers and acquisitions. Find out the reasons why they occur, how the companies involved stand to gain from them and how they are financed.

Chapter 18

Assessing Financial Performance

• •

In This Chapter

▶ Doing vertical, horizontal and cross comparisons

▶ Making comparisons over time and against competitors

▶ Judging the quality of profits

▶ Calculating how well your investments are paying off

• •

*Y*ou can analyse an organisation's finances in many ways – by looking at its cash flows, equity, debt, assets and so forth – but one vitally important consideration worth knowing is whether or not the company you're looking at is financially successful. Is it primed to be the next shooting star destined to be a global sensation, or is it doomed to disaster? Understanding the extent of a particular company's financial success (or otherwise) is crucial, whether you're an investor, a manager, a regulator, an employee, a supplier, a partner, a competitor or just some Tom, Dick or Harry who writes introductory corporate finance and accountancy books.

In this chapter, we explain how to evaluate whether a company is managing its finances effectively and whether or not it's improving over time.

Understanding the Importance of Analysing Financial Success

Determining how financially successful a business is provides a lot more information about the company than simply how well it manages money. Financial performance analyses are how people pull apart, quantify and measure every aspect of the success of the company. After all, the ultimate goal of a company is to generate wealth for its shareholders (to make money), and so every element of the company's activities is assessed in financial terms.

The nature of money (which we discuss in Chapter 1) combined with the objective of companies to maximise shareholder wealth make finance the ideal medium to assess how successful the company is, what activities are contributing to or detracting from that success and how the business compares to others in the market – as well as how it compares to itself over time.

A significant number of people are paid based on the financial performance of whatever they're responsible for managing, for example:

- ✔ **Corporate executives:** Often paid bonuses based on the financial performance of the company (which isn't necessarily a good thing when you consider that financial information can be manipulated in the short term to generate high bonuses, but at the cost of the long-term financial stability of the company).

- ✔ **Hedge fund managers:** Typically paid based on how the portfolio they're managing compares to the market.

- ✔ **Investment bankers, account managers, and mergers and acquisitions (M&A) consultants:** Paid based on the success of the transactions made or sales closed.

In addition, everyone else in society relies on companies to be financially successful, because when they're not firms go bust, forcing people to lose their jobs, suppliers to lose a customer and the world as a whole to lose a value-generating organisation. This failure contributes to more unemployment, more people struggling to find new jobs (because fewer jobs are available in the market) and a stagnating economy.

If an organisation isn't operating efficiently, it's wasting resources that can be better allocated to a more competitive firm. Analysing the financial performance of a company is how you determine whether it's competitive or is going to be lost to the natural selection of the market.

Using Common-Size Comparisons

Common-size comparisons – analyses used to do data comparisons – are some of the most valuable tools in assessing the financial performance of a company. They come in two forms, vertical and horizontal, which provide a unique series of detailed information regarding each of the three primary financial statements:

- ✔ **Balance sheet:** Sometimes referred to as the *statement of financial position* (refer to Chapter 4).

✔ **Cash flow statement:** Sometimes referred to as the *statement of cash flows* (refer to Chapter 6).

✔ **Profit and loss account:** Sometimes referred to as the *income statement, statement of comprehensive income* or *statement of profit or loss* (refer to Chapter 5).

Although the vertical and horizontal are valuable in their own right, yielding insights into how effectively the business is being financially managed, you can also use them in conjunction with each other to provide even more information, producing so-called cross comparisons.

Common-size comparison analyses are used to determine how effectively the value of an organisation is being managed and whether or not trends are improving. These comparisons are unique because everything in them is broken down to a percentage value of a single reference point, allowing you to account for changes and proportions of a company's finances, for example:

✔ **Vertical analyses** reference the sum of the value of the company and track how a company is using its assets as a proportion of the total assets available.

✔ **Horizontal analyses** track changes over time as a proportion of a specific date used as a reference to determine how a company has improved (or not).

Used together, you can track changes in the proportions of value allocations throughout the company.

Looking at vertical common-size comparisons

Each vertical common-size comparison uses a single financial statement from a single year. In other words, you can do a vertical comparison of a company's 2013 profit and loss account, and then another one for its 2012 profit and loss account.

These comparisons are intended to calculate the allocation and usage of value within the organisation by measuring the proportion of total value that's being distributed in each entry of the financial statement. They're called vertical comparisons because the items you're comparing on a profit and loss account appear in a vertical list, instead of next to each other.

The following example takes you on a quick walk through a vertical common-size comparison of a profit and loss account to show you how this process works.

You start at the top of the profit and loss account with turnover (which can also be called sales or revenue), because that's the total amount of money the company brings in during the period being examined. From here, you can break down any other part of the profit and loss account as a percentage of turnover (sales). So if your sales are £100,000 and your cost of sales (COS) are £65,000, according to your vertical comparison COS represents 65 per cent of sales. That means that 65 per cent of all sales are going into the cost of production, leaving 35 per cent (the *gross profit*) to pay for other expenses.

Therefore, if earnings before interest and tax (EBIT) is 5 per cent, administrative costs are taking up 30 per cent of the sales, leaving only 5 per cent to be taxed on. By the end, the net profit is 1 per cent. The following table puts this data in order so that you can see what this scenario looks like (by *nominal* we mean the stated monetary value).

Profit and Loss Account	Nominal Value (£)	Turnover (%)
Turnover	100,000	100
COS	65,000	65
Gross profit (margin)	35,000	35
Administrative costs	30,000	30
EBIT	5,000	5
Interest and tax	4,000	4
Net profit	1,000	1

By doing this analysis, you can easily compare items in the profit and loss account as a proportion of total profit. Of course, you can do the same in a balance sheet as a percentage of total assets, or in the cash flow statement by breaking down each type of activity (for example, cash flow from operating activities) as a percentage of the total cash flows. This analysis allows you easily to determine how a company's value is being used and whether each item in the financial statements is being managed efficiently.

The ability to perform such an analysis is particularly useful when talking about horizontal comparisons, industry comparisons and time comparisons (see the following two sections). You can compare your vertical analyses to other companies in the same industry to see how the value of your company is being managed. You can also track vertical analyses over time to see whether individual items are improving over a period of several years, thus allowing you to track trends.

Handling horizontal common-size comparisons

Horizontal common-size comparisons are a bit different from their vertical counterparts (see the preceding section). They still use only one type of financial statement at a time, but instead of using that statement from just one year, they use several consecutive years' worth of the same type of financial statement. For example, when a company does a horizontal analysis on its profit and loss account, it uses the profit and loss accounts for 2011, 2012 and 2013. Three years of comparisons is pretty much the norm for horizontal analyses, but doing extended analyses to measure long-term trends and searching for patterns or cycles in the company's performance is very common.

In the UK, the Companies Act 2006 requires statutory financial statements to show the current year financial results together with the previous year's financial results as a comparative.

For consistency's sake between the different types of comparisons, we use the profit and loss account to illustrate how the horizontal common-size analysis works. Remember that you can use each analysis for every one of the major financial statements, but the profit and loss account works particularly well for examples because it's easy to illustrate and explain.

Profit and Loss Account	Reference Year (£)	Next Year (%)	Last Year (%)
Turnover	100,000	104	110
COS	65,000	108	115
Gross profit (margin)	35,000	99	101
Administrative costs	30,000	113	127
EBIT	5,000	70	46
Interest and tax	4,000	70	46
Net profit	1,000	70	46

The reference year is always considered 100 per cent, and the following years are measured as a proportion of that 100 per cent value. For a horizontal analysis, you're not that worried about how value is being used or distributed throughout the organisation, only how those values change over time. So the percentages shown are a percentage of a single reference year.

Turnover, for example, is £100,000 in the first year, and then changed in the following two years, referencing the first year rather than the year before (in other words, the column 'Last Year' is measured as a percentage of the 'Reference Year' rather than 'Next Year').

This horizontal analysis allows you to track changes in financial management over time to determine whether the company's financial management is getting better or worse, as well as where the changes are being experienced. In the preceding example, for instance, turnover increased over a three-year period, meaning that the company increased its sales during that period. That wouldn't matter if its costs increased more than its sales did, but this company did a very good job, increasing sales and cutting costs of production to a fraction of what they were in the reference year. More sales plus lower costs means that the company is using its resources more efficiently.

Still, the horizontal analysis tells you how things are changing only in a nominal sense, which isn't entirely useful.

Considering cross comparisons

The horizontal common-size comparison (see the preceding section) does a lot to help you understand changes in a company's finances over time by comparing financial reports from several consecutive years. A vertical comparison (the subject of the earlier 'Looking at vertical common-size comparisons' section), by contrast, tells you how efficiently corporate value is being allocated and used. But you can get the best of both worlds, because two types of comparisons use data from both these analyses, producing *cross comparisons*.

Cross comparisons come in two flavours, neither of which has a formal name and so we call them the 'rate-of-change' cross comparison and the 'time-distribution' cross comparison.

Rate-of-change cross comparison

Before you can perform a rate-of-change cross comparison, you first need to do vertical common-size comparisons for several consecutive years (we describe how in the earlier 'Looking at vertical common-size comparisons' section). After the vertical comparisons are done, you can measure the amount that each comparison has changed over time. In other words, you measure the rate of change of each proportion. If COS increases from 10 per cent of turnover in 2012 to 20 per cent of turnover in 2013, you can say that COS has increased as a proportion of sales by 100 per cent in one year. That this situation would be a very bad thing is certainly worth knowing.

You're doing a horizontal comparison of several vertical comparisons. The reference year to which other years are being compared is adjusted to 100 per cent, and then the following years are a percentage change of the different vertical comparison proportions. The result tells you whether the asset use and allocation is improving over time, which is a very important indicator of changes in corporate financial efficiency and trends in corporate financial management.

Here's a short example to illustrate the point.

Profit and Loss Account	*Vertical Reference (%)*	*Next Year Vertical (%)*	*Final Vertical (%)*
Turnover	100	101	102
COS	65	—	—
Gross profit (margin)	35	—	—
Administrative costs	30	—	—
EBIT	5	—	—
Interest and tax	4	—	—
Net profit	1	—	—

The Next Year Vertical and Final Vertical fields are left blank until the percentage of change values are known. It could be that COS is 75 per cent, which would be bad because that would mean gross profit margin would only be 25 per cent (100 per cent less 75 per cent), which is a ten per cent decrease.

Time-distribution cross comparison

This cross comparison is similar to the one in the preceding section except in reverse. You start by doing horizontal cross-comparison analyses, but pick only two of them – the one for the first year of the period you're analysing and the one for the last year of the period you're analysing. Realistically, you can do them for every year in between as well, but you're only carrying out this exercise two years at a time. So, for this example, you're doing a horizontal comparison for the years 2012 and 2013.

After you finish the horizontal comparisons, you're left with a series of percentages showing how 2013 changed from 2012. Now you move onto the vertical analysis. Remember that, unlike a standard vertical analysis, these percentages don't add up to 100 per cent of turnover. But you're still setting turnover (or total assets or total cash flows) to 100 per cent and then comparing all other entries in the analysis to that. By doing so, you're collecting information on the degree to which each changed relative to turnover. So, if COS is 101 per cent of turnover in your cross comparison, COS increased by 1 per cent more than turnover.

The goal is to measure how much each entry changes relative to a reference point. This process allows you to understand better how allocations are changing over time and whether they're becoming more or less efficient.

Here's a quick example to show how this analysis looks.

Profit and Loss Account	Horizontal Change (%)	Percentage of Turnover (%)
Turnover	100	100
COS	100	99
Gross profit (margin)	100	101
Administrative costs	100	98
EBIT	100	102
Interest and tax	100	103
Net profit	100	101

Providing Context by Performing Comparatives

Each of the financial calculations we discuss in this book is valuable in its own right, but, like financial statements, each is limited in the information it provides without some sort of context (a bit like a ratio: on its own it's useless without something to compare it to). What you really want is to take each of those calculations and work out how it compares to some reference point; otherwise, it doesn't have much meaning. It's just an abstract number that tells you about the company, but you have no idea whether the number attributed to the company is good or bad.

For example, a company may have an asset turnover of 3 (flick to Chapter 7 for more on asset turnover), which provides some information about the company but not whether the number is a good or a bad thing. To understand that, you have to analyse *performance comparatives,* which is the process by which you add context to your calculations by comparing them to some other standard.

Such calculations are commonly compared against two standards: the same company in a different year, or other companies in the same year. We look at both in the following sections.

Contrasting over time

A lot of what we talk about in this book (particularly in Chapters 4–8) is considered *spot analysis:* analysis for a single point (or spot) in time, as opposed to assessing trends. Spot analysis is great if you live in a time-loop that repeats the same point in time over and over again; otherwise, the amount of useful information you can derive from a single moment in time is limited. So, instead of looking at your financial ratios and calculations by themselves, you want to compare them to the previous years' ratios and calculations to see how they've changed, if at all.

The goal is to judge the current performance of a company based on the past performance of the same company. This analysis allows you to look for patterns in performance ratios, identify cyclical changes, note patterns in these changes over time and determine whether the overall trend is good or bad. Identifying many of these patterns, such as whether cycles exist, allows you to begin identifying the causes of those patterns. Being able to recognise what influences your financial performance allows you to be more proactive in responding to those influences, as well as potentially even managing the influences themselves to react in your own favour.

In addition, watching for patterns, cycles and current trends allows you to project future financial performance.

But bear in mind that these figures are estimates, because human error tends to be a frequent cause of problems. Even when that's not an issue, you need to recognise that as you attempt to project farther into the future, your estimates become less accurate. Projecting what your finances are going to look like tomorrow is far easier than forecasting what they'll look like in ten years' time. (Chapter 19 delves deeper into financial forecasting.)

Take a look at the following couple of examples, which show how a time analysis of financial ratios and calculations can make a big difference compared to just a single calculation of any financial ratio or calculation.

The *quick ratio* is a measure of liquidity that calculates a company's ability to pay off debt that will become due in the next year. You calculate it as follows:

(Current assets − Stock) ÷ Current liabilities

With that in mind, here's the first example.

Company A in 2013: Quick ratio = 0.7

That doesn't sound so bad, does it? In a worst-case scenario where the company can't sell any of its current stock, it's still able to account for 70 per cent of its current liabilities using its highly liquid assets. But, is that really a good thing? Compare that against time.

Company A in 2012: Quick ratio = 0.9

Company A in 2011: Quick ratio = 1.2

Uh oh! The company appears to be losing liquidity at a rate of about 26 per cent annually – which is very fast! It may have a lot of debt coming to maturity this year, it may not be collecting money owed from customers quickly enough or it may simply not be making as many sales. In any case, this situation doesn't look good for the company.

Don't take this example the wrong way, though. Take a look at a second, almost identical example to see how they differ in important ways.

Company A in 2013: Quick ratio = 1.0

Company A in 2012: Quick ratio = 1.3

Company A in 2011: Quick ratio = 1.7

The company is still losing liquidity at a rate of about 26 per cent annually during the same three years, but the significant difference is that the ratio is much higher. The firm is still able to cover all its current liabilities using only highly liquid assets. Not only is this example not as severe as the other one, but it may also be considered a good thing! Holding all your assets in a highly liquid form means that you're not using them to generate more revenues. The company in this example may be intentionally lowering its liquidity in order to increase its returns on investment or increase the efficiency of its asset management.

As you can see, finding trends is much easier than interpreting them. Whether a reduction in liquidity is helping or harming the company's financial wellbeing depends greatly on a number of other factors.

In this example, you may want to consider combining it with a horizontal common-size comparison (check out the earlier section 'Handling horizontal common-size comparisons') of the company's balance sheet and profit and loss account to see whether it's having trouble generating revenues or turning sales into cash. You can do the same via a time-comparison of trade debtors turnover (which we explain in Chapter 7) or turnover in days to determine whether the company is collecting money owed or taking longer than normal to do so.

The key to understanding the context in these time-comparison calculations is to look at what variables are going to influence or be influenced by the change. In the liquidity example, the important aspects are how much debt is changing, how much revenue is changing, projections of revenue collection on old sales, projections of new sales and the amount of debt the company can pay off after other bills are also accounted for. This type of analysis is a great way to understand the state of a company and what to expect out of it in the future.

Comparing against industry competitors

Imagine that a company you're analysing has improved dramatically over the years. The common-size analyses make its asset allocations seem to be steadily improving, supported by a comparison of its financial ratios over the last ten years that shows improved financial health.

Is the company really doing well, though? How can you even tell if you're looking at only one firm? If a company has a current ratio of 1.5, which is up from 5 years ago when its current ratio was 0.5, what does that even mean for its operations (check out Chapter 7 for more about current ratios)? If other companies in the same industry (competitors) are maintaining current ratios of 5.5, the improvement from 0.5 to 1.5 still sounds pretty risky. The firm may simply be better at managing its assets, or perhaps the industry it competes in takes a long time to collect monies owed from customers, requiring businesses to maintain a lot of cash or other liquid assets or else risk insolvency.

In any case, whether it's good or bad, you never know whether the company is strange unless you compare it to other companies in the same industry.

Using industry averages

Frequently you don't compare the company against just one other competitor, or even several other competitors individually. When you're comparing the financial performance of your company against the industry, typically you use industry averages, which are calculated using a simple mean. If you want to know what the industry average is for current ratios, you find out the current ratio for all the competitors in the industry, add them up and then divide by the number of competitors. For example:

> Current ratios in industry: 0.5 + 0.6 + 0.6 + 0.9 + 1.0 = 3.6
>
> Divided by the number of competitors in the industry (5) = 0.72

In this way you discover that the industry average current ratio is 0.72. You don't yet know why it's 0.72, but you do know that companies in this industry commonly maintain very low liquidity at any given point. You also know that your company has a current ratio of 0.75, which is very close to the industry average and probably doesn't indicate anything important.

Therefore, using a company that maintains pretty average liquidity, you decide to take a look at its stock turnover in days and trade debtors turnovers in days (refer to Chapter 7). You find that this company sells its stock and even collects its money very quickly. This fast inflow of cash means that it doesn't need to maintain very high liquidity because it can safely assume that it will be getting more very quickly, allowing it to invest a greater proportion of its assets in longer-term investments that generate high yields. Spectacular!

If your company has a current ratio of 1.5, it isn't efficiently using its assets to generate income. If it has a current ratio of 0.2, it may be at huge risk of becoming insolvent.

Even though by themselves these numbers are rather vague, when you add in the context of the industry average, you can see how your company is doing compared to the competition. This analysis gives you a chance to understand why the industry attempts to maintain certain ratios, why the company in question deviates from the average and whether that's indicative of something good or bad.

Comparing changes in the industry

One additional thing to take into consideration is a comparison of changes in the industry over time. After you know what the industry average is for a particular ratio or calculation and you know how your company compares, you can also track how this relationship changes over time. Is your company increasing its liquidity faster than the industry average? Is it decreasing its profitability slower than average? Is it improving its asset management at exactly the same rate as the industry average? All these questions are relevant to understanding how a company is doing in a competitive market. Like other time-based data, this analysis helps you to project future performance as well as evaluate the health of the business compared to the industry as a whole.

Keep in mind that an entire industry can quite possibly be sporadic, so don't rely exclusively on industry-based comparisons. Look at how an individual company is changing over time (as we discuss in the earlier section 'Contrasting over time') as well as the spot rates. The use of *benchmarks* – which means comparing the profits of a company with its competitors or industry sector – is a fairly common way of doing this.

Don't forget to check the quality of the earnings a company is making, too. Just because it's generating earnings now doesn't mean that those earnings have any quality; they may be one-off payments that disappear in the next cycle.

Determining the Quality of Profits

Not all profits are created equally; sometimes a source of profit is volatile, temporary or uncertain, which can result in poor-quality profits. In contrast, *quality* profits could be where a company rents out properties and are receiving a continuing profit through these rentals, so the profit they receive is stable and continuous.

As we describe in this section, two primary aspects can undermine the quality of the profit listed in the financial statement: the use of different accounting methods and the sources of revenues and costs. You can then break down each of these groups into more detailed concerns, with each influencing whether the profits a company is generating are sustainable, maintainable or retainable.

Just because a company seems to be profitable doesn't mean that the business itself is successful or even that it isn't at risk of going out of business.

Tackling accounting concerns

Despite the reputation of accounting as a field of relentlessly stiff regulations and methodologies, in fact companies are given freedom to decide their preferred method of valuation on several issues. Sometimes they're allowed to decide the accounting period to use for a particular cost or revenue (within the parameters of Generally Accepted Accounting Practice); other times they can choose from several options the manner in which they value their costs, revenues or assets.

Naturally, with companies recording these things using differing methods, variances occur, and as a result the exact manner in which you view or interpret the financial statements also changes. For example, a company may appear to have unusually high profits one year, until you realise that it deferred certain costs until the next year in order to better use its tax deductions; otherwise, it would've lost money in the current year (even though, of course, this goes against the 'matching' principle in which costs should be matched against their respective revenues).

With financial statements, things aren't always as they seem. Your ability to understand the implications of the accounting decisions that companies make can be just as critical as your ability to calculate the financial ratios themselves. Here are some of the more common accounting issues to bear in mind.

Stock accounting

Three primary methods of stock accounting exist:

- ✔ **FIFO:** Stands for first-in, first-out, which means that whatever stock was produced first is considered to be the first stock sold. When measuring the cost of sales, the company measures the cost of producing the first items made rather than the most recent items made.

- ✔ **LIFO:** Stands for last-in, first-out, which means that the last items to become stock are considered the first to be sold. So when measuring the cost of sales, the company measures the cost of producing the most recent stock made rather than the first stock made.

This method is shortly to be outlawed in the UK when the new UK Generally Accepted Accounting Practice (FRS 102) comes into play for accounting periods commencing on or after 1 January 2015.

✔ **AVCO:** Stands for weighted average cost. Using the AVCO method, you calculate the weighted average cost of items held at the beginning of the year with the following formula:

Weighted average cost = Total cost of goods in stock ÷ Number of items in stock

The weighted average cost is then used to value goods sold. You need to calculate a new weighted average cost, however, each time more stocks are bought during the year.

Several other methods are available, many of which attempt to use the best of LIFO, FIFO and AVCO; others account for costs in a manner related to project management (the amount of the project completed). For the purposes of this section, though, LIFO, FIFO and AVCO illustrate well what you need to know about this particular subject. Just remember that costs change over time. (For more information about LIFO, FIFO and AVCO, refer to Chapter 5.)

During *inflationary periods* (when costs, overall, are increasing), using the LIFO method results in the appearance of higher costs, because the most recent stock has cost more to produce. Using the FIFO method, on the other hand, gives the illusion of costs being lower than they really are, because the company is accounting for the cheaper historical cost of production.

The flip side to this issue is that during *deflationary periods* (when costs are decreasing, which rarely ever happens except in deep recessions), using the LIFO method makes the company appear to have lower costs whereas the FIFO method makes costs appear more expensive. Neither one of these methods is inherently bad, but you do have to take these aspects into account when studying the costs, liabilities and profits that a company generates. Be sure to understand that just because a company appears to be 'safe' right now doesn't mean that this situation can't be artificially generated.

During a deflationary period, companies using LIFO may see that they appear to be incurring lower costs and make the improper decision of lowering price or attempt to use the appearance of higher profitability to take on new loans. Although such companies appear to be more profitable, the true costs of production are simply in past stocks, putting the company at serious risk due to actions taken on false pretences.

Depreciation

As we explain in Chapter 4, several different methods of accounting for depreciation exist: the straight-line and reducing-balance methods are the most popular sorts in the UK. The method of depreciation a company chooses has an influence on the profit and loss account (because depreciation is included as a cost) and the balance sheet (because depreciation influences the total value of the company's fixed assets).

Therefore, knowing what type of depreciation the company uses helps you to understand how to interpret financial statements and their respective ratios. Particularly for organisations with a large amount of fixed assets with depreciation to account for, the chosen method of accounting can have a significant impact on how those companies' profits look to analysts who don't consider this fact.

The exact influence that each depreciation method has depends on the method you're looking at:

- **Methods that depreciate the value of an asset more quickly**: These account for a higher amount of depreciation cost in the early years of the life of the asset (the reducing-balance method is an example of such a method). They also reduce the total asset value of the company on the balance sheet more quickly when accounting for that particular asset.

- **Methods that last longer:** These attribute a greater amount of the depreciation cost later on, not only recording the total asset value of the company as artificially high (the market value of assets decreases quickly early on and then levels out over time), but also giving potential to account for greater depreciation costs in the profit and loss account than were experienced, causing artificially high net profit.

Cost recognition

Sometimes companies don't have to recognise their costs in the year in which those costs are incurred, which poses certain tax benefits. A company that has already used all the tax deductions it wants for one year can sometimes use some in the following year.

For particularly large costs, companies can use *amortisation,* whereby the expense of an asset (especially for intangible assets such as goodwill) is recognised over a period of time, usually the lifetime of the asset. Like depreciation, those methods of amortising or recognising costs that account for the entirety of the expense sooner tend to be more conservative and, therefore, contribute to higher quality in financial reports.

Thinking about sources of cash flows

Looking at the source of cash flows can help to determine the quality of a company's profits. The amount of profit during any single year doesn't tell you whether a firm can expect those earnings again in the future or even whether it maintained them consistently throughout a single period. (The latter implies that profits may have been cyclical or that the company generated high revenues during one part of the period and made no sales at all during another part.)

Although many potential sources of low-quality cash flows exist, we cover just two of the most common: temporary transactions and volatile income sources. This discussion helps you to watch for other similar problems that may arise when analysing financial statements and making corporate financial decisions.

Temporary transactions

In a lot of profit and loss accounts, you may see categories called something along the lines of 'exceptional items', 'extraordinary items' or anything indicating that the source of the cost/income isn't to be expected in the future. Such items may include revenues from a lawsuit won, payments to rebuild part of an office building following a fire or a bad debt that the company incurred.

The problem is that these things aren't necessarily listed as separate items in the financial statements (though they often are), and so trying to find out about any of these items is a good idea.

Transactions that are longer than a single period is one common source of temporary transactions that can be significant if you're to avoid having the wool pulled over your eyes. Amortising the costs of intangible assets over long periods of time can be deceptive, and if you don't watch out long-term repayments and fixed-income sources of revenues (annuities, for example) can also end suddenly, reducing revenues.

Often, instead of being listed as temporary transactions, these sorts of cash flows are listed as 'sundry income' or 'miscellaneous expenses', which isn't exactly useful when you're attempting to evaluate the quality and duration of those revenues and costs.

If you're a shareholder, you have the right to request information regarding those items listed in the 'other' categories. Doing so may also be a good idea if you're considering investing in such a company – and it's an even better idea if you're the manager of one.

Volatile income sources

When you're looking at the annual report of a company, you may well see that it lists just the end-of-year financial information for the current year, with the previous year for comparison and perhaps projections for the next couple of years disclosed in the supporting notes to the financial statements.

Be on the lookout for the cash flow statement, because that helps you identify where all the money is coming from and where it's going, though often only one year at a time.

Having several years' worth of these statements helps you determine how consistent revenues and costs are over time. If any items appear to be increasing, decreasing or both to extreme degrees, they may not be the kind of revenues or costs you can count on being consistent or continuing at all. Deeper investigation into what the company is doing may be helpful in determining whether a problem's lurking somewhere. Perhaps a source of income just stops being collected entirely, or maybe a cost increases dramatically one year without revenues increasing proportionally to make up for that cost, thus causing liquidity problems.

Another volatility issue to be concerned with is within-year cyclical volatility: a number of industries have extremely cyclical sales depending on the season within a single year. The tourism industry (for example, hotels, resorts and so forth) is highly cyclical and tends to have a slow off-season.

To identify these issues, you often have to resort to evaluating the company's *quarterly reports:* financial reports that are issued at the end of each quarter (every three months). These reports can help you identify something that's going on within a single year that may not be easily identified in the annual reports.

Assessing Investment Performance

Much of corporate finance is focused on how you get money and how that money is then used. No surprise, therefore, that companies are extremely concerned about whether or not they're using their money effectively. Of course, all sorts of different views exists on what constitutes the effective use of money, and at least twice as many measures of success, but the general idea is that any money spent needs to generate value for the company.

This aspect is usually determined, at the bare minimum, by whether or not the spent money creates a positive return on investment. If you spend money on something, you hope that it contributes to the creation of revenues greater than the amount spent; otherwise, that particular purchase is contributing to your company losing money, which is never a good thing.

Determining whether a company is successfully using its money to invest in assets and operations isn't always that easy, however, and so to help the following sections take a look at some useful methods.

Employing conventional evaluations of success

You can measure the degrees of success companies are generating in far more ways than we can hope to cover in a single chapter. Nevertheless, we go over a few different methods for evaluating the success of standard capital investments as well as financial or portfolio investments.

Each chapter of this book that discusses how to assess the value and price of an investment (check out Chapters 10–12) helps to establish some of the fundamentals of evaluation. For example, if you purchase an investment with the expectation that it's going to yield a certain percentage as returns and it doesn't, you did something wrong. Remember that your ability to compare the actual returns against the projected returns is a huge part of your ability to establish what success is and whether you've been successful in your investments.

Put simply, if you analyse the value of something and fail to extract that value from it, you've failed either in your assessment of its value or in your attempt to extract that value. If you extract equal or greater value from that expenditure than anticipated, you've succeeded. You can measure the degree of failure or success in these cases simply as the percentage over or under the projected rate of return. If you're expecting 10 per cent returns and you get 20 per cent returns, you've succeeded by a margin of 200 per cent, which may result in a big, fat, end-of-year bonus!

Arithmetic rate of return

The *arithmetic rate of return* on a specific asset is pretty simple. It's a spot measurement that measures only the total rate of return over the life of the investment, as follows:

$$R = (V_t - P) \div P$$

where V_t is the value of the asset at time t and P is the purchase price.

You take the value of your asset at any point in history, subtract your purchase price to determine your gain or loss and then divide that by your purchase price to determine the rate of return *(R)*. This simple calculation provides important information about how well you're using your purchases, assets, investments . . . and pretty much everything you own. For those assets that don't increase in value but produce things of value (such as machinery), you can include the value produced as a part of your value at time, *t*.

A variation on this equation includes calculations that account for reinvestment of the cash flows generated on the investment, for those investments that generate cash flows, or which can be reinvested after maturity (for example, capital, bonds, dividend-generating shares and money-market investments).

Average rate of returns

The *average rate of returns* starts with the arithmetic rate of return (see the preceding section) and measures that for every year you're dealing with (the years you're including in your calculation). You add up the rate of return from each year, and then divide it by the number of years you're measuring to get the average rate of returns.

If you happen to care, the calculation looks like this – though it makes the process much more intimidating than it is:

$$\bar{r}_{arithmetic} = \frac{1}{n}\sum_{i=1}^{n} r_{arith,i} = \frac{1}{n}\left(r_{arith,i} + \cdots + r_{arith,n} \right)$$

Time-weighted rate of returns

The average rate of returns from the preceding section distributes all returns equally so that the rate is the same each year. Using the *time-weighted* approach gives you a better understanding about how performance changes by weighting the returns from each year being included. You carry out this calculation as follows:

$$\bar{r}_{geometric} = \left(\prod_{i=1}^{n}\left(1 + r_{arith,i}\right) \right)^{\frac{1}{n}} - 1$$

This method of determining your rate of return is more accurate than the previous two methods because it accounts for changes in the rate of returns over time. The equation may look intimidating, but it really isn't. Here's the procedure:

1. **Find the arithmetic rate of returns from each year and add 1 to each.**

2. **Multiply the answers together.**

3. **Divide your answer from Step 2 by 1 ÷ *n*, where *n* is the number of years.**

4. **Subtract 1 from your answer in Step 3.**

5. **Multiply the answer from Step 4 by 100 to get your answer as a percentage.**

Risk-adjusted return on capital

The return on capital assets generated per pound of economic capital is called the *risk-adjusted return on capital* (RAROC):

RAROC = Rate of return ÷ Economic capital

Economic capital is the amount of liquid assets that a company needs to keep on hand so that it can handle risk concerns: credit risk, liquidity risk and so on. Therefore, the RAROC method of calculating the rate of returns accounts for risk generated by measuring the amount or return per pound of capital the company must keep on hand to compensate for the additional risk generated. This is a measure that is used by banks in particular.

Perusing portfolio manager evaluations

Another concept that you can use with any expenditure or investment is generally applied to evaluations of the success of investment portfolio managers. These evaluations involve (surprise, surprise) the actual returns, risk and average market returns. As with evaluating the estimated price and value of assets compared to the market, the degree of success is also evaluated in such a manner.

Besides seeing a trend in gradually increasing the complications among the ratios described in the following sections, you may also notice that they're all similar but with subtle yet important differences. In fact, loads more ratios also work on the same basic premise, with each one using certain measures, expectations, parameters, probabilities and so on. With a little bit of maths savvy, you can easily create your own equation that's some slight variation of an existing one and then name it after yourself!

Alpha

To help understand some of these analyses, we begin with the ratio α (alpha), which you calculate as follows:

$$\alpha_s = R_s - [R_f + \beta_s(R_m - R_f)]$$

This equation may look familiar, because it's almost identical to the CAPM equation from Chapter 15 – with just one key difference: you start with the actual returns on an investment and then subtract the value of the investment as calculated by the CAPM model.

This equation then tells you that alpha is equal to the amount of returns generated (R_s) over the market anticipated returns based on the level of risk (R_f)

over the market average returns (R_m) (usually measured using some related index or other benchmark) and the risk-free rate. If you anticipate returns of $100 on an investment and you generate $101, your alpha is $1 because you generated returns of $1 over the CAPM anticipated rate, so this formula can tell you about individual performance (or performance of a portfolio) as opposed to the market.

Hedge fund and other portfolio managers are often evaluated on their ability to generate a consistently high alpha value on a given portfolio, or some variation of alpha. In fact, the amount these managers are paid is often based on alpha, a variation of alpha or some equation that incorporates alpha. Bet you want to take another look at the equation now.

Sharpe ratio

The *Sharpe ratio* is a way to look at the returns of an investment or portfolio, which measures the amount of returns for each unit of volatility that's generated in a portfolio. In other words, higher returns and lower volatility mean more returns per unit of volatility.

Here's how you calculate the Sharpe ratio:

$$S = [E(R - R_f)] \div \sigma$$

where $[E(R - R_f)]$ is the expected value of the excess of the asset return over the benchmark return.

The equation's not that hard, but the little σ (sigma) may be unfamiliar unless you're well-versed in statistics. All you need to worry about for the purposes of this book is that it's a measure of variability: a higher σ indicates a wider dispersion among the rates of return. Other than that, basically the equation says that any returns over the risk-free rate are divided by the amount of dispersion of those returns, to give you the Sharpe ratio.

Measuring performance this way incentivises portfolio managers to take risk but ensures that they're generating greater returns for the portfolio than volatility. Yes, this measure is based on the faulty notion that volatility is the same as risk, working on the assumptions of CAPM, but whether it's right, wrong or indifferent, this is the Sharpe ratio.

Sterling ratio

The *Sterling ratio* is very similar to the Sharpe ratio, but instead of measuring risk using dispersion of returns, it measures risk using the average drawdown of the portfolio (*drawdown* is an economic term that means a decline from peak performance).

You calculate the Sterling ratio very simply:

$$SR = (R_p - R_f) \div \text{Average drawdown}$$

where (R_p) is the portfolio return.

Therefore, you take all the major drawdowns (losses of value) of the portfolio, add them together and then divide the sum by the number of drawdowns. As a result, this calculation rewards risk of lost value but only if the returns on investment are higher than the risk incurred.

V2 ratio

The *V2 ratio* works on a similar premise to the Sterling ratio but is slightly more complicated. It uses drawdowns in excess of market drawdowns measured by the average drawdowns of some benchmark index:

$$V_R^2 = \frac{\left(\dfrac{V_n}{V_0}\right)^{\frac{P}{n}} - 1}{\sqrt{\dfrac{\Sigma_{i=0}^{n}\left(\dfrac{V_i}{V_i^P} - 1\right)^2}{n}} + 1}$$

Chapter 19

Forecasting Finances Is Easier than Predicting the Weather

*T*his chapter concerns finding a way to clear your mind of preconceptions. If that sounds more like a self-help book, bear with us, because financial forecasting really does involve the ability to look past what you think you already know. Past and future can speak to you effectively only when you're living exclusively in the present.

We discuss using current and historical data about the company, the industry and the economy to predict the future. Of course, your predictions may be wrong, but you can also use the data to determine the probability of being wrong and by how much you may be off the mark. As a result, we use a lot of foundation-level statistics and probability, but we show you some short-cuts too. The statistics we explain includes much that we use in equations throughout this book, and so if you don't fully understand how to do any of it, don't worry, because we refer you to those equations.

Seeing with Eyes Analytical

To forecast finances successfully, you have to let go of your preconceived notions about what you *think* the future will look like and instead allow the information you have available to guide your ideas. Too many people working in forecasting and projections let their established ideas and beliefs get in the way of what may otherwise be very promising data.

To start, disregard what you think you know about the company you're study-ing and discover everything afresh, starting with the company's historical data. After you understand the data, you can then use everything you already know about the company to determine the reason it's performing in that manner and only then can you predict what's going to happen.

One common mistake, known as *confirmation bias,* is that people tend to look at data simply to confirm what they think they already know. Confirmation bias is the normal result of the human tendency to rely on patterns and trends to make sense of the world, but it can also cause you to be fooled relatively easily. So, analyse the data first and then worry about using what you know to explain that data.

Collecting data

Before you can analyse any of the data that's going to help you project your company's future financial performance, you need to collect that data. Thankfully, in the age of the Internet, this task is fairly easy. (For more infor-mation on assembling data, check out Chapter 2.)

If you don't have Internet access, we're afraid that you need to spend a lot of time collecting the required data by requesting it directly from the company concerned or going to the local library or a financial adviser to get the infor-mation you require.

To be honest, data collection can be a pretty tedious and sometimes long, drawn-out process. Narrowing down the exact type of information you're looking for helps a lot and results in people generally being more forthcoming with the information. Otherwise, you just end up collecting everything that may be relevant and sorting it out later.

The great thing about financial data is that everything about the data itself is the same. It's all measured in money, and so you don't have to worry about the technical details of the different types of data or anything.

Knowing where to look

The vast majority of financial data you want about any business comes from just a handful of locations:

   ✔ **Financial reports:** Financial reports are usually the first place to look because they're easy to find and already formatted in a way that's relatively simple to analyse. We don't just mean the annual reports – quarterly reports, monthly reports and everything else are important as well.

Sometimes you can just go to the relevant company's website and download all the financial information directly free of charge. Published annual reports are a reliable source of information.

✔ **Reports regarding stock, production and employment:** Companies, particularly larger ones, occasionally distribute reports on stock, production and employment, especially when prompted by organisations that are attempting to compile economic reports.

✔ **Accounting records:** If you're able to acquire the company's accounting books and records, these sources are easily the most comprehensive and detailed data you can find. Admittedly, though, getting your hands on such information is quite often difficult.

✔ **Internet sources:** For information about share prices (critical for many of the financial calculations we discuss in Chapter 8), our favourite source is www.google.com/finance, but lots of websites are available, all providing basically the same information. For other corporate financial information, you can look at the Companies House website (the place where all UK company accounts are filed) (www.companieshouse.gov.uk). Some of the information on this website is free of charge; for other information you may have to pay a nominal fee (sometimes just £1).

Comparing your data

As with any financial data, you probably benefit by collecting the same information from several other companies in the same industry for comparison.

Research data on the national economy. Fortunately, you don't have to compile this data yourself, because a variety of sources provide decent quality reports on this issue:

✔ **Office for National Statistics:** Offers several sources for economic data, including information about the economy, crime and justice, and the government itself. You can access the website at www.statistics.gov.uk.

✔ **International Monetary Fund:** You can find its research at www.imf.org/external/data.htm.

✔ **World Bank:** Features economic data at http://datacatalog.worldbank.org.

Finding an average

After you gather all your information, you need to work out what to do with it. You have to do some simple descriptive calculations of statistics and *probability,* which is the mathematics of uncertainty. In other words, you measure the likelihood of an event occurring using information about performance and relationships between *variables* (that is, information that is subject to change).

When you have a lot of different values for a variable, finding an average tells you the middle value – in other words, what's typical. Averages fall into different types, each with its own strengths and weaknesses, but in financial equations the vast majority of averages are the *mean average.*

To calculate the mean average, you need to add up all the values and divide that total by the number of values. In the example, $1 + 2 + 3 + 4 + 5 = 15 \div 5 = 3$, the mean is 3.

To look at a *weighted average* (an average that takes into account differences in the importance of each value), you attach a weight to each value. For instance, if one of the values in the preceding example was worth 60 per cent of the entire sample and the rest weighted equally at 10 per cent each, the average changes a bit:

$$1(0.1) + 2(0.1) + 3(0.1) + 4(0.1) + 5(0.6) = 0.1 + 0.2 + 0.3 + 0.4 + 3.0 = 4$$

The weighted average is 4 because the value 5 has more weight than the other values, bringing the average up a bit compared to the standard mean average. The total weight is 100 per cent, which is just 1 as a decimal and why each value is being multiplied by a decimal – 0.1 is 10 per cent, 0.6 is 60 per cent and so on. So whatever proportion a specific value consists of, you multiple that by its decimal (for example, 75 per cent is 0.75).

Most people use the weighted average in situations where an investment portfolio has different proportions of investments or when they're accounting for time-weighted averages, where more recent values are more important than historical ones.

A more common method used in financial analysis and projections is *moving averages,* which takes the average from a predetermined number of days prior to a given day. For example, for a three-day moving average on Wednesday, you include data going back to Monday; for Thursday, you collect all the data going as far back as Tuesday; and for Friday, you go back to Wednesday. This data helps illustrate whether the mean is increasing or decreasing over time.

Measuring data distribution

Obviously, not all the numbers in a data set are going to be exactly the same as the average. You can measure the manner in which data is distributed around the average in different ways. Say that the average net profit of a company is £10,000. That's great, but it doesn't tell you whether that number changes much: the company may consistently earn £10,000 every year, or it may earn £0 in the year before and £20,000 the year after. This information is the sort of thing worth knowing, and we describe two ways in which you can measure it.

Range

Range is very simple: it's simply the difference between the largest and smallest values. So, if a company has profits of £10,000 and £20,000, you can say that it has a two-year range of £10,000, or 100 per cent.

If you're looking at the range for the company's profits over the last 20 years, you may want to pay attention to its *interquartile range* (which simply means the range of the middle 50 per cent of values). This approach allows you to make sure that the company didn't experience unusually high or low profits in certain years, which would throw a spanner in the works where your data's concerned.

To find the interquartile range, you take the profits from all the years and put them in numerical order, divide them into four equal pieces and then take the range of the middle two pieces. So, if a company's profits have a range of £100,000 but an interquartile range of only £20,000, you may think that the company had extreme variation in its profits in some of those years.

These ranges are often illustrated on graphs in a couple ways:

- ✔ **Box plots:** To compare changes in specified time intervals, you can use box plots to show changes in the mean and distribution of financial data. Figure 19-1 shows range and interquartile range in the form of vertical rectangles with lines coming out the top and bottom. The box is white if the closing value is higher than the opening value, and black if the closing value is lower than the opening value.

- ✔ **Bollinger bands:** Changing trends in dispersion are often included in Bollinger bands. The three horizontal lines in Figure 19-1 illustrate the maximum (top), mean (middle) and minimum (lower) values in a range over time.

Figure 19-1:
Box plots and Bollinger bands.

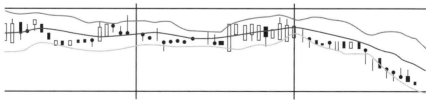

Standard deviation

Standard deviation is another measure of distribution, this time represented by the letter σ (sigma). It's a concept used quite frequently in equations, and here's how you calculate it:

1. **Calculate the mean average (as we describe in the earlier section 'Finding an average').**

   For example:

   1, 2, 3, 4, 5; Mean = 3

2. **Subtract each value from the mean.**

   For example:

   3 − 1 = 2, 3 − 2 = 1, 3 − 3 = 0 and so on

3. **Square each difference.**

   For example:

   $2^2 = 4$, $1^2 = 1$, $0^2 = 0$, $-1^2 = 1$, $-2^2 = 4$

4. **Add the squares together.**

   For example:

   4 + 1 + 0 + 1 + 4 = 10

5. **Divide the answer by the number of values.**

   For example:

   10 ÷ 5 = 2

6. **Take the square root of the answer from Step 5.**

   For example:

   $\sqrt{2} = 1.41$

The standard deviation is 1.41, meaning that the variation of the values away from the mean is measured in units worth 1.41 each.

What standard deviation tells you is the extent to which results are spread out from the average – for example, if the temperature in one month stays about the same each day, the standard deviation will be low.

Understanding probability

Probability theory is pretty easy (hurray!). The total probabilities of an event occurring or not always equal 100 per cent. If you have a 10 per cent probability that something may happen, you have a 90 per cent probability that it won't.

The simplest example is the coin toss. You have a 50 per cent probability that the coin is going to land on either side because only two options exist. Take 100 per cent probability, divide it by two options and each option has only 50 per cent probability. Each time you flip that coin, you have a 50 per cent probability of it being heads or tails. Just because it lands on heads 100 times in a row doesn't mean that the coin has a better chance of landing on tails: on flip 101, you still have a 50 per cent probability that it will land on tails. (A lot of gamblers get stuck in that trap.)

Normal distribution

When you apply probability theory to the standard deviation (see the preceding section), you end up with something called a normal distribution.

The *normal distribution,* shown in Figure 19-2, has a lot of very important traits, but all you really need to know is the relationship between standard deviation, probability and the distribution of data. The percentages in the curve itself tell you what percentages of the data are included within the number of standard deviation units listed at the bottom. After you calculate the standard deviation and the mean (see the earlier sections 'Finding an average' and 'Standard deviation'), you can work out probability pretty easily. For example, say that you have a mean of 4 and a standard deviation of 1. According to the graph, 34 per cent of all values will be between 5 and 6, 68 per cent of all cases will be between 4 and 6 and so on.

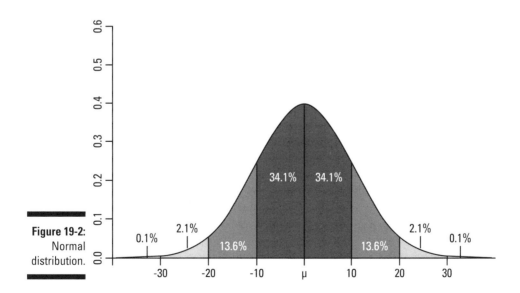

Figure 19-2:
Normal
distribution.

You care about normal distribution because probability calculations are used frequently in financial forecasts. Imagine that you want to predict the most probable percentage drop in the stock market as a result of an increase in interest rates. By collecting historical data and determining the mean and standard deviations, you can estimate the likely range to any percentage of probability you like. You may say that the stock market has a 68 per cent probability of dropping by 1 to 2 per cent or a 95 per cent probability that it'll drop between 0.8 to 2.2 per cent.

TIP

The more certain you want to be, the wider your range is going to be, because you have to account for a greater range of data that encompasses a particular level of probability.

Bayesian Probability

You can take the normal distribution calculation in the preceding section a step further. Imagine that you want to know the probability that, given the event that the stock market drops by 1 to 2 per cent, a specific company's share price is also going to drop by 1 to 2 per cent? You can come up with the answer to this interesting question by using something called *Bayesian Probability:*

$$P(A|B) = \frac{P(B|A)P(A)}{P(B)}$$

This equation says that in order to calculate the probability of thing A happening conditionally of thing B, you carry out the following steps:

1. **Take the probability of thing B happening as a result of thing A and multiply that amount by the probability of thing A.**

2. **Divide the answer by the probability of thing B happening.**

In other words, if a 68 per cent chance exists of the stock market decreasing by 1 to 2 per cent (thing B) and there's only a 50 per cent chance of a share price drop happening without B (thing A), but a 95 per cent probability exists that interest rates will rise given a share price drop, you can calculate the total probability of your share price dropping as follows:

$$P = (0.95 \times 0.50) \div 0.68 = 0.698 \text{ or } 70\%$$

The probability *(P)* of a drop in share price given a drop in the market occurs is 70 per cent.

After you get a chance to practise these conditional probabilities, they're quite simple to perform and can even be modified to your own purposes. Conditional probabilities are used frequently in financial forecasting, often being incorporated in Arbitrage Pricing Theory models (refer to Chapter 15 for more on this).

Viewing the Past as New

Most people are obsessed with their money and spend a lot of time and resources tracking and recording data. That's a good thing, because as a result just about all the historical data you can ever want regarding corporate finance is already collected and compiled. You don't have to do any of that time-consuming research; you just need to collect the data that others have found.

When reviewing historical data you need to shut off everything you think you know. In Chapter 22, we discuss a bit about behavioural finance, and behavioural mistakes tend to be amplified when you're dealing with issues of uncertainty, such as forecasting. So go into your research with an open mind, allow the data to surprise you and always be looking for something new and interesting that others may not have noticed in order to give yourself a financial edge.

Finding trends and patterns

When reviewing historical data, your first job is to look for trends and patterns. If you can identify trends that are occurring and any cyclical patterns that have happened in the past, you gain important insight into what will (or at least may) happen in the future.

Start with patterns, for example. You can usually best explore patterns by plotting your data on a graph (though nowadays it's much easier because Microsoft Excel does the job for you). Try several different graphs and really look at each of them to see whether you can recognise any patterns that begin to emerge. For instance, if you randomly pick a set of revenue information without knowing which company they belong to and see a pattern where sales go up in the summer and down in the winter, you can easily determine that the company's sales follow a cyclical pattern based on the seasons. You can probably take a good guess at what type of company it is, perhaps even naming the company without being told.

Not all patterns are as obvious or simple as this example, but the basic premise is the same: you're looking for any patterns that allow you to predict what's going to happen in the future of your company's finances.

Looking for short- and long-term trends is also important. Here's a perfect example. Have a look at any graph of the stock market online (for example, check out www.google.com/finance). Looks pretty jagged, right, with lots of ups and downs? Now zoom out to increase the time duration you're looking at on the graph. Keep zooming out and you start to see a bigger trend. Overall, the stock market has been increasing in value relatively smoothly over time. That long-term positive trend is certainly made up of short-term upward and downward trends, but overall they're leading to an increase in value over the course of many decades.

Find trends like this one in all your financial forecasting. Understand how long each short-term trend lasts, try to predict when it will change direction and then work out what the trends are doing in the long run.

Looking at regression

By regression, we don't mean returning to the state of a knuckle-dragging cave-dweller. No, the goal of *regression* is to look at historical information to determine whether any variables are influencing financial movements.

Today this process typically uses highly advanced computer programmes, such as analytics software and databases, to perform something called *data mining*. Basically, data mining works by including all the data you can possibly get your hands on and letting a computer programme decide whether any correlation exists between the thing you're trying to forecast and other variables. You can do data mining on your own, but unless you already have some idea of what you may be looking for, it's just all guesswork, which isn't ideal at all.

For example, you may find that your company's costs increase with the temperature outside. As the temperature increases, so do total costs; as temperature decreases, the company's costs also decrease. You may even find that, on average, costs change by 1 per cent for every 3 per cent change in temperature. This relationship is called a *correlation*.

Note that a correlation doesn't mean that the temperature is causing a price increase – just that the two are related. You can think of a correlation like this: if *all* relationships were causational, you'd be able to say that Bono from U2 kills people, because a high correlation exists between short life expectancies and countries that Bono visits. But obviously, although a correlation exists, the short life expectancy and the visits by Bono are caused by poverty.

If temperature and cost are correlated, the relationship may look something like Figure 19-3.

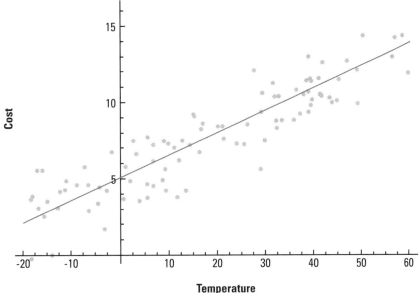

Figure 19-3:
Regression
analysis.

The dots in Figure 19-3 are the actual values included. You plot them as you would on any graph: find the correct spot on the horizontal axis (temperature), move up to the correct spot on the vertical axis (cost) and place the dot where the two intersect. The line going through them illustrates the proportion of the relationship. (In this case, a one-third slope indicates that for every 1 unit increase in cost, temperature increases by 3 units.)

Consider the following attributes in Figure 19-3:

  ✔ **Positive correlation:** As one factor increases, the other increases as well.

  ✔ **Negative correlation:** One factor decreases as the other increases.

The closer the dots are to the line, the stronger the relationship. If the dots are far away from the line and don't look like they're in a pattern, the relationship is very weak. In Figure 19-3, the relationship is fairly strong, because you can see the pattern even without the line present.

Knowing what to do with correlations

Ideally, if you can find a relationship, you want to be able to use it to make financial predictions. For example, if determining what your costs will look like next week is possible by measuring the temperature today, temperature is a good thing to know. If the weather forecast says that it's going to be 30 degrees Celsius next week (unlikely where the great British weather is concerned), perhaps you can use that to predict your corporate costs.

Creating greater accuracy

You can also use multiple variables to create more accurate correlations. These *multivariate regressions* attempt to show how each variable has an influence on the thing you're measuring. When used together, you can create an even more accurate model that not only explains what's causing changes in the thing you're measuring, but also how much of a role each variable plays and how you can use that to predict what will happen in the future. For this book, we stick with just a simple regression, though.

With regards to investing, any correlations that allow you to predict movements in the share price are highly prized.

Performing a regression analysis

You can carry out a regression analysis using Microsoft Excel:

1. **Title each column in cells A1 and A2 with the label of the type of data that you're going to use in each.**

   For example, you can use labels such as 'Temp' and 'Costs'.

2. **Start inputting the appropriate data below the title in column A.**

   For example, you can include the temperature on a given day with a new value in each cell.

3. **Input the proper data below the title in column B as well.**

   Be very careful to match the proper data together. For example, if you're putting the cost for a particular day in a cell of column B, make sure that it's next to the correct temperature for the same day.

4. **Use the Excel function LINEST.**

   For 'Known_y's' include all one column, including the title. For 'Known_x's', use all the other column.

5. **Press Enter to get a decimal value.**

   The closer to 1 that value is, the stronger the relationship. The closer to 0 that value is, the weaker the relationship. A value of 1 means that a perfect positive correlation exists, whereas a value of 0 indicates that no correlation exists at all and a value of –1 indicates a perfect negative correlation. If the number is positive, it's a positive correlation; if it's negative, you have a negative correlation.

If you can identify the influences on your finances, you can manage those influences to make them work in your favour. You're empowered to change your financial future.

Seeing the Future Unclouded: Forecasting

Financial forecasts are used in just about every aspect of corporate finance. Budgeting, investing, risk assessment, financing, stock management, production schedules, hiring . . . basically anything that involves money is going to be subject to financial forecasting. We're serious when we say that people obsess over money, and they want to know everything about it, including what will happen in the future. After you analyse your data, you can provide them with predictions of the future.

The forecast itself is often nothing more than a prediction of what's going to happen, typically including the probability of the prediction being correct and a range of other values that may also occur, with an explanation for the deviation. Often, you can explain these forecasts to someone in under a minute, if really necessary, but forecasters prefer to try and provide more information than just the basics.

 Include any information that may be potentially useful for making decisions or back-up plans. Forecasting finances is a bit like forecasting the weather; you like to know if the probability of rain is low, but unless it's 0 per cent probability, you should probably make back-up arrangements as well.

Using statistics and probability

Simply put, to forecast your finances you look out for trends, patterns and relationships, determine the probability of these factors influencing a particular outcome and use that to model your forecast. For instance, if government indicators predict that the economy is going to grow by 4 per cent next year and you've assessed a correlative relationship (as we describe in the earlier section 'Looking at regression') of economic and sales growth predicted by indices at half of the government indicators, you should predict that the economic growth will contribute to a 2 per cent sales increase next year. Does that mean that sales will increase 2 per cent next year? Only if nothing else influences your sales at all, because other factors may make sales higher or lower, but the economic growth will have a bit of a positive influence on your sales.

Based on consistent trends over each month of the last three years of a steady 1 per cent monthly sales increase, you may predict that you'll continue to see steady growth over the next several years, but with a 68 per cent probability of slowed growth because you find patterns where sales slowed down every fourth year. Even if you can't work out what variables influenced that slowed growth, after calculating the probability of it you can determine that your sales have a definite possibility of a temporary slow-down.

Predicting movements

In the stock market, the two things that are most commonly used to predict movements are earnings and price. We honestly believe that using these two items as predictors is completely insane, because both tend to be too volatile and too easily manipulated to be useful indicators.

So what are good indicators? A joke passed around by American economist Paul Samuelson says, 'The market has predicted eight of the last five recessions'. Another, somewhat more accurate indicator, is the yield on Treasury bonds. This yield tends to increase and decrease in a generally similar way to national gross domestic product, but two to four years earlier. Still, ratios such as price-to-earnings are quite popular for predicting stock-market movements.

Calculating the Altman's Z-score

An interesting case of statistical financial projections is the *Altman's Z-score*. This calculation is 72 per cent accurate in predicting that a company will go bust within the next two years. Although not spectacularly accurate (better models are now available), the Altman's Z-score is a very simple equation to use and is accurate enough to prove a point. Here's how the equation works:

$$Z = 1.2T_1 + 1.4T_2 + 3.3T_3 + 0.6T_4 + 0.99T_5$$

where:

T_1 = Working capital/Total assets

T_2 = Retained earnings/Total assets

T_3 = EBIT/Total assets (EBIT is earnings before interest and taxes)

T_4 = Market value of equity/Total liabilities

T_5 = Sales/Total assets

Here are the risk score ratings:

>3 = as risky as slipping in snow in an Indian summer (very low risk of liquidation).

1.81–2.99 = as risky as slipping in snow in Britain in the month of March (moderate risk of liquidation).

<1.80 = as risky as slipping in snow in Britain in the month of January (high risk of liquidation).

When using statistics and probability, you take several different variables (the components of the different financial calculations), weight each one by the amount it can predict liquidation in a standard deviation and then add them together to give something called a *z-score* (a measure of observed distance from the mean for a particular value). Together, they provide the 72 per cent accuracy.

Seeking a precedent: Reference class forecasting

Reference class forecasting involves finding a similar precedent set in the past for the thing you're trying to predict and then using the outcome of that scenario to check whether your forecast is reasonable compared to what happened historically. Because reference class forecasting is very prone to variations, given that not each situation is exactly the same, performing the forecast first helps you avoid *bias* or *guiding scenarios* (where your opinion is shaped by preconceived notions rather than the data itself).

When you do the reference class forecast and the data doesn't match expectations based on your reference, you can determine why it's different and alter your forecast as necessary.

Evaluating forecast performance

You can use two primary methods to evaluate financial forecasting performance: time and accuracy. A forecaster is considered more successful when he's able to predict very closely when something will occur or very closely the degree to which something is going to change. If a forecaster predicts that revenues will jump in July, but sales drop in July only to jump in August, the forecaster isn't very accurate. If the forecaster predicts that sales will jump by 10 per cent and sales in fact jump by 11 per cent, that's bad as well.

Of course, a few variables (such as production capacity, for example) influence how those differences in forecasts should be interpreted. If sales jump by 11 per cent instead of 10 per cent and the company isn't ready to handle that extra 1 per cent jump, its management will be angry at the forecaster, even though he was only 1 per cent out in his forecast.

Chapter 20

Spelling out the ABC of M&A

....

....

Many people associate mergers and acquisitions (M&A) with the under-hand business practices of the 1980s, when methods such as hostile takeovers and the liquidation of otherwise successful companies came into prominence. This perception isn't entirely fair, though: the 1980s have been unduly targeted because business practices of large organisations have been accused of being underhand.

Still, the stereotype that the M&A industry is filled with corruption and sociopaths is an idea perpetuated mostly by such films as Oliver Stone's *Wall Street* (whose characters become involved in the hostile takeover of an airline with the intention of liquidating all its assets) or Bret Easton Ellis's book *American Psycho* (whose main character is an executive at an M&A firm who also just happens to be a serial killer). If you ask people to define exactly what M&A consists of, what an M&A firm does or why companies pursue M&A (or even what M&A stands for), the chances are that a large percentage of people can't answer any of these questions correctly.

In this chapter, we shed light on this topic, discussing the details of the different types of M&A activities. These differences are often subtle, with overlaps between them, or at least the terms are often used incorrectly/interchangeably, and so we define exactly what each activity is and provide examples to illustrate. We also look at the motives for M&A activity and how companies stand to benefit. In addition, we go over how companies are valued and priced for potential M&A integration, whether a company is considered under- or overvalued and how companies finance their M&A activities. You may be surprised to discover that integrating organisations is an expensive process, and so when the asking price has been determined, companies need to establish whether or not they can afford it.

Getting the Lowdown on M&A

Mergers and acquisitions are both forms of integration between companies. Although M&A isn't the only type of corporate integration, the term has entered the popular vocabulary to cover a number of corporate integration options, despite referring to only two. M&A can also refer to the splitting up of companies: selling, stopping or otherwise parting with operations that used to be part of a single company.

Therefore, on the whole, M&A is a field that deals with an odd trait inherent in companies – that is, their ability to combine, divide, become each other, become something else and otherwise interact in a very permeable manner with other organisations.

M&A is a complicated issue that involves a lot of consideration about the potential for a number of different things to integrate well, including the company's operations, its management, corporate culture, branding, marketing and distribution, and a great number of other issues. M&A isn't purely a financial concern, not by a long shot, but these are all secondary considerations for executives, because they determine whether or not a merger is going to work only *after* they've already determined the potential for financial benefit.

In other words, the primary motivation for M&A is always money. After a company establishes that money's to be made, it does all the extra work to determine whether or not it can tap into this metaphorical gold mine.

Having said that, a company can make money through M&A in a number of different ways. Two businesses that are individual from each other don't stand to benefit if they integrate their two respective organisations only to keep earnings and market share between them unchanged. Some form of gain needs to exist from the synergy between the two companies.

Yes, we know *synergy* (the idea that the two combined companies can gain benefits beyond what they can produce individually) is one of those seemingly nonsensical management terms that never seems to work out for the combined company, but that's primarily the result of ineffective M&A. A great number of motivations lie behind M&A, but far too many companies are overly anxious to participate in such activities. As a result they underestimate the difficulty of making the M&A happen or assume that any M&A is sure to benefit the company, without evaluating the value of the proposed integration. In other words, synergy has become a bad word because it's used too often as the sole justification for M&A, instead of determining what exact synergy is going to come out of the decision: and that's just bad management.

As regards M&A, you have to make one big consideration: the legal position. A lot of legislation around the world says that companies can't integrate their operations in certain ways, or sometimes at all, if doing so significantly changes competition in the industry. If two companies decide that they want to merge, but, say, only three companies offer that particular product, the chances are that the government (or the Competition Commission in the UK) is going to stop them from merging, sometimes fining them for predatory business practices. (If the companies are based in one nation that allows the merger but they also have operations overseas, they're likely to end up getting fined in only one of those nations.)

The result can be extremely expensive in terms of fines and expenditures on the M&A-in-progress, and so make sure that you assess the legal implications of any M&A before even making the attempt.

Differentiating Between the M and the A

The differences between mergers, acquisitions and other forms of company integration can be subtle on an operational level and yet still result in significant financial differences in the long run. These small but crucial variations in integration techniques are, more than anything, legal variances that define exactly who has ownership over what and the assets and resources to which people are entitled, including company profits.

The following sections look at each of the most common forms of corporate integration, what makes each unique and helps you recognise the different form of corporate integration. We also look at some real-world examples of each form of integration carried out by large organisations and see how things worked out for them.

Joining together: Mergers

Mergers are rather strange events. A *merger* occurs when two companies 'become' each other or, more specifically, both companies cease to exist and a new company is formed out of their operations. The shareholders have their shares reorganised under the new company, and all operations fall under a new set of executive management, which usually consists of a combination of the management from the two individual organisations prior to the merger. This type of arrangement is usually considered to be a *merger of equals,* or a combining of companies on equal terms. In reality, though, the larger or more financially healthy company tends to assimilate the other.

The Compaq/HP merger

In 2002, the computer companies Compaq and Hewlett–Packard (HP) merged. This merger was done, financially, by exchanging equity shares of Compaq for a proportion of shares of HP. The two companies held a shareholder meeting during which equity holders for both companies voted on whether the merger should take place. Of course it did, and so the share symbols CPQ (Compaq) and HWP (HP) disappeared and formed the new company's share symbol HPQ. A brand new company formed from two companies dying in a collision of happy partnership.

Or was it so happy? Even before the merger took place, several news sources questioned whether Compaq was being overvalued. The company was already having difficulty maintaining sales while competing against other companies, such as HP, Dell, Apple and others in the industry. After some controversy about conflicts of interest and vote-buying, in the post-merger company the dominant firm became apparent. The company kept the name Hewlett–Packard (at least the Daimler AG merger we discuss in the later section 'Clearing up the Mess: Divestitures' was called Daimler–Chrysler, allowing the image of both companies to remain intact) and HP's CEO maintained control over the new company – a role that forced the ex-Compaq CEO and new HP president to resign from his position after complaints that he was merely a figurehead to ease the transition. The operations merger was smooth and the shares maintained their value, but Compaq computers are no longer made and HP maintains total control. This merger was quite clearly an assimilation that avoided the negative connotations of an 'acquisition'.

Although a merger is, technically, a combination of companies to form a new one, which may imply a level legal playing field in the terms of the merger, the reality isn't so simple. Typically mergers tend to occur between companies where one has a dominant place in the market, allowing that company more leverage to maintain managerial control over not only the merger process, but also how operations are run after the merger is complete. This control includes how finances are managed and representation in management.

Mergers happen so frequently because of financial strategy. For companies of all sizes, certain other forms of M&A (such as a *vertical acquisition*, which is when a company acquires another company – for example, a large construction company may acquire a small, owner-managed builders merchants) carry negative connotations. Calling an integration a 'merger' implies equality in the integration, allowing both companies to maintain a positive image and their shares' market value. If one company is seen to be 'acquiring' the other, investors may infer that the acquired company was in trouble or overvalued, causing the market value of the shares to drop and reducing confidence in the newly integrated entity.

Purchasing a company: Acquisitions

An *acquisition* differs from a merger (check out the preceding section) because it doesn't combine two companies. Instead, one company purchases the other as you'd purchase a car.

Acquisitions are a bit more flexible than mergers in respect of the legal organisation of each company, but the true hallmark of an acquisition is that one company then owns another after the acquisition process is complete.

Not all acquisitions are considered bad. When a smaller company (the *target*) is being acquired by a much larger company (the *bidder*), the latter quite frequently appreciates the value of the smaller company, especially for businesses that are already known to be in financial trouble and whose share price has dropped in value as a result. In this case, even rumours of an acquisition can raise the price of the company's shares, because investors believe that being acquired by a company with more assets or better management may give the struggling company the jump start it needs to be more successful, as well as the fact that for those staff in the target company who manage to survive the acquisition, it can lead to greater opportunities.

Here are two of the possible options that may influence an acquisition:

- ✔ **Organisational sovereignty:** An odd term that refers to whether or not the acquired company remains a company in its own right. Remember that companies can own other companies and the acquiring company has the option merely to make the acquired company a single branch or division of its other operations as opposed to allowing it to stay an independent entity. So, in many cases, a company may just purchase a controlling share of the acquired company's equity (usually more than 50 per cent to gain control), giving it the ability to manage the acquired company from a distance but never fully integrating the two organisations. On the other hand, the acquired company may simply cease to exist, becoming a single division of the acquiring company.

- ✔ **Partial acquisition:** The acquiring company is required to purchase more than 50 per cent of the equity in the acquired company. This amount gives the acquiring company a controlling shareholding, allowing it to manage the acquired business however it wants. A partial acquisition does, however, limit the acquiring company's ability to integrate completely the company's operations, because private shareholders still remain (sometimes called *minority* shareholders or *non-controlling interests*).

    In other words, in partial acquisitions, the acquired company remains a business. In a *full acquisition,* the acquiring company purchases the total value of the acquired company and has the option to make that company a part of its own operations.

Bank of America acquires Merrill Lynch

In 2008, Bank of America (BoA) acquired Merrill Lynch, a securities firm. Merrill Lynch now no longer exists, technically. It doesn't have shares, and it's not a company. Instead, Merrill Lynch exists as the wealth management arm of BoA, which maintains the Merrill Lynch name for these operations. It has a separate website for Merrill Lynch customers and even keeps much of the same branding. BoA even attempted to keep many of the same executives managing the operations of the newly acquired division, but they soon left (taking the demotion from CEO to branch director is a hard pill to swallow). This particular acquisition was a full acquisition despite BoA's decision to allow Merrill Lynch to maintain much of its previous public image as a separate entity.

This particular acquisition very much helped Merrill Lynch as well. Sometimes acquisitions can harm the acquired company, because investors tend to believe that it has become overvalued. In the case of Merrill Lynch, however, everyone already knew the company was in trouble. Merrill Lynch was literally just days away from going bust. The only reason Merrill Lynch still exists is that BoA acquired it. Whether or not the acquisition was a good idea is still a matter of some controversy, though, owing to the lack of disclosure regarding exactly how much bad debt Merrill Lynch had incurred.

Taking control: Buyouts

A *buyout* occurs when one company buys a controlling shareholding in another. A buyout is very similar to the partial acquisition approach (which we discuss in the preceding section). In fact, some people argue that no difference exists, which isn't surprising because the difference is subtle at best.

The primary difference between a buyout and other forms of M&A is that a controlling shareholding is used, rather than a share swap (which we explain in Chapter 13), purchase of other forms of equity or other possibilities of acquisition. So, in a buyout, a controlling share of equity is purchased. Another subtle nuance occurs when that controlling share is purchased by borrowing more money or by having an Initial Public Offering (IPO; refer to Chapter 3). When a company raises additional money for the sole purpose of controlling another company, it's called a *leveraged buyout*.

The use of the buyout is popular among *venture capitalists* (a company or third party who provides capital to high-potential, high risk or new companies) and investors, and is used for gaining control and expanding one's operations very quickly without the intention of ever integrating those additional operations.

A buyout is sort of an arm's-length approach, where the purchased company is expected to maintain the high degree of autonomy it always had, but the purchasing entity intends to take advantage of the increased reach or earnings potential after the buyout because it will have access to more business through more customers and more contacts.

Considering other forms of integration

At the core of all M&A is the idea of corporate integration, but companies can make corporate integration happen in several ways that aren't technically mergers or acquisitions. To use a phrase we heard from Kent Kedl of Technomic Asia (a firm of Chinese business consultants), M&A has been extended to 'M,A&A: Mergers, Acquisitions and Alliances'.

Hostile takeover

A *hostile takeover* is really the same thing as a regular buyout or acquisition (see the earlier 'Taking control: Buyouts' and 'Purchasing a company: Acquisitions' sections, respectively) except that it occurs without the consent of the management of the acquired company.

A hostile takeover occurs in a few ways:

- ✔ A *proxy fight* occurs whereby a majority of shareholders of the target company are convinced to vote out the current board of directors and replace it with a board that agrees to the takeover.

- ✔ A company buys up a controlling share of equity on the *secondary market* (the financial market in which previously issued shares are bought and sold).

- ✔ A company purchases the debt of a troubled company and gains control over its assets through liquidation (which we describe in Chapter 14).

In any case, the end result of a hostile takeover is the same as a normal acquisition or buyout, but it's done by force.

Factoring

Factoring is a much less integrated way to integrate. It's a one-time deal (which can be repeated in the future, but each deal takes place only once rather than being ongoing) that's relatively short term and keeps both organisations totally independent of each other.

The Toys 'R' Us buyout

In 2005, a *consortium of investing companies* (several organisations working together) purchased Toys 'R' Us in a leveraged buyout, making the company privately owned but by several parties. This followed an unsuccessful and expensive plan to remodel and relaunch the chain, which was blamed on market pressures (namely competition from companies like Walmart and Target). As a buyout, Toys 'R' Us remains its own company, an entity in its own right, but it's owned by several others who share ownership.

Factoring works by one company selling its *sales ledger* (that is, the record of all customers who owe the company money) to another at a discount. So, in essence, the acquiring company (known as the *factoring company*) is only acquiring the future cash flows on the acquired company's *trade debtors* (customers who owe the business money because they've bought goods or services on credit), meaning that it's purchasing part of the company's future revenues. Usually, the purchase price on such a deal is only 5–20 per cent of the total value, depending on the quality of the trade debtors, *trade debtor days* (days the customers take to pay eventually) and other variables.

In this way, one company can acquire another's specific operations and within a limited timeframe, instead of carrying out a permanent and total acquisition.

Joint ventures and partnerships

Sometimes companies want to work together on a specific operation but don't want to merge their other operations. These joint ventures and partnerships come in several different forms, the exact details of which aren't entirely relevant to this book. What does matter is that the exact nature of the contributions to these agreements, as well as the allocation of earnings, are established during the contract negotiations to form the agreement.

Joint ventures and partnerships tend to be far more popular than any other form of corporate integration – usually because it gives an opportunity to go into another market and in some cases it may even be the only way in which local regulations allow you to operate in that market – but they're also less involved in finance and more in corporate management, and so we don't spend a whole lot of time on them.

Clearing up the Mess: Divestitures

We don't want to give you bad dreams, but imagine for a moment that you've done awful, terrible things during your time managing M&A, and as a result of your incompetence, not only are you likely to have nightmares for the rest of your life, but also the company you worked for now needs to get rid of your acquisitions. Well, maybe your huge executive severance package eases the pain, but the reality is that the company now owns operations it doesn't want anymore. In such cases, or anywhere a company is looking to get rid of some of its operations, it goes through something called a divestiture.

Divestiture is a broad term that can include several different potential methods for accomplishing the same thing: getting rid of assets. In the case of M&A, if a division/branch/operation within the company can't stand alone as a company it probably needs to shut down those operations and liquidate the hard assets for whatever it can get for them. If that division or whatever has the potential to operate independently of the company, it probably spins off into its own company. In other words, it stops being a part of the larger company and operates independently.

Here's a perfect example of a merger-gone-wrong that resulted in a divestiture. In 2007, Daimler sold its Chrysler operations to a capital investing firm, following weak sales by Chrysler and an inability by Daimler to do anything successful with it. Chrysler was sold and later repurchased by another car manufacturer (Fiat). Daimler decided it was better to sell the division for what it could get and take the loss on the chin, instead of lose everything trying to sort out a company it didn't have the ability to help. As you can see, the proverbial 'money pit' applies to all levels of investments, not just homes or cars. It just goes to show that sometimes entire enterprises change hands for just a few pounds if someone really wants to get rid of them.

Identifying Motives for M&A

The ultimate goal for any M&A activity is to make money, but then that's the primary motivation behind all businesses' activities. But you don't simply sign an M&A agreement and money appears out of nowhere. The M&A fairy doesn't appear in the middle of the night and fill your pockets with cash when you integrate companies. No, the top brass in charge need to know how to extract that money from the arrangement and derive value from integrating – to milk that cow for all it's worth!

M&A can improve a company's financial performance in several different ways. The financial aftermath of any M&A is where you make the distinction between managers who know what they're doing and those that are just pretending, which is all highly dependent on the ability of managers to recognise in advance that money can be made by integrating companies. If an M&A results in the company losing money hand over fist, this is because of a bad managerial decision.

If you agree to integration under the simple assumption that it's for the best, you're probably guessing and should look for a different job. If you can define exactly how your company's going to make money (and how much), you truly understand your motivations for M&A and can move forward with the deal – isn't it nice knowing that we approve?

The following sections cover some of the most common motivations for M&A, and talk about how money can be made from each of the individual motivations and exactly who makes that money.

Discovering diversification

Diversification means the same thing in this context as it does with investment portfolios: it's the process of making something more varied. With investment portfolios, diversification means holding unrelated investments to avoid risk and volatility for the whole portfolio that may otherwise be caused by just one or two investments. In M&A, diversification refers to attempts to make the product portfolio or operations more varied.

Diversification can be financially beneficial because it enables a company to operate in different areas of the market (or even a different market), but you need to be careful to make sure diversification is appropriate for the company. There's no point investing in diversification if doing so isn't going to reap rewards (in other words, make money).

Imagine that you own a stationery company. Your business does pretty well, but you make the majority of your sales during the back-to-school season and the school year. You're profitable on average, but during the school holidays, you simply aren't selling enough to make up for the cost of operations during those months. Then you spot a manufacturer of paper plates and napkins with the exact opposite problem; sales during spring and summer months because people tend to have barbecues, but nothing during the winter.

After some discussions, you realise that the manufacturing processes for both products are almost identical and the two companies can merge, diversifying both product lines into a single manufacturing facility. You've just doubled your product portfolio (stationery and now paper dinnerware) and are now generating more consistent revenues. Instead of reinventing the wheel, so to speak, you simply merge with another company, allowing everyone to take advantage of the skills of the other.

Financially, this merger means greater revenues, less volatile earnings and more efficient operations through lower average overhead per unit of output. Congratulations: your M&A is a success!

Expanding geographically

M&A is a popular way to expand into foreign markets or new areas within the same nation that are already dominated by established competitors. The approach allows the company to expand into these territories while using a name that's already recognisable and people who already have expertise in the area. M&A is a great way to enter into new markets and increase total sales. If you're lucky, M&A can also mean generating economies of scale (see the next section).

Daimler's merger with Chrysler (check out 'Clearing up the Mess: Divestitures' earlier in this chapter) was primarily motivated by geographic expansion. Daimler is a German company with very little presence in the United States, while Chrysler was faltering but still had a prominent US presence. Daimler saw merging with Chrysler as an opportunity to enter into the highly lucrative American automotive market, going as far as beginning to label certain lines such as the Jeep Grand Cherokee with Daimler branding.

The Daimler and Chrysler merger failed, however, because of cultural differences and organisational culture. Daimler was a very hierarchical company with a clear chain of command and respect for authority. Chrysler, on the other hand, favoured a more team-oriented approach. This example shows that there's more to consider in an M&A than simply profit – a target company (the potential acquiree) may do things a lot differently than the bidding company (the potential acquirer) and managing these differences ineffectively can doom an M&A to failure.

Benefiting from economies of scale

Buying in bulk saves money. If you've ever shopped at a cash-and-carry retailer such as Costco or Makro, you've no doubt bought things in large quantities to save cash. Many people buy kitchen rolls in cases of 12 rolls (with larger families you almost have to) because it's cheaper per roll than buying one or two at a time, and kitchen rolls don't have a sell-by date on them (as far as we know) so you know that you'll use them. Well, that's basically how *economies of scale* works: you operate in larger quantities to make production cheaper per unit.

Say that you have a machine that produces 1,000 units per year (units of what doesn't matter). You sell only 500 units per year, though. So, if you have overhead of £1,000 per year and you're only selling 500 units per year, you have an average overhead of £2 per unit (£1,000 in overhead ÷ 500 units = £2 per unit).

You decide to perform a little M&A to get into a foreign market, which increases sales to 1,000 units per year. Your overall overhead stays the same, which means that your average overhead reduces to just £1 per unit (£1,000 in overhead ÷ 1,000 units = £1 per unit). You've just reduced your overhead per unit by 50 per cent through M&A. Well done!

Enjoying economies of scope

Economies of scope is about reducing average cost of production, but unlike economies of scale (see the preceding section) you're attempting to reduce average costs by offering different product lines that use much of the same resources.

If two companies that manufacture stationery and paper plates merge, the new company is working out of a single manufacturing facility, which greatly reduces the overhead to produce the products both firms were making using two facilities. This increase in production for equivalent fixed costs is also a form of economies of scale.

An example is Kimberly Clark, a conglomerate that sells a huge range of personal care goods. These products all use the same branding, marketing, design and things of that nature, and so the indirect costs associated with the supporting activities (for example, marketing, finance and so on) can be applied to a wider range of products, reducing their cost per unit.

Integrating up, down and all around

Companies can integrate in different directions, within the same supply chain or even across industries.

Vertical integration

Vertical integration occurs when a company acquires another company that is up or down the supply chain in the same industry:

- ✔ **Backward integration:** When a company acquires a company from which it buys.
- ✔ **Forward integration:** The acquisition of a company to which it sells.

For example, take an imaginary company. Theoretical Paper Limited (aka: TP) decides that the time is right for a little M&A. It wants to do some vertical integration – no real reason other than the CEO's son read about it in the newspaper. So TP looks up the supply chain to see whether it can acquire a packager, distributor or retailer. Nothing would be financially feasible for them integrating upstream, and so TP looks downstream and finds a timber company with the rights to tree farms that provide timber to all the paper companies in its market. Oh, glorious day!

The acquisition of this company gives TP greater control over the market – the capability of profiting from the efforts of its competitors and accessing the best wood before anyone else! This acquisition puts TP in a position to increase sales through a better quality product than the competition, lower prices by gaining access to wood cheaper than the competition or simply put the competition out of business by refusing to provide them with wood.

Horizontal integration

Horizontal integration focuses on combining different companies at the same level in the supply chain. It's extremely common in technology companies, where developers acquire other developers or manufacturers acquire differ-ent manufacturers.

They do so not only to get rid of competitors (see the later section 'Eliminating competitors'), but also to gain the rights to new ideas and patents and to increase market share to compete against more established companies. In all cases, the point is to cut costs or increase revenues.

Conglomerate integration

Conglomerate integration is the acquisition by one company of a company that's nowhere in the same supply chain, horizontally or vertically. The untrained eye may think that these forms of integration have no more benefit than simply the additional revenues generated by investing in another company. If you look a little bit closer, though, you can often see much, much more.

Say that a bank buys a car dealership. Many people may see this move as a simple case of diversification (for details, flip to the earlier section 'Discovering diversification'). If you examine the types of loans that the bank makes, however, you spot that the number of car loans it issues increases dramatically. This integration is conglomerate integration because the two companies aren't in the same business, but they do complement each other. The bank continues to operate normally but provides loans to the dealership it owns at lower rates than would be possible with a standard financing agreement.

Eliminating competitors

M&A is a common way for larger companies to eliminate potential competitors from the pool of smaller but quickly growing companies (and we don't mean sending them 'to swim with the fishes').

In 2007, for example, Coca Cola acquired Energy Brands, a company that produces several lines of bottled water. Coca Cola recognised the growing demand for bottled water and other non-sugar based beverages as a replacement for soda as populations around the world become more health-conscious, and so it picked one of the more promising companies in that trend and bought it. Coca Cola eliminated one of its competitors by purchasing it, while also diversifying its product portfolio with a product competing with its primary line of products.

Seeking manager compensation

Although not exactly the most financially sound motivation, or the most honest, compensation packages have been a primary motivation for far more than one case of M&A. Instead of making the best decision for the companies involved, these actions are taken by individuals seeking self-benefit, such as the following:

- ✔ Getting bonuses for short-term performance manipulation.
- ✔ Receiving *golden parachutes* (huge benefits that top executives receive when the company is taken over by another company and the executive leaves the company being taken over).
- ✔ Manipulating *greenmail circumstances* (purchasing enough shares to threaten a takeover so that the company buys them back at a higher value).

Yes, it stinks, but such motives are unfortunately around.

M&A is a big deal, even for large companies, and a lot of money gets shifted around very quickly during M&A deals. As a result of the deals themselves and the short-term aftermath, frequently executives are in a position of personally making a huge amount of money. We don't entirely blame them; who can't stand to benefit from an extra two or three digits on their salary? Of course, this extra income is usually at the cost of the long-term financial health of the company; but, rightly or wrongly, income is often a primary motivator in decisions to participate in M&A, or at least the decision to start looking for M&A partners.

Gaining synergies

The world is increasingly seeing M&A based on operations between companies that match well, but not for the usual supply chain or competitive reasons. A lot of these integrations focus on the philosophy of 'one person's rubbish is another's treasure', all designed, of course, to cut costs and generate revenues between both firms.

For example, more integration between manufacturing firms and energy companies is occurring whereby the heat or smoke from a processing plant that normally gets disbursed into the air is used to produce electricity and sold back to the utility companies. Similarly, transportation infrastructure companies that specialise in bridges are partnering with wind-farm energy companies to incorporate turbines into their designs.

Measuring What a Business Is Worth to You

Imagine that you find a company with which you want to dance the M&A mambo. You know exactly what benefits you hope to gain from the integration of operations, you're confident in your financial projections for the return on investment, you pick the best company with whom to integrate and you even know the type of M&A in which you want to participate. So, you give the CEO a call and say that you're ready to buy. The first question the CEO asks you, besides whether or not you're crazy (no-one rings up a CEO and asks for a merger), is how much you're willing to offer! Uh oh. Now what?

Assessing a price

Walk down any street in your own industrial or commercial districts (areas with a lot of industrial estates rather than homes) and look at the buildings. Do you see a price tag for the sale of any businesses? Of course not; that would be silly. Businesses often don't advertise that they're for sale and at what price. These transactions are handled through careful financial valuations, usually done separately by both parties who then meet to negotiate price.

For companies, this transaction almost always includes a shareholder vote as well. The shareholders have the right to reject the acquisition or, if they don't want to turn it down outright, voice their concern about pricing so that the price can be renegotiated. Often, the price is set as a proportion exchange in shares, the purchase price of a controlling interest in the equity at an agreed-upon price per share, the exchange of assets or liabilities, or simply an outright purchase.

Exactly how companies assess the price they're willing to pay for an acquisition is extremely involved. The purchase isn't expensive in the same way that paying £100 for a pair of shoes is expensive; this is far, far, far more money. So, unsurprisingly, when you're dealing with millions or billions of pounds, companies tend to be meticulous in their financial evaluations of value and price. Typically, they use several methods to compare, evaluate and compare again the purchase price of a company, and then they develop some average or estimate using a combination of those evaluation methods.

The truth is, though, that each individual method isn't all that difficult. The tricky part is trusting whether or not you're correct. If you have *differentials* (variations that occur according to circumstances) in the estimated price between the different methods you've used, you need to determine why that differential exists and what price to use.

Choosing an evaluation method

The methods used to evaluate prices for an M&A depend a lot on the type of M&A. For factoring (see the earlier section 'Considering other forms of integration'), it's almost exclusively a discounted price of the book value on future cash flows. In other words, if the future cash flows are worth £100 in nominal value, the price of purchase is likely to be around £85 to account for the time value of money and credit risk.

Partnerships and joint ventures don't really have a purchase price; instead, the businesses tend to come to an agreement regarding the amount of investment, types of investment and relative proportion share of the income earned. For example, if both companies are contributing 50 per cent of the investment, they each probably earn 50 per cent of the income generated from the venture.

The deals tend to get a little more complicated, however, when one company is investing *intangible assets* (things you can't touch) such as expertise, but then the market value of consulting or outsourcing that expertise or the market value of wages for hiring a similar position are all common measures of the contribution of such intangible assets. Even for buyouts and hostile takeovers (see the earlier sections 'Taking control: Buyouts' and 'Considering other forms of integration', respectively), often the analysis is no more complex than that used for investing in the shares of these companies using the investor equations we discuss in Chapters 7 and 8. The book value of the company, the market value or combinations thereof are used in conjunction with these calculations in order to determine whether the company is over- or underpriced as regards what that company is asking for as payment in the acquisition.

The other forms of valuations, the ones really worth discussing in detail, are the mergers and the acquisitions. How does one company place a value on another company in these cases? Typically, professional reports developed by M&A firms are extremely detailed, assessing every aspect of the business. These reports are always done from the perspective of the acquiring company because the benefits that are generated for such a firm are indefinite, whereas the sale price is a one-off transaction (potentially broken up into several payments).

For this reason, companies often pay something called a *control premium* – an amount paid for a company that's more than the actual value of the company. This payment is made when the acquiring firm believes that it can generate more value from the acquired company than the acquired company is currently able to produce on its own. For example, a company may be worth £1 million, but the acquiring company feels that it can make that company more successful by using economies of scope (flick to the earlier 'Enjoying economies of scope' section for details), and so it's willing to pay £1.25 million instead, expecting to generate positive returns on investment beginning in five years and continuing each year indefinitely. Sounds like a good plan, but how did they work that out?

Balancing book and market value

The easiest method of evaluating a company's value is comparing its book value and its market value. You find the book value in the balance sheet and it's just the total value of all the firm's assets minus the value of intangible assets and liabilities: the sum of all the physical assets the company owns less the debt it holds. That number tells you what you can receive for that company if you just decide to sell it, based on the total amount paid by the company for its assets (which can be optimistically high if the company is doing poorly, or pessimistically low if the company has a lot of future potential for earnings). Of course, most M&A isn't motivated by this intention.

Next, you compare book value to the market value of the business – that is, the total number of shares it has issued multiplied by the market price per share. If nothing else, the result tells you what market sentiment is for this company, as well as what you can make from selling its assets in a worst-case scenario.

Comparing with other companies

Another method is simply to compare the company in question to the sale price of other comparable companies. Even if, as is likely, no other companies perfectly match for such a comparison, this analysis still provides valuable information. Just as when you're buying a house and you want a baseline value to compare one house to another, working out what companies of the same relative size are worth tells you how much over or under the average company in question is selling for.

In addition, working out how much companies in the same industry, but of different size, are worth helps provide valuable information of market expectations of price relative to their size, industry, earnings or similar evaluations.

Using cash flow

Another method of evaluating a company is the cash-flow approach, and it's a little trickier. With the use of historical data and sales projections for the next several years, you can determine the future cash flows for the company. Using the present value of future cash flows, the company can estimate exactly how much money it'll generate from the business.

This evaluation becomes so tricky because the company also has to consider how cash flows are going to change under the ownership of the company. What is the nature of the changes, and how are they going to influence costs, revenues and profits? If you can determine this information within a reasonable range, estimating the value of the company becomes easier. If nothing else, you discover how long you're going to take to start generating a positive return on investment, if at all. Are you going to have to wait 100 years? Is the price set so high that you'll never generate a return? Price negotiations for M&A frequently measure price in years rather than in pounds, which may sound strange to some but it's done this way because taking account of the time value of money (known as the *net present value*, which we talk about in Chapter 10) gives an indication of how long it will take to generate a return (or determine the *payback period,* which we also talk about in Chapter 10).

Measuring market share

Larger organisations may also use measures of market share to evaluate companies. This method still eventually comes down to what that market share is worth, how much additional revenues can be generated using that market share and the ability to expand on the newly acquired share. But particularly for highly competitive industries, such as the mobile phone sector, the value of market share can be high. If you're dealing with sky-high brand loyalty, say the competition between Vodafone and Orange, taking market share can be like digging through concrete using a plastic spoon.

Looking at other aspects

Price isn't just set by valuation, however. The amount that the acquiring company can afford plays a big role. It's not simply about what value the firm can extract out of the other company if it simply can't afford the high price. The company being acquired must also be convinced that the price is fair, because if it's too low it has little incentive to agree to M&A. This consideration is more a matter of the company's own asset availability than valuation, but it still plays a significant role in price-setting negotiations.

A number of other methods are also used to value a business, such as the P/E ratio, which we discuss in Chapter 8, and Asset Based Valuation, which relies on knowing the value of a business's assets and what its outstanding liabilities are.

Financing M&A

Like all investments, the method of payment plays a highly significant role in whether or not making that investment at all is feasible. A number of methods are available to pay for M&A, each with its own pros and cons.

- ✔ **Cash:** Cash is great. It's cheap compared to other methods, is an instant transaction and is mess-free (meaning that when it's done, you don't have to mess with the transaction again). The problem is that you're not talking about a small amount of cash. These sums are typically huge and not always available. Not many companies, much less individuals, carry around millions or billions in an easily accessible bank account.

- ✔ **Debt:** Debt is expensive. If you're taking out a loan or making payments over a longer period of time to the old owners, the chances are that you're paying interest. Doing so increases the cost of the purchase significantly, which you need to take into consideration during the pricing process. The positive part is that debt is relatively easy to come by and is more flexible than cash as regards repayment plans.

Here's a look at debt from the purchaser's perspective. For companies that are in a lot of financial distress, agreeing to accept the debt that the company has incurred is also an issue that can be accounted for in the price. If a company is worth £100 but owes £200 in debt, agreeing to accept that debt certainly lowers or potentially eliminates the price of the purchase.

✓ **Equity:** Having an Initial Public Offering (IPO) to afford M&A isn't entirely unheard of. It has the same benefits and drawbacks as having an IPO for any other reason (refer to Chapter 3), though with less investor backlash. Having an IPO just for fun tends to make investors believe that the share price is overvalued and causes the market price to drop, making the IPO generate fewer funds and depreciating the value of existing shares. But if it's done in conjunction with M&A, often investors are more forgiving or even excited about the prospect, increasing the value of the IPO and existing shares – not a bad option if your shareholding can handle the extra shares in issue (in other words, your shareholding isn't diluted too much).

You can also buy a company by swapping shares. The shareholders agree to give up their shares in exchange for a set number of the acquiring company's shares. For example, shareholders of Company A may receive 1.5 shares from the acquiring company for every 1 share they hold of the acquired company. This transition of ownership in shares is quite common for mergers.

Part VI

The Part of Tens

To get to grips with ten key points about Islamic finance, head online to www.dummies.com/extras/corporatefinanceuk for a bonus Part of Tens chapter.

In this part . . .

✔ Spread your wings (and expand your potential) and dive into the diverse and ever-changing world of international finance.

✔ Attempt to understand people better by looking at their actions and reactions, in order to understand why they make the particular decisions they do and to appreciate the roles that different types of behaviour play in financial decision making.

Chapter 21

Ten Things You Need to Know about International Finance

In This Chapter

▶ Getting familiar with international currency

▶ Considering the opportunities and risks of international investments

▶ Sourcing capital and distributing products globally

. . . .

*T*he world is extremely large, and the people within it vary quite a bit from each other. Although this diversity makes the world a fascinating place, these differences do cause some unique circumstances in corporate finance that you need to understand, anticipate and use to your benefit in order for a company to remain competitive.

As advances in global communication, information and transportation occur, simply remaining domestically-minded is no longer sufficient, because 'sticking your head in the sand' does nothing more than blind you to the manner in which businesses around the world are already influencing your own company and your own life. This chapter discusses some of those things that are uniquely related to international finance.

Understanding that Trade Imbalances Don't Exist

When you visit an electronics outlet to buy a computer, you give the shop assistant money and, in return, the store gives you ownership of a laptop. At no point in this exchange do you or the store have a trade imbalance, because the value of goods and money being exchanged are equal. The shop, having given a thing of value to you, is now in possession of a piece of paper that represents the value of debt that society owes it in the form of goods and services. (Money is meaningless except as a measure of how many goods and services are owed.) The shop holds onto the money you gave it for a while and then uses it to purchase goods and services.

National trade works in a similar way. Nations keep track of all the trades they make in their balance of payments, with the two primary accounts being as follows:

- **Current account:** Measures the amount of consumable goods entering or leaving a country. (The current account is what people are talking about when they discuss trade deficits and surpluses.) These goods may include food, cars, machinery, customer service, employment or anything else being purchased. A *current account deficit* means that a nation imports more goods than it exports and a *current account surplus* indicates that a nation exports more goods than it imports.

- **Capital account:** Consists of investments one nation makes in another nation's economy, such as the value of new business start-ups, the value of stocks, shares and bond purchases, and even the transfer of money related to imports and exports. So when Nation A exports goods to Nation B, it does so with the expectation that it will later trade the currency Nation B gives it for a greater amount of resources than Nation B gave it this time. In other words, the whole process of exporting is an investment.

  Here's a more personal example: if a person tries to buy something from you using a type of money that you can't spend or convert into a useable type of money, would you still sell to that person? Of course not.

An increase in one of these accounts always results in a decrease in the other. So when a nation has a current account deficit, it also has a capital account surplus.

A nation can sustain a current account deficit as long as the people of other nations are confident that they'll be able to use the currency they receive for their exports to purchase other goods and services from the importing nation or other nations interested in the importing nation's currency.

The real issue is whether or not the value of the nation's exports are going to increase over time relative to the value of its imports. In other words, a nation wants to know whether all the money it's spending will boost the total value of its productivity in a manner that allows it to meet its export obligations later (because other nations now hold its currency) while still maintaining enough production to meet domestic demand, and whether companies are treating imports as capital investments (hence, a capital account surplus) or mere consumption. Take a look at the nearby sidebar 'Cheap labour and the US trade deficit' to see what we mean.

Cheap labour and the US trade deficit

At the time of writing this book, the United States has the largest current account deficit and the largest capital account surplus in the world. China is in the opposite position with the largest current account surplus and the largest capital account deficit. (Current and capital accounts are very nearly exact opposites of each other.) In the US, many people are afraid that their country is buying too much from China, but what they don't understand is that it's buying things from China for very little US currency.

In 2007, a deep recession hit the US and much of Europe (the UK is taking much longer to get over it than originally hoped), causing prices to go down because people were unable to afford them. During that same period, China was virtually untouched by the recession, and people bought up more of its products because China kept the exchange rate low. As a result, prices in China increased along with wages (a process called *inflation*).

If wages and prices in China continue to increase faster than in the US, China will eventually be purchasing from the US by using its huge US currency reserves and a large middle class with tendencies to spend the majority of its earnings (due to its newfound ability to pursue previously unavailable comfort goods). At the point where neither nation can achieve the benefits of cheap labour and resources, they'll trade with each other based on their relative advantages (the things each can produce more efficiently and, as a result, more cheaply than the other) rather than simply on low income. The process by which this occurs between trade partners is called *factor price equalisation*.

Revealing that Purchasing Power Is Different to Exchange Rate

The *purchasing power* of a nation's currency refers to that nation's ability to purchase goods. Usually purchasing power is measured using a list of necessities, such as certain groceries, utilities and other requirements for daily life, but for simplicity's sake assume that purchasing power is measured in beer. (Economists are fond of using beer as an example; can't imagine why.) Purchasing power by itself doesn't really mean anything, but when used to track changes over time, it helps measure inflation. For example, if the price of beer goes up from £100 per keg to £101 in a year, the nation experiences 1 per cent inflation that year.

Purchasing power also comes into play when you're comparing the ability of your money to buy something in your home country and the ability of a foreign currency to buy the same something in the foreign nation. This comparison is called *purchasing power parity* (PPP). For example, if £100 buys a keg of beer in the UK, but that exact same keg of beer bought in the US costs $124, the PPP of the dollar in the States to the pound in the UK is £100 = $124 (£1 = $1.24).

Probably the most famous way of measuring PPP is by using the Big Mac Index (published in *The Economist*). If you're thinking that it sounds like a burger, you're right! The Index does indeed use the price of a McDonalds' Big Mac in every nation to determine PPP.

Exchange rate, on the other hand, refers to how much foreign money you can buy with your money. At the time of writing, £1 gets you $1.55 in the US. Note that the exchange rate is different from the PPP. If a nation has a very low exchange rate (so that you can buy a lot of its money cheaply), but the PPP in that nation is higher than your country's PPP, the two measurements tend to balance each other out as far as exports go. For instance, if the US has a purchasing power 1 per cent higher than the UK and an exchange rate 1 per cent lower than the UK, US prices would be the same as UK prices for any UK sterling that you exchange into dollars.

Examining Eurobonds (which Aren't Necessarily from Europe)

The term *Eurobonds* refers to bonds in one nation that are denominated in another nation's currency. So a Japanese-currency bond owned in Canada and subject to Canadian interest rates is a type of Eurobond even though it has nothing to do with Europe. (Specifically, this particular bond is called a *Euroyen bond,* because it's a Eurobond denominated in the Japanese yen.)

Eurobonds have the same basic function as a traditional bond in a given nation, but they incorporate elements of other nations in that they're denominated in a foreign currency. People like Eurobonds because, although they don't typically pay better interest rates than other bonds, they do allow investors to earn money on fluctuations in exchange rates as well as on interest.

Pretend for a moment that you're a college student in the UK with £10,000 to invest (hey, we told you this was pretend). You can earn 5 per cent on a traditional treasury bond, or you can earn 5 per cent on a US dollar Eurobond plus any speculative earnings that you make if the dollar increases in value compared to the UK pound. If the exchange rate changes so that the dollar is 1 per cent more valuable than it was before you invested, you make 6 per cent on a 5 per cent bond.

Of course, you're also taking a big risk because the exchange rate fluctuation can just as easily go the other way, as well as the fact that you'll be charged to get your money back into your domestic currency. See Part IV for details on risk management and its role in corporate finance.

Sorting the Muddled Relationship of Interest and Exchange Rates

Particularly if you manage a multi-national company, anticipating fluctuations in exchange rates can be an extremely important part of your company's financial management success. So what influences exchange rates?

The *International Fisher Effect* (IFE; an hypothesis in international finance) says that for every 1 per cent variation that a nation has in its *nominal interest rates* (that is, interest rates before adjustments are made for inflation) over another nation, the currency of that nation experiences a 1 per cent decrease in exchange rate via inflationary pressures associated with increased interest, increased consumption and investment speculation. For example, if the UK has an interest rate of 10 per cent and Germany has an interest rate of 11 per cent, according to the IFE the exchange rate of the Euro drops by 1 per cent relative to the UK pound. This drop occurs because the United Kingdom's relatively lower interest rates stimulate consumption and capital investment in the nation, causing inflationary pressure to depreciate the value of the currency to foreign investors and foreign traders.

That being said, the IFE is more of a 'jumping-off point' intended to prove a point, and more elaborate models based on it have improved accuracy and usefulness. The IFE tends to hold true only in *cluster formation* (that is, small groups or bunches) soon after the interest rate differential occurs, because a change in interest rates happens only once whereas exchange rates are in a continuing state of fluctuation, and so you end up seeing a J curve when you graph the two rates. (With the *J curve,* the exchange rate drops at first before rising up higher than the original point, forming a J shape when graphed.) This pattern occurs as the exchange rate goes down at first but then goes back up as the lower exchange rate and devalued currency causes a nation's exports to be relatively cheaper for people in other nations, attracting more trade in the long run.

In addition, many large nations, such as the US, have very stable economies. US treasury bills, for instance, are considered 'risk-free' investments, and US treasury bonds are considered to be extremely low risk, except in that interest rates may fluctuate, causing the future value of a low-interest bond to decrease. Even during record government debt, the US Government can still issue bills and bonds that yield next to 0 per cent interest without too much trouble, because when interest rates rise the broad market infrastructure and openness to foreign investors maintains high levels of capital investment. On the other hand, some nations with smaller or more volatile economies lose a significant number of investors with lower interest rates, because investors don't want the additional risk without higher returns. Plus, such nations typically don't have stable capital investments.

In essence, the IFE allows companies to forecast changes in exchange rates and international markets using current interest rate differentials, but they may have to play about with the maths to make their forecasts accurate enough to be really useful.

Spotting the Spot Rate and Other Currency Transactions

A number of things influence exchange rates, but in the end, how are exchange rates decided when a floating currency is involved? The process actually works a lot like buying shares. The organisations that have foreign currency and are willing to sell it for domestic currency (or another foreign currency) tell people how much of the domestic currency they want to receive for their foreign currency (called the *ask price*). For example, the organisations may ask for 1.5 of the domestic currency for every 1 of their foreign currency.

When people want to buy that foreign currency, the amount they're willing to pay for it is called the *bid price.* For example, a person may bid 1.3 of the domestic currency for every 1 of the foreign currency. The difference between the ask price and the bid price is called the *spread,* and no exchange can take place until buyer or seller (sometimes both) compromises on the final transaction price.

The price that's agreed upon in this type of transaction is called the *spot rate,* because it's the exchange rate that occurred right there on the spot. The majority of all foreign exchanges in which individuals participate are spot exchanges. For example, in all major international airports, you can exchange money in foreign exchange booths, where you get the spot rate of exchange. Because individual people don't exchange enough to influence the exchange rate, you're pretty much at the mercy of whatever price the booth is asking for the currency you want.

Even though the airport exchange broker rips you off after charging brokerage rates plus the exchange spread, as an individual you're not dealing with a vast amount of money. So you're not risking much of a loss even if the exchange rate of the currency you buy drops suddenly, making your purchase worth much less than when you paid for it.

International companies and institutional investors, on the other hand, have quite a bit to be worried about. When these organisations exchange currency, they often do so in very large quantities.

To mitigate risk or (all too often) to generate more income by speculating on the exchange, professionals rely on other types of exchanges than the spot transaction. Most of these exchanges are similar to the other risk management transactions that we describe in Chapter 13. Here's a quick look at some of them:

- **Currency swaps:** These exchanges occur when two organisations agree to exchange currency with each other and then exchange back at a later date, typically at the same rate. This arrangement allows each organisa-tion to have some foreign currency on hand for temporary use without foreign exchange risk. When available, swaps are extremely effective at mitigating risk.

- **Future and forward transactions:** These exchanges are contracted to take place in the future at a price agreed upon immediately, giving a guaranteed transaction rate regardless of what happens to the market rate between the contract signing and the delivery date. The difference between forward transactions and future transactions (sometimes called *futures*) is primarily that futures are standardised contracts that are traded in a similar way to stocks and shares, whereas forward transac-tions are individually customised between the parties of the transaction.

- **Options contracts:** Some companies prefer to purchase options contracts, which give them the option to buy or sell a currency at a specific rate but doesn't oblige them to do so.

Diversifying Can't Completely Eliminate Risk Exposure

Diversifying your investments means buying stocks and shares in several dif-ferent companies. In an ideal world, if one of those companies does poorly the others mitigate your losses. But even this strategy can't eliminate *systematic risk* (from the fact that any given nation's market constantly jumps around in different directions). For instance, if you were to buy up all the same shares in the FTSE 100, the value of your portfolio increases and decreases exactly the same as the overall FTSE 100. Despite diversifying your portfolio, you're still vulnerable to systematic risk.

For this reason, some investors look to other nations to mitigate risk. After all, on many occasions one nation's markets are crashing while another's economy is booming. For example, if you owned shares in only US companies at the end of 2007, you'd have lost quite a bit because the value of pretty much all US shares crashed. If, on the other hand, you held investments in China as well, the amount of your portfolio's total value that was lost wouldn't have been nearly as large, because China's equities didn't crash in 2007 like most of the Western world.

Investing internationally, however, has its own inherent risks not otherwise found in traditional equity investing. Here are just a few of them:

- **Foreign exchange risk:** Foreign equities are denominated in the currency of their nation, and so even when the value of your equity stays the same, if the exchange rate drops your investment is worth less to you.

- **Foreign regulations:** These regulations may restrict you from taking your money out of the country.

- **Political instability:** The government may fall apart altogether after a rebel coup. (A lot of US investments in Cuba were seized and lost during the Cuban Revolution.) Or a nation in which you have investments may have culturally engrained nepotism or corruption within executive management that results in poor competitiveness.

As with any investment or serious business venture, when you're diversifying your investments internationally, you absolutely must do your research on the risks so that you continue to stay knowledgeable of any changes. But even though you can mitigate quite a bit of systematic risk by diversifying internationally, inevitably you take on a degree of unsystematic global risk at the same time: it's a trade-off.

Cross-Listing Allows Companies to Tap the World's Resources

As companies reach out in search of capital to fund start-ups and expansion, they often look beyond their own borders for investors and lenders. Here are the three main reasons why:

- Domestic availability of capital is limited and can be relatively homogeneous.

- Issuing bonds abroad increases a company's access to the number and types of lenders interested, reducing the amount of interest the company has to pay to attract investors.

✔ Issuing shares abroad increases a company's access to investors, increasing the amount of capital raised in share issues for a given expected rate of return for the estimated corporate risk.

In other words, companies look to international investors in order to raise more money at cheaper rates.

Companies usually start by sourcing capital from their domestic markets. From there, they often move to sourcing capital internationally by issuing foreign bonds, which work a lot like regular financial bonds. With a little added sophistication, companies can choose to issue Eurobonds to raise their domestic currency in a global market (check out the earlier section 'Examining Eurobonds (which Aren't Necessarily from Europe)' for more on these bonds).

If a company wants to issue equity internationally, the best method of attracting the attention of investors is usually to list equity on a foreign exchange. Doing so doesn't issue new shares in the other country but allows people from that nation to purchase shares in secondary transactions (which can still raise capital for the company if it holds any treasury shares). This process of having shares listed in more than one equity market is called *cross-listing,* and it allows foreign investors to purchase a company's shares in a number of ways, including the following:

✔ **Depository receipts:** These receipts are traded like equity but are in fact representative of the equity held by another organisation. They allow foreigners to invest without giving them direct foreign ownership.

✔ **Global registered shares:** These traditional shares of equity can be traded on multiple markets worldwide rather than a single equity market.

If a company already cross-lists or feels that it's large enough to attract investors, it can issue equity in multiple countries simultaneously during an initial public offering.

As with all international operations, sourcing capital globally comes with some additional risks that increase the costs of capital to some extent. For instance, companies often have to cover agency costs associated with staying within foreign financial accounting and reporting standards. Plus, foreign exchange risk usually becomes an issue when companies deal with bonds or equity denominated in foreign currencies, and you can't rule out the potential for additional risk whenever politics (and two or more governments) are involved (flip to the later section 'Complicating Your Life with Politics').

The central question is whether these risks result in costs that are greater than the original benefits of sourcing internationally. In general, when raising funds internationally, companies need to try to source capital from low-risk nations with greater potential to provide cheap and plentiful access to investors and avoid listing in nations that hold little benefit but high-cost requirements or other forms of risk.

Outsourcing as a Taxing Issue

The decision to *outsource* (or transfer certain operations to an outside company) is a financial one that many companies have to deal with at some point. Basically, a company has to decide whether another company can perform one or more of its operations comparably and more cheaply than it currently performs them. The risks associated with outsourcing translate into potential costs, but as long as the amount the company saves by outsourcing the operation exceeds the expected costs associated with risk, outsourcing makes sense.

To decide whether outsourcing is right for your company, you can use a practice known as *transfer pricing,* in which each function of the company essentially 'purchases' and 'sells' to the other functions in the company.

As an example, imagine a UK motor-vehicle manufacturing plant in which all the functions of building a car occur in the same plant. One of the functions is to put tyres on each car. So the tyre-installation function of the plant purchases each car, finished up until the point of adding tyres, from the function before it. When that function finishes installing the tyres, it sells the car with its tyres installed to the next function in the process at an established profit margin. The plant's overhead costs are attributed to each function in the proportion that the particular function uses them.

Companies go to all this trouble – treating every function of their operations as independent customers and sellers to each other – because doing so allows them to determine whether they have competitive pricing in each of their functions. For example if, through transfer pricing, the UK company discovers that an overseas firm is capable of selling cars with tyres on them cheaper than the UK company can do itself, even including the cost of shipping, that company may decide to outsource the tyre-installation function. It ships the cars to the foreign firm to have the tyres put on, and then that overseas company ships the cars with tyres back to the UK company for the next phase of production.

Transfer pricing is pretty standard in the form of accounting called *activity-based costing,* but many companies prefer to use other accounting methods and rely on this form of analysis only when considering outsourcing.

Although outsourcing sounds like a win–win situation in the preceding example, it often comes with additional costs. Here are a couple of the big ones:

✔ **In international finance, outsourcing any function overseas requires the transfer of assets over international boundaries.** This can mean a company having to forgo assets, because sometimes outsourcing requires a company to export or import an item, or (in the case of customer service or accounting) to transfer funds to pay the other company. If the other company is providing goods or services to the end user, outsourcing may also require bringing funds back to the parent company.

✔ **Outsourcing to another country involves taxation for companies and governments.** Companies have to pay tariffs on goods they send to another country, and then they have to pay more tariffs on those goods when they receive them back again. These costs can add up very quickly, discouraging outsourcing and trade.

In order to ease the burden on companies some nations set up trade agreements that allow for reduced or eliminated taxation on the transition of goods across national borders. Others allow tax-free capital movement under certain circumstances. For example, free-trade zones in China allow businesses to send goods to China, tax-free, for the purpose of altering those goods and then re-exporting them. So if the car company from the preceding example is from the UK and sends its cars to China for tyre installation, it pays taxes only on the cars sold to customers in China. At the same time, the UK car manufacturer has to pay import taxes only on the value of the work done in China, not the value of the entire car.

Not all nations are as sensitive as China to the needs of businesses. Some nations even go so far as to limit or prohibit any money from leaving the country. In these cases, companies have to manage their capital movement carefully to make outsourcing work for them. For instance, they can choose to acquire resources from within the foreign nation and send the resources back to their headquarters in their own country, allowing them to allocate their foreign earned income as costs instead of attempting to transfer the money itself at high tax rates or even illegally. If these transfers occur between related companies (for example, subsidiary and parent), they can even alter the total amount that they're taxed on their earnings by transferring assets to countries with low tax rates.

Complicating Your Life with Politics

Governments and politicians seem to have an uncanny way of knowing exactly how to make your life as complicated as possible. When you're dealing with international finance, you have to be aware of not only your own nation's international policies, but also the policies of at least one other nation, plus how each nation involved interacts with the others. (It's all really rather annoying sometimes, except when you make your living in international finance or by writing finance books.)

Compared to companies that operate on a purely domestic level, firms that operate internationally tend to be the target of more government concern as politicians attempt to cater to the needs of individual industries or adhere to some form of national idealism. This concern may come in any number of forms, including regulations or requirements placed on foreign companies and protectionist policies put in place to restrict or hinder trade. Here are a few examples:

- **Embargoes** prohibit outright any goods from being imported at all, usually from a specific nation but sometimes broadly to specific industries. For example, businesses involved in defence, energy and telecommunications, as well as other areas critical to national infrastructure or safety, are often restricted to local companies or organisations with close ties to government officials.

- **Quotas** limit the quantity of a particular product that can be legally imported into a country.

- **Tariffs** (sometimes referred to as *duties*) are taxes on goods being imported into a nation, which make them more expensive to foreign customers. Who bears the burden of the tax depends on whether any of the companies in the supply chain are willing and able to drop their price or forfeit profitability; otherwise, the end user sees the higher prices.

These concerns are relatively common for international companies, and each one limits the potential financial performance that a company can achieve within a nation. But some governments enforce more unusual requirements as well:

- Developing nations and those with more restrictive government control may require a minimum value of investment in order to operate within the nation. For example, a nation may require an investor or company to spend at least £1 million in order to start a company or purchase equity in a company.

- Government regulations may require a company to recruit a minimum number of local nationals or maintain a minimum proportion of local nationals within the workforce. These regulations can impact workforce efficiency if meeting them requires the company to choose local nationals over those workers who may have more merit.

- Government regulations may require a company to source raw materials from local companies, which can result in cost inefficiencies.

Trading across borders

Countries often make exceptions for companies that want to work in particular industries that are intended to contribute to the development of the nation or that focus exclusively on hiring locals to produce exports.

In addition, international agreements have helped pave the way for more integration. The North American Free Trade Agreement (NAFTA) between the US, Canada and Mexico strongly

reduced the limitations to trade between these three nations. Similarly, members of the European Union have severely limited economic and political restrictions between them. The Association of Southeast Asian Nations (ASEAN) has done the same for many Southeast Asian countries as has Mercado Común del Sur (MERCOSUR) for South American nations.

The world of international politics is highly dynamic and not always completely transparent, and so international companies have to keep up with relevant regulations and maintain a level of flexibility in all their international relations.

Knowing Your Neighbours: Cultural Understanding Is Vital

Not all financial infrastructures work the same way. Culture plays a big role in how a nation's government, companies and even individual transactions operate. Therefore, when you're dealing with a company involved in international finance, you absolutely must know a bit about the nation(s) in which the company operates in order to understand the context of its overall financial position.

In many nations with a prominent Muslim presence in government, Sharia law forbids companies from lending money and then requesting more money in return above what was originally issued. As a result, throughout much of the Middle East, companies don't charge or earn interest in financial transactions, such as with loans or savings accounts. In order to account for the time value of money (where increasing inflation causes an equal amount of money to be worth less over time), companies have come up with some novel solutions, which resemble equity ownership and/or rent-to-own programmes.

As a result, when financial analysts from a Western nation analyse the finances of a bank or other financial institution in these Muslim nations, the calculations can appear very different from what they're used to seeing. This difference results from the lack of interest-bearing loans and the way that depository accounts are treated more as equity than liabilities. Without an understanding of the cultural and financial context in which a company operates, you're prone to making some serious mistakes during any assessment.

Many attempts have been made worldwide to quantify cultural variations and develop simple, standardised methods of interpreting financial information across differing systems. For instance, many nations have adopted a method of financial accounting called the *International Financial Reporting Standards* (IFRS), which was developed by the International Accounting Standards Board. IFRS is like a common language across all nations that helps them analyse the same financial reports in the same way. If you want more information about IFRS, have a read of *IFRS For Dummies* (Wiley) written by Steve Collings (you may know the name from somewhere; he's pretty good).

Even with a common financial reporting regime such as IFRS, however, culture can still influence the context in which financial transactions take place. For example, a culture in which people tend to accept higher levels of risk tends also to have higher price-to-earnings ratios, because the investors are willing to accept a higher price relative to the potential for future earnings. In contrast, a culture that tends to avoid risk may have a lower average price-to-earnings ratio. Without being aware of these differences, you can end up investing in an overvalued company or avoiding a great deal in an undervalued investment.

Companies can use the main dimensions of culture (as researched by Geert Hofstede, an influential Dutch researcher) to help them identify financial trends that may seem unusual, or even to find opportunities hidden by cultural norms unfamiliar to those outside the nation in question. These cultural dimensions include:

- **Context (or 'time horizon'):** The degree to which people generally recognise things as having inherent traits, or the set of circumstances or facts surrounding a particular event.

- **Growth versus development:** The degree to which the people of a nation generally prescribe values in growth (for example, status, wealth and power) or development (for example, quality of life and intersocial connections).

- **Individualism:** The degree to which people generally view themselves as being individuals or being a part of a group.

- **Power distance:** The amount of social and professional equality generally recognised between individuals and their authority figures.

- **Risk aversion:** The degree to which people generally avoid uncertainty.

Chapter 22

Ten Things You Need to Understand about Behavioural Finance

*T*he practice of behavioural finance developed from the need to explain how companies and the people within them behave, steering a course between the fields of finance and psychology. Broadly speaking, *behavioural finance* looks at people's actions and reactions, in order to determine how to better understand them and so make better decisions. In this chapter we give you a nod and wink towards some of the irrational and emotional decision-making to watch out for.

Anomalies in behaviour develop for good reasons, but frequently they put people in a position of lower efficiency, weaker returns or higher risk. So you need to go out of your way to study what these behaviours are and what causes them, measure their impact on financial performance and seek to use these behaviours more effectively (or at least minimise them as much as possible).

In your pursuit to be rational in your financial decisions, whether personal or corporate, don't get so bogged down doing a raft of analysis and preplanning that you become paralysed and unable to make decisions. In many situations, you can end up costing a company (or yourself) more money by waiting far too long to make decisions. In such cases, the level of detail and rationality used in your analysis becomes counter-productive. For example, to be a successful manager of finance, you have to be able to make decisions based on partial information to meet time constraints. In other words, you have to maintain a balance between being as accurate as possible and taking ages to make a decision.

Making Financial Decisions Is Rarely Entirely Rational

Studies in corporate finance make the assumption that people are rational decision-makers. In fact, most economic models, financial and otherwise, assume that people act unemotionally and with a certain degree of competence. Here's the reality, though: people are emotional, illogical, impulsive and ignorant. That's where behavioural finance comes into play. It defines what's rational, identifies the causes of irrational financial behaviour and measures the financial impact of that behaviour.

People rarely make any decisions, much less financial ones, entirely rationally. Four primary factors (other than corruption) lead people to forgo rationality in favour of some other reasoning technique:

- ✔ Lack of information
- ✔ Lack of time to collect or process the information
- ✔ Lack of ability to understand the information
- ✔ Emotional impulse

When people have a limited ability to take stock of a situation, they often use reasoning methods that rely on experience-based judgements (known as *heuristic methods*), because people generally trust experience. Maybe they rely on their 'gut instinct', an emotional response with no precisely identifiable cause, or perhaps they choose to employ some loosely applicable general 'rule'. Whatever alternative method they use, each one is subjective and, therefore, highly subject to irrationality.

Executing Sound Financial Decisions Involves Identifying Logical Fallacies

Logic can be really complicated. Common sense may get you through the day unscathed, but when you're dealing with finances, what you really want is good sense. The problem is that human brains have a tendency to try and find patterns in the world around them. Although this pattern-seeking behaviour is necessary for people to function (you assume that you won't fall into oblivion with every step you take based on the pattern that the ground stopped you from falling before), sometimes it can lead to making incorrect conclusions. When you rely on faulty logic, you're relying on a *fallacy*.

Logical fallacies can be based on flawed logic structure, distractions, emotional responses or any number of other factors that use information that isn't related to the decision at hand. In finance, a fallacy can lead to a massive mistake resulting from improper judgement. For example, you may think that a company is a bad investment because the owner is a 20-year-old college dropout, but if every investor had given in to that fallacy, no one would've invested in a new company called Microsoft. Fortunately for Microsoft, its investors relied on logical decisions in which they used data in a proper manner, without letting outside sources and unrelated information interfere.

Here are two common fallacies that you may come across in corporate finance:

- ✔ **Gambler's Fallacy:** Involves irrationally measuring the probability of an outcome. Imagine that you bought some shares in a company and the share price is spiralling downwards. Instead of selling those shares and investing in something else, you hold onto them because you keep thinking that the share price has to go up eventually, that statistically it can't go down every single day. That's naive thinking. Even assuming an equal probability of increase or decrease in value – that each new day brings a 50 per cent chance that the company's share price will increase – isn't accurate, because a poorly performing company has a greater probability of decreasing in value.

- ✔ **Sunk Cost Fallacy (or 'money pit'):** Refers to the idea that a company (or individual) has already put so much money or effort into a project that it has to continue to pursue it at any additional cost. The fallacy is in value assessment and tends to be highly emotionally charged. In investing, it's called the *disposition effect,* which is when investors are more willing to accept gains than losses and end up owning poorly performing shares in a company because they think that the share price is going to go back up eventually.

  To see this fallacy in action, imagine that you're an entrepreneur and you start a company that sells CDs on the high street against all advice not to do so: such companies are going down the pan because too few people are buying CDs. Needless to say, the company does terribly, and so you continue to pump money into advertising to try to get sales up. You've put so much money into the start-up costs (now considered *sunk costs* because you can't recover them), and you refuse to accept that investing in this company was a bad idea. Even though the original costs may be sunk already, continuing to put money into the poorly performing company is just making things worse for you.

Getting Emotional about Financial Decisions Can Leave You Crying

Your personal financial decisions can be some of the most emotionally charged decisions you make in your life, which is why many people prefer to let professionals handle their money. They believe that professionals with no personal attachment to their money are better placed to make rational decisions.

The world of corporate finance is similar in that people are typically dealing with someone else's (the company's) money, and so you may think that emotions run low in corporate finance. But that's not always the case. Even though they don't realise it, people working in corporate finance sometimes let their emotions influence their decisions, at least to some extent.

Consider this real-life example: when England won the world cup in 1966, UK share prices jumped significantly. Winning the world cup had absolutely nothing to do with the value of these companies, and yet the value of their shares jumped. Why? Because the mood people are in when making financial decisions influences the decisions they make. When people hear good news, they're prone to accepting additional risk in their investments. When people receive bad news, they tend to be more wary and avoid risk as much as possible (assuming that they're not prone to extreme acts of self-destructive behaviour that would lead them to do something crazy).

No matter how far removed you are from the person who owns the money you're working with, when you're forced to make a decision your mood and emotions influence that decision to some extent. Although this doesn't change your entire financial strategy (only those with extreme emotional volatility allow an emotional state to dictate their major decisions), when your mood influences your willingness to deviate from rationality, financial inefficiencies do occur, resulting in increased costs or decreased income. In a single incident, this deviation from rationality may not be entirely damaging, but as more and more people in a company are influenced in this way or a single person is continuously influenced, over time the company can face significant decreases in total financial effectiveness.

Stampeding in Finance Can Get You Trampled

Investors have a tendency to get caught up in a stampede of other investors, believing that they're running like the bulls in the stock exchange when, in reality, they're just mice jumping off a cliff. As soon as some trend starts to occur, investors follow it as quickly as possible, often without even fully understanding why. All they know is that they don't want to miss out on something big.

Like other forms of behavioural anomaly, this stampeding scenario is influenced by the imperfect distribution of information. In other words, not everyone receives all the same information at the same time. So when someone sees an individual or group, particularly one that has developed some form of credibility in the person's mind, participating confidently in a transaction that seems unusual, that person is likely to wonder if the individual or group knows something she doesn't. The person may even know that an investment isn't worth what people are paying for it, and yet she happily pays the same price because the investment has already increased in value so much that she starts to question her original opinion.

You need just two situations to create this stampeding scenario:

- ✔ Someone deciding whether the return on a purchase or investment is worth the cost plus risk.
- ✔ At least one other person who decides that the return is worth the risk (leading the first person to question the second person's judgement).

When these two things are in place, you have a behavioural time-bomb of poor financial judgement. This sort of situation is what often leads to bank insolvency, where customers withdraw all their money after losing confidence in the banks (such as what happened in Cyprus). It also leads to investment bubbles, where a category of investments is highly overvalued when people overestimate how far above book value per share a company can sustain its share price using earnings, driven by other investors' confidence in the shares. This situation occurred extremely frequently during the dot com bubble in the 1990s, where many investors lost lots of money when Internet companies crashed.

Letting Relationships Influence Finances Can Be Dangerous

The idea that the people you know are more important than what you know carries weight all over the world. In Chinese it's called *guanxi,* in Arabic it's called *wasta* and in Russian it's *blat,* but it all means the same thing: showing favouritism based on personal relationships rather than merit or qualifications. This form of favouritism is called *cronyism* (or *nepotism* when you're dealing with relatives).

Here's how cronyism works. You're in charge of something at your company, and you make decisions to spend money on goods and services based on the personal relationships you have with people instead of their merit compared to those competing with them.

Maybe you're in charge of recruiting staff or you know someone who is, and you push for a particular person to get the job based on the fact that you know her and you want to maintain good relations with her or you think that working with her would be fun. As a result, wages are paid to an employee who has lower productivity and less potential to contribute to the company in the long run compared to other candidates.

Or maybe you purchase supplies from the company where one of your family members works, because you trust that person over someone you don't know. In this case, you end up paying more for the company's supplies by simply accepting the higher price or by not performing a full evaluation of market prices and quality.

Cronyism isn't the same as networking. Although you're attempting to do business with people you know in both cases, in *networking* you're attempting to use social opportunities to find people who can benefit your business. In cronyism, you're looking to use professional opportunities to benefit your social connections.

Preventing cronyism from occurring in a company is relatively simple at all levels of management except the highest. You just have to require individuals to use predetermined evaluation criteria when making important decisions and then hold them accountable for proper recording and analysis using those criteria. Doing so helps a company maintain a business network based on quality, price and other forms of merit instead of personal relationships, thus improving financial performance at all levels and across all departments.

Satisficing Can Optimise Your Time and Energy

Remember that old saying 'time is money'? Well, you're about to find out that people naturally apply a value to their time. This value isn't so much about money as it is about using your limited amount of time doing things you need or want to do.

As a simple example, imagine that you're spending your day off lounging around the house playing computer games, and you decide that you can't be bothered to cook dinner. So you decide to order a pizza. You could probably make something healthier, cheaper and more delicious, but you settle for something that's 'good enough' and doesn't require any additional time or effort on your part.

In corporate finance, the application and measurement of what's 'good enough' is called *satisficing*. In a more practical sense, the term refers to humans' inability to know what's truly rational.

Say that you own a veterinary surgery. When you're shopping for flea powder for your patients' dogs, you probably don't know what price every shop in the city centre charges and so you just go to whatever shop you've visited before, believing them to have prices reasonably below retail or with whom you have a working rapport. Even if that shop doesn't have enough flea powder, you probably end up buying whatever they do have available with the mindset that you can always go back out shopping when you run out.

In fact, a shop a couple of miles away has plenty and the powder is £1 cheaper per box, but you don't know that and you don't intend to run around the entire city, because the measure of time needed to collect fully all the information and the resources required to make a rational decision aren't available. In the time it took you to go back out and pick up more flea powder, you would've been better off going to the other shop, but being unaware that the other shop even has flea powder you determined that this option was good enough for your immediate needs.

You can also apply this same response to an employee who doesn't have anything else to do, and so financially her time is theoretically worthless. Yet this person places a certain value on her time so that she'd rather be doing something other than working out what the flea-powder market looks like.

In these examples, satisficing behaviour causes people to make less-than-optimal decisions, but they do so based on the decision that their time's worth more than the potential benefits. As with all financial decisions, satisficing comes with a degree of uncertainty and risk, and so the results can be good or bad. Therefore, we aren't saying that satisficing itself is good or bad, just that you need to recognise that it happens and in certain cases it may need addressing.

Explaining Life in the Improbable: Prospect Theory

People prefer to live their lives in a fantasy: they fear what they don't understand and dream of what they (probably) can't achieve. Unsurprisingly, this same view influences people's financial decisions in a behavioural fluke described as the *prospect theory,* which basically says this:

> When making financial decisions that aren't certain (meaning that the outcomes aren't certain, but the probability of success can be estimated), people look at the potential for gain or loss instead of relying on rational thinking using the probable outcomes.

Consider medical insurance as an example of this theory in action. Insurance companies have so much data available to them that they can determine with extreme accuracy the probability of a person getting sick or hurt based on ancestry, geographical location, job, lifestyle habits and a number of other variables that they research when people apply for cover. As a result, insurance companies can also accurately estimate the amount they have to pay every year in medical benefits. They then charge a percentage over that amount to maintain profits. (In other words, people pay more for medical services every year than they're worth in the amount equal to the overhead costs and profits of the entire medical insurance industry.)

Why on Earth do people pay so much for medical insurance when they'd more than likely be better off just paying the hospital directly? Because people make decisions in the world of the improbable, thanks to the prospect theory. Insurance salesmen are trained to prey on this fact. They tell you horror stories about what may happen to you and your family if you don't have medical cover. Although a small probability does exist of you receiving more benefits from your cover than you pay, that probability is very small, as proved by the fact that insurance companies increase in profitability nearly every year. Still, people focus on that small probability of the worst-case scenario, and then they act on it.

Prospect theory has two extremes:

- ✔ **Highly cautious people who fear potential loss significantly more than they desire potential gain.** These people have a difficult time investing at all for the fear that they may lose their money. They purchase the maximum amount of insurance they can buy and are definitely not investing in the stock market.

- ✔ **Risk-takers who desire the potential gains far more than they fear the potential losses.** These people take extreme risks in the hopes of receiving a huge financial return. They're often traders, bank executives or hopeless gambling addicts.

The people who make the most rational decisions attempt to measure potential gains and losses objectively, weighted by probability. Many of them end up working as value investors or finance underwriters.

Accepting that People Are Subject to Behavioural Biases

When you're dealing with corporate finance, you rely on the collection and analysis of data to help you answer questions and make decisions. Even though all the data you need to make the best decision may be available, how you perceive and use that data can be an erroneous process thanks to the following two types of bias:

✔ **Statistical bias:** This type of bias occurs when people collect data from a sample rather than from an entire set of data and then assume that the data they collect represents the entire set of data. Say that a financial analyst wants to assess the returns on capital investment that a company is able to generate. If she takes data only from the marketing department of the company rather than from every department, her analysis is going to be biased.

✔ **Cognitive bias:** This bias occurs during the processing of information, when people choose to use their own personal judgement rather than the data results. Cognitive biases come in a variety of shapes and sizes:

- *Status quo bias* refers to the tendency of people to avoid changing established methods, such as when a team of employees refuses to implement a more efficient management accounts system just because they don't want to learn the new system.

- *Self-serving bias* refers to the tendency of people to give themselves credit for successes but blame outside factors for failure. This type of bias contributes to wrong self-assessments of investing performance.

- *Confirmation bias* refers to the tendency of people to acknowledge only data that confirms their preconceived beliefs, resulting in the rejection of factual information that challenges their beliefs. This bias can devastate a company when it leads to management ignoring their analysts or professional advisers.

 Corporate finance relies heavily on the accuracy of data and the precision of analysis. Although individuals are constantly subject to multiple types of bias, companies can reduce the rate of error due to bias by maintaining proper data collection methods and using full analyses. The key is to interpret only what actually occurs instead of letting personal judgement influence decisions.

Analysing and Presenting Information Is Fraught with Problems

How people process the data available to them is subject to behavioural errors based on the context in which the information is presented. For instance, when some expression of judgement makes its way into the presentation of data or information, that judgement influences how others analyse and understand the information.

The process of introducing your own interpretation of a subjective measure or event is called *framing.* Everything you witness is processed through a filter, called a *frame,* which is composed of everything you've come to assume about the world around you, including the behaviour of people. These frames cause you to understand and interpret things in a different manner from the people around you and, as a result, alter how you each respond.

Say that the manager of the marketing department sends you a proposal of a project and asks whether the project fits within the department's remaining budget. As you research the marketing budget, you discover that the entire budget has been drained because a marketing staff member called Geoff spent it all purchasing a jet ski for 'team building' purposes. The following two options demonstrate that how you present information greatly influences the way people react to it:

- ✔ **Scenario 1:** You tell the marketing manager that Geoff stole the funds, thus putting it in the manager's mind to press criminal charges against him.
- ✔ **Scenario 2:** You simply say that the project exceeds the remaining budget.

Both cases are likely to be true, but in Scenario 1 you assume that Geoff was stealing company money, adding an element of personal judgement and essentially planting that idea in someone's head. In Scenario 2, however, you're only presenting information likely to be considered out of the ordinary; after all, Geoff may have been told to develop a team-building outing and made a really stupid decision.

In the first scenario, Geoff's going to prison. In the second, the marketing department is likely to rework the project for lower costs until the new quarter when its budget is replenished while Geoff simply gets fired for incompetence instead of going to prison.

For another example of framing, consider the following two sentences:

- ✔ The price of Hang-ups Picture Framing Ltd's shares have plummeted 75 per cent, causing devastating losses.
- ✔ The price of Hang-ups Picture Framing Ltd's shares have plummeted 75 per cent, causing them to be a great buy!

In both cases, the price of Hang-ups' shares lost 75 per cent of their value, but the action that a person is likely to take in response to this information changes depending on how the information is presented. Even so, what really matters in this situation is whether or not the company is valuable according to the analyses, not how someone explains what happened to the share price.

Ethnocentrism is another form of framing, in which you judge the occurrences of one nation by the standards of another. For example, when an analyst from a nation of people who are culturally more comfortable taking risk analyses the shares of a company from a nation of people who are culturally averse to risk, the analyst is likely to see the company's price to earnings ratio as being extremely low for the value of the company. As a result, the analyst may think that the company is undervalued.

The problem is that the analyst is judging another nation's company based on the frame of her own ethnocentrism. Unless those shares *cross-lists* (which is where a company trades its shares on one or more foreign stock markets in addition to its own domestic stock market), the price isn't likely to increase as the analyst predicts, simply because the people of the nation where the shares are from aren't willing to take the additional risk compared to the company's future potential earnings.

 Framing can influence all sorts of financial decisions. Keep in mind that *data* is the term used for raw results and *information* is used when those raw results have been processed in some way. You have to be very careful to apply relevant contextual information along with any analysis you give and ensure that the manner in which you present information remains objective, neutral and free of judgements that contribute to framing.

Measuring Irrationality in Finance Is Rational Behavioural Finance

Understanding how irrational financial behaviour works is only half the job. You also have to determine the value of irrationality. That is to say, you need to work out how much your own inherent irrationality costs you (and your company) financially.

To see what we mean, consider how you'd measure the cost of satisficing behaviour (see the earlier section 'Satisficing Can Optimise Your Time and Energy' for details):

1. **A person goes shopping, intending to purchase ten loaves of bread:**

   • Shop A has only five loaves at £2 per loaf.

   • Store B has ten loaves at £1 per loaf.

2. **The person spends £1 in fuel each direction getting to and from Shop A, not knowing that Shop B has more loaves of bread at a cheaper price.**

   So she goes to Shop A twice, buying five loaves of bread each time.

3. The person spends £24 on bread and travel.

If she'd checked out Shop B's stocks, she would've spent only £10 for the bread, £2 for fuel plus an additional £1 for going between stores.

The cost of being lazy (sorry, we mean satisficing) in this example is £11.

Satisficing isn't the only behaviour that has a measurable influence on finance. Although some are easier to quantify than others, all behaviours are measurable, but not all necessarily have a negative influence. For instance, people who were too worried about their finances to invest in an Internet company may have saved themselves from the crash in the late 1990s, giving that behaviour a positive value. That doesn't mean that it was good behaviour, however, because it was still based on irrationality. The decisions to refrain from investing were based on an emotional response rather than a calculated determination of the level of risk, and so the decisions were just lucky and could just as easily have resulted in missing out on important investment opportunities.

After identifying the role that an individual plays in the financial world and recognising what behavioural anomalies each individual is subject to, you can make estimates on the cost of behavioural anomalies and take steps to minimise the risk that such behaviours occur. Formalising and quantifying the role of human behaviour in causing deviations from rational financial decisions is a relatively new but very important step not only to understanding but also improving upon the current financial infrastructure of organisations.

Index

• *P* •

• S •

About the Authors

Steve Collings, FMAAT FCCA is the audit and technical director at Leavitt Walmsley Associates, a firm of Chartered Certified Accountants based in Sale, Manchester in the United Kingdom. Steve trained and qualified with the firm and is also the firm's Senior Statutory Auditor. Steve qualified with the Association of Accounting Technicians in 2000 and then went on to qualify as an Associate Chartered Certified Accountant (ACCA) in 2005. In 2010 Steve became a Fellow of the Association of Chartered Certified Accountants (FCCA). Steve also holds the Diploma in IFRS from ACCA which he obtained in 2008 as well as their Certificates in IFRS and Certificates in International Standards on Auditing.

Steve specialises in financial reporting and auditing issues and has been writing professionally for several years. Steve is the author of *The Interpretation and Application of International Standards on Auditing* also published by John Wiley & Sons, Ltd. in March 2011 as well as the author of other publications on the subjects of UK accounting standards, International Financial Reporting Standards and International Standards on Auditing and the author of several articles which have been published in the various accounting media, primarily *AccountingWEB.co.uk*. Steve also lectures to professional accountants on financial reporting, auditing and Solicitors Accounts Rules. Steve won *Accounting Technician of the Year* at the British Accountancy Awards in November 2011.

Michael Taillard's other works include *Economics and Modern Warfare* (published by Palgrave Macmillan), and *101 Things Everyone Should Know About the Global Economy* (published by Adams Media). After spending several years as a university economics instructor at several locations in the United States and China, Mike decided to leave and become a freelance research experimentalist. Mike's work so far includes economic research projects for The American Red Cross, a theoretical study for the United States Strategic Command (STRATCOM), and award-winning research through a private school and tutoring company designed as a philanthropic experiment in macroeconomic cash flows as a form of urban renewal. Mike has also appeared in documentaries such as *Dead Man Working*. Mike received his PhD of financial economics and has an academic background that includes a master's degree in international finance with a dual concentration in international management, as well as a bachelor's degree in international economics.

Dedications

This book is dedicated to all my family and friends.

– Steve Collings

This book is dedicated to my family back in Michigan.

– Michael Taillard

Author's Acknowledgements

Writing a book is a project which brings with it a whole host of challenges and is certainly not a one-person project; the production of a *For Dummies* book requires the skill and expertise of an entire publishing team and this book, and my previous title, *IFRS For Dummies*, was certainly no exception. Writing the UK edition of *Corporate Finance For Dummies* has been a pleasure and therefore my most sincere thanks and gratitude goes to the Commissioning Editor, Claire Ruston, who got this project off the ground.

Every author of a book needs a strong and supporting publishing team behind them and the team behind *Corporate Finance For Dummies* have been just that. I would like to express my sincere thanks to Steve Edwards (my project editor) for all his help and advice during the writing process. Caroline Fox (my technical reviewer) has, once again, done an outstanding job on the review of the manuscript with helpful advice and guidance throughout. The other guys on the publishing team also deserve a huge thank-you from me for all their help in taking the manuscript through the editing and publishing process and turning it into the finished product.

The support I have received from family and friends – particularly when deadlines are approaching, does not go unnoticed. My thanks go to Les Leavitt, the managing partner at Leavitt Walmsley Associates for his support and enthusiasm for this (and my other) book projects and for accommodating deadlines in with the work projects.

Finally, my sincere thanks go to you, the reader, who has picked up this book. I sincerely hope you find it helpful and a good reference guide to the world of financial accounting. Make notes in the margin and keep it close to hand to guide you through any complex issues you stumble upon during your journey through the world of financial accounting.

– Steve Collings

Publisher's Acknowledgements

Project Editor: Steve Edwards

Commissioning Editor: Claire Ruston

Assistant Editor: Ben Kemble

Development Editor: Andy Finch

Copy Editor: Andy Finch

Technical Editor: Caroline Fox

Proofreader: Kerry Laundon

Production Manager: Daniel Mersey

Publisher: Miles Kendall

Cover Photos: © iStockphoto.com/zentilia

Project Coordinator: Kristie Rees

UK editions

BUSINESS

Bookkeeping For Dummies

978-1-118-34689-1

Pop Up Business For Dummies

978-1-118-44349-1

Starting & Running a Business All-in-One For Dummies

978-1-119-97527-4

MUSIC

Mandolin For Dummies

978-1-119-94276-4

Ukulele For Dummies

978-0-470-97799-6

DJing For Dummies

978-0-470-66372-1

HOBBIES

Stargazing For Dummies

978-1-118-41156-8

Keeping Chickens For Dummies

978-1-119-99417-6

Beekeeping For Dummies

978-1-119-97250-1

Asperger's Syndrome For Dummies
978-0-470-66087-4

Basic Maths For Dummies
978-1-119-97452-9

Body Language For Dummies, 2nd Edition
978-1-119-95351-7

Boosting Self-Esteem For Dummies
978-0-470-74193-1

Business Continuity For Dummies
978-1-118-32683-1

Cricket For Dummies
978-0-470-03454-5

Diabetes For Dummies, 3rd Edition
978-0-470-97711-8

eBay For Dummies, 3rd Edition
978-1-119-94122-4

English Grammar For Dummies
978-0-470-05752-0

Flirting For Dummies
978-0-470-74259-4

IBS For Dummies
978-0-470-51737-6

ITIL For Dummies
978-1-119-95013-4

Management For Dummies, 2nd Edition
978-0-470-97769-9

Managing Anxiety with CBT For Dummies
978-1-118-36606-6

Neuro-linguistic Programming For Dummies, 2nd Edition
978-0-470-66543-5

Nutrition For Dummies, 2nd Edition
978-0-470-97276-2

Organic Gardening For Dummies
978-1-119-97706-3

FOR DUMMIES®

Making Everything Easier! ™

UK editions

SELF-HELP

Cognitive Behavioural Therapy For Dummies
978-0-470-66541-1

Creative Visualization For Dummies
978-1-119-99264-6

Mindfulness For Dummies
978-0-470-66086-7

LANGUAGES

Spanish For Dummies
978-0-470-68815-1

Polish For Dummies
978-1-119-97959-3

British Sign Language For Dummies
978-0-470-69477-0

HISTORY

The Tudors For Dummies
978-0-470-68792-5

Medieval History For Dummies
978-0-470-74783-4

British History For Dummies
978-0-470-97819-1

Origami Kit For Dummies
978-0-470-75857-1

Overcoming Depression For Dummies
978-0-470-69430-5

Positive Psychology For Dummies
978-0-470-72136-0

PRINCE2 For Dummies, 2009 Edition
978-0-470-71025-8

Project Management For Dummies
978-0-470-71119-4

Psychology Statistics For Dummies
978-1-119-95287-9

Psychometric Tests For Dummies
978-0-470-75366-8

Renting Out Your Property For Dummies, 3rd Edition
978-1-119-97640-0

Rugby Union For Dummies, 3rd Edition
978-1-119-99092-5

Sage One For Dummies
978-1-119-95236-7

Self-Hypnosis For Dummies
978-0-470-66073-7

Storing and Preserving Garden Produce For Dummies
978-1-119-95156-8

Teaching English as a Foreign Language For Dummies
978-0-470-74576-2

Time Management For Dummies
978-0-470-77765-7

Training Your Brain For Dummies
978-0-470-97449-0

Voice and Speaking Skills For Dummies
978-1-119-94512-3

Work-Life Balance For Dummies
978-0-470-71380-8

Making Everything Easier!™

COMPUTER BASICS

978-1-118-11533-6

978-0-470-61454-9

Windows 7

978-0-470-49743-2

DIGITAL PHOTOGRAPHY

978-1-118-09203-3

978-0-470-76878-5

978-1-118-00472-2

SCIENCE AND MATHS

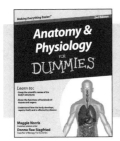

978-0-470-92326-9

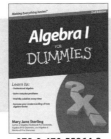

978-0-470-55964-2

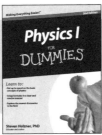

978-0-470-90324-7

Art For Dummies
978-0-7645-5104-8

Computers For Seniors For Dummies, 3rd Edition
978-1-118-11553-4

Criminology For Dummies
978-0-470-39696-4

Currency Trading For Dummies, 2nd Edition
978-0-470-01851-4

Drawing For Dummies, 2nd Edition
978-0-470-61842-4

Forensics For Dummies
978-0-7645-5580-0

French For Dummies, 2nd Edition
978-1-118-00464-7

Guitar For Dummies, 2nd Edition
978-0-7645-9904-0

Hinduism For Dummies
978-0-470-87858-3

Index Investing For Dummies
978-0-470-29406-2

Islamic Finance For Dummies
978-0-470-43069-9

Knitting For Dummies, 2nd Edition
978-0-470-28747-7

Music Theory For Dummies, 2nd Edition
978-1-118-09550-8

Office 2010 For Dummies
978-0-470-48998-7

Piano For Dummies, 2nd Edition
978-0-470-49644-2

Photoshop CS6 For Dummies
978-1-118-17457-9

Schizophrenia For Dummies
978-0-470-25927-6

WordPress For Dummies, 5th Edition
978-1-118-38318-6

Think you can't learn it in a day? Think again!

The *In a Day* e-book series from *For Dummies* gives you quick and easy access to learn a new skill, brush up on a hobby, or enhance your personal or professional life — all in a day. Easy!

Football Rules & Positions FOR DUMMIES *in a day*

Improving Your **Golf Swing** FOR DUMMIES *in a day*

Buying & Serving **Wine** FOR DUMMIES *in a day*

Getting Started with **Crowdfund Investing** FOR DUMMIES *in a day*

Boost Your Confidence FOR DUMMIES *in a day*

Giving a **Presentation** FOR DUMMIES *in a day*

Launch a WordPress.com **Blog** FOR DUMMIES *in a day*

Rugby Union Basics FOR DUMMIES *in a day*

Cricket Rules FOR DUMMIES *in a day*

Become More Mindful FOR DUMMIES *in a day*

Running a **Great Meeting** FOR DUMMIES *in a day*

Knitting a Scarf FOR DUMMIES *in a day*

Planning a **PRINCE2** Project FOR DUMMIES *in a day*

Building Rapport with NLP FOR DUMMIES *in a day*

Ukulele FOR DUMMIES *in a day*

Become More **Relaxed** FOR DUMMIES *in a day*

Available as PDF, eMobi and Kindle